THE ESSENTIAL
INSTANT POT®
KETO
COOKBOOK

THE ESSENTIAL
INSTANT POT®
KETO
COOKBOOK

210 Delicious Ketogenic Recipes
To Fuel You Every Day

CASEY THALER
NASM-CPT, FNS

Authorized by Instant Pot®

GRAND CENTRAL
Life & Style

NEW YORK • BOSTON

INSTANT POT® and associated logos are owned by Instant Brands Inc. and are used under license.

Cover design by Jen Wang
Cover photograph copyright © 2019 by Ali Donzé
Cover copyright © 2019 by Hachette Book Group, Inc.

Grand Central Life & Style
Hachette Book Group
1290 Avenue of the Americas, New York, NY 10104
grandcentrallifeandstyle.com
twitter.com/grandcentralpub

First Edition: January 2019

Grand Central Life & Style is an imprint of Grand Central Publishing.
The Grand Central Life & Style name and logo are trademarks of Hachette Book Group, Inc.

Additional Credits, for insert photos, can be found on page 239.

The Hachette Speakers Bureau provides a wide range of authors for speaking events. To find out more, go to www.hachettespeakersbureau.com or call (866) 376-6591.

Production by Stonesong; interior design by studio2pt0; illustrations by Andrew Mayer

Library of Congress Control Number: 2018958459
ISBNs: 978-1-5387-3256-4 (trade paperback); 978-1-5387-3255-7 (ebook)

Printed in the United States of America
LSC-C
10 9 8 7 6 5 4 3 2 1

CONTENTS

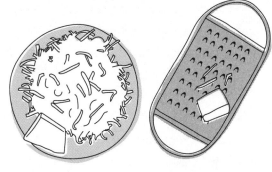

LUNCH

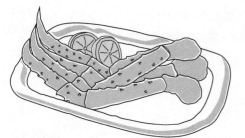

DINNER

DESSERT

SIDES

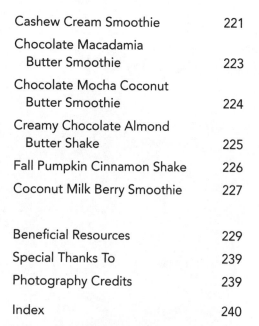

INTRODUCTION

The keto diet and the Instant Pot have both exploded in popularity over the last few years. Many have found that cutting out sugar is a life-changing experience, and can lead to better health, sustained weight loss, increased mental clarity, and a longer lifespan. The Instant Pot, in a different way, has been just as revolutionary. By offering a faster, easier, and cleaner way to make healthy meals, the Instant Pot has sold more than five million units since 2014. It is truly a game-changing phenomenon.

In my daily life, I find myself more often making meals that are not quite as fancy as what you may find in a gourmet, five-star restaurant. While complex meals *sound* great, by the time Wednesday night rolls around, I'm one step away from ordering pizza, just because I am so crunched for time.

This is where the magic of the ketogenic diet and the Instant Pot come together. In no time at all, I can throw some vegetables and meat into the inner pot, set the timer, and keep on doing whatever else I need to do. Within 30 minutes, I have dinner! No fuss, no hassle, and barely any clean up. A truly perfect solution for my busy life, and one which also allows me to stay healthy.

I am far from alone in discovering both of these groundbreaking trends. The online Reddit community for keto now has more than 700,000 members.

And the Instant Pot? Well, in just one day, on Amazon's Prime Day 2018, the Instant Pot sold more than 300,000 units. While that statistic is incredible on its own, what's more incredible is that there seems to be no sign of it slowing down. Buckle up, because it looks like the keto diet and the Instant Pot are both here to stay.

Inside this book, you will find 210 keto Instant Pot recipes, all designed to help you live your best life, lose weight, and feel absolutely amazing. There are recipes for lasagna, cookies, cakes, pies, muffins, quiche, lobster bisque, crème brûlée, mahi mahi, mac and cheese, pizza, baby back ribs—and so much more.

Each recipe will fit the macronutrient requirements of a ketogenic diet, and the nutritional information is listed for easy reference. I have designed every recipe to be as easy to follow and as quick to prepare as possible. As I've learned by directly helping individuals in the gym (and in the kitchen), ease of use is paramount. It is hard enough eating healthy; if you don't have quick, delicious, easy recipes, it is almost impossible. Fortunately, every recipe in this cookbook can help you lose weight, build muscle, and stay away from junk food. Simply try one of the easy-to-make keto desserts if you feel a craving for something sweet coming on. Or make a whole chicken or baby back ribs for dinner—that way you will have leftovers for a few days more of healthy, low-carb eating.

As I have seen firsthand with my personal training clients, sugar is not only inflammatory, it causes you to gain weight. While some sugar is okay, anything more than small amounts can quickly lead to problems. By adopting a ketogenic approach, you will cut out sugar drastically, and watch as the pounds fall away. Even though I constantly get the question "What is the best thing to do in the gym to lose weight?," the real answer is that it's actually what you do in the *kitchen* that helps to move the needle.

I hope you enjoy reading this book as much as I enjoyed writing it. Here's to a newer, healthier you—and an entirely new way of preparing and eating meals!

KETO BASICS

The keto diet has been rapidly increasing in popularity over the last few years. In fact, *Cosmopolitan* and *Forbes* have deemed it the most popular weight-loss trend. According to Google, currently more than one million people search for the term "keto diet" every month. This previously obscure dietary approach leaves out almost all carbohydrates and sugar and retrains your body and brain to run off dietary and stored fat, not carbs and sugar. Some scientific research (most notably from the *New England Journal of Medicine* and Harvard University) has even shown that a keto approach may be associated with health benefits like slower aging, sustained and better weight loss, a decreased risk of developing Alzheimer's, and a longer lifespan. From a nutrition standpoint, a keto approach is particularly beneficial because it lowers your daily intake of sugar and trains your body to burn fat, rather than glucose.

A keto approach is also noteworthy for its improved hormonal response, compared to the Standard American Diet (SAD). One of the biggest culprits in this equation is insulin. Sugar intake (especially in excess) causes insulin to spike, then to fall rapidly. You likely know this phenomenon as a "sugar crash." But insulin is a big problem when it comes to weight loss, and the more insulin we are releasing, the less fat we are burning. Therefore, to oversimplify just a bit, the more carbs and sugar you are consuming, the less likely your body is to burn off its stored fat. There are exceptions to this rule—ironman athletes, marathon runners, etc.—but they are exceedingly rare. For the large majority of us, too many carbs and too much sugar is a direct recipe for weight gain.

A keto approach fixes all of this, as instead of slamming down carb-heavy favorites, we instead take in large amounts of healthy fats. These fats let our bodies and brains run smoothly and efficiently via ketone bodies, instead of using glucose. Ketone bodies are produced by our liver when our carbohydrate intake drops low, and our body starts shifting to fat as its preferred fuel source. When our carbohydrate intake drops to less than 100 grams per day (and often less than 50, or even 20 grams), we enter a metabolic state called ketosis. This is a great place to be if your goal is to lose weight and body fat.

With a keto approach, protein intake is kept at moderate levels, as too much protein can actually kick us out of ketosis. Sometimes you can also pair a keto approach with intermittent fasting, which is another dietary approach that has been rapidly increasing in popularity in recent years. With intermittent fasting, by not eating for prolonged periods of time, we are actually increasing our insulin sensitivity.

Keto recipes are filled with flavor, which is a big relief, as when most of my clients first hear that they are going to be eliminating almost all carbs and sugar, they go into a mini panic. But inside this cookbook you will find delicious recipes for keto donuts, keto ice cream, keto mac and cheese—and even keto fudge. Just because you might be eliminating carbs, does not mean you will be eliminating flavor.

The first few days shifting from the Standard American Diet (which is extremely heavy on carbohydrates) to a very low-carb keto diet, may be fairly tough. The difficulty of this "keto flu" period is directly proportional to how many carbs you were taking in before you made the switch. The more carbs and sugar you were taking in, the more pronounced the keto flu will feel. But do not worry—this period does not last long.

Luckily, there are also a few ways to combat the keto flu. You may want to try a variety of things, like getting more sleep, exercising lightly, drinking plenty of water, making sure you are still getting enough carbs, ramping up your fat intake, being mindful of your electrolytes, and possibly even taking supplements (usually electrolyte or ketone supplements work best).

Once you shift into fat-burning ketosis, you will find that your body starts to burn fat more efficiently and is running on ketones. This happens once you stop taking in so much glucose (sugar). There are even some scholars and researchers, like Dr. Loren Cordain (*New York Times* bestselling author and founder of the paleo diet), who believe a keto diet more closely mimics the way our ancestors may have eaten. This is because it allows for long periods of survival between meals and allows the body and brain to thrive without large amounts of glucose (or any food at all, really).

It is important to note that the keto diet should be adopted and followed fairly

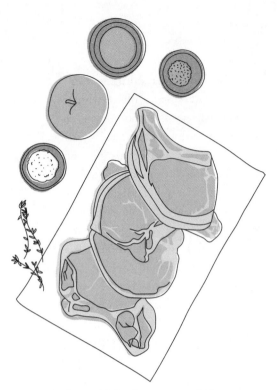

carb intake, usually between 20 and 50 grams of net carbs, per day. This brings us to the important point of differentiating between carbs and net carbs. When you are pursuing a keto diet, it is important to count net carbs, not total carbs.

To get an accurate net carb count, simply subtract any fiber grams from your carb intake. Fiber does not raise your blood sugar or cause insulin to be released, so we do not need to worry about it for optimal ketosis. Vegetables are particularly high in fiber, so do not be too worried about eating lots of vegetables while maintaining a keto approach.

However, one important caveat—do not overconsume root vegetables. The most popular root veggies that are often accidentally overconsumed with a keto approach are yams, carrots, sweet potatoes, pumpkin, spaghetti squash, and turnips. These starchier vegetables are typically higher in carbs, with less fiber, and sometimes even have a little sugar in them. Tread lightly with these.

Every recipe in this cookbook will provide you with a very small amount of net carbs and is extremely low (or completely devoid) of sugar, moderate in protein, and full of healthy fats. If you feel like an expert after reading this cookbook and want to make your own keto Instant Pot recipes, make sure you keep the ideal keto macronutrient ratios in mind. Mix and match from the following foods listed on page xx and xxi to create your own keto Instant Pot recipes.

precisely, and it is always a good idea to get your doctor's input before drastically changing your dietary intake. It is crucial to note your macronutrient intake when adopting a keto approach. The macronutrients we will be concerned with are fat, protein, and carbohydrates.

Typically, a keto diet will allow for about 60–70% of dietary intake to come from fat, 20–30% to come from protein, and the remaining intake to come from carbohydrates. It is obviously almost impossible to maintain these exact percentages at every meal, but they are key numbers to keep in mind for the big picture. Though the exact grams of carbohydrate intake per day will vary per person, typically, ketosis is achieved at 20 to 100 grams of carbs, per day. However, typically, ketosis is maintained with lower

The Essential Instant Pot® Keto Cookbook

INSTANT POT BASICS

The Instant Pot has become a bestseller in just a couple of years—and for good reason. It can make a cheesecake, make tough meats palatable in less than an hour, and cook a few days' worth of food with minimal clean up. Once you try the Instant Pot a few times, you will definitely be hooked. The Instant Pot is also perfectly suited for the meat- and vegetable-centric keto diet.

One of the hidden bonuses of the Instant Pot is more flavorful cooking. That's because pressure-cooking allows more of the herbs and spices to be absorbed into your food. Since a keto diet lacks large amounts of sugar, it is extremely important to keep things interesting by using a large variety of herbs and spices. An Instant Pot is also great for keto cooking because you can batch-prepare food for the week ahead, meaning you won't resort to reaching for the sugary snacks.

One of my favorite features of the Instant Pot is the very simple cleanup. No one likes having to do a lot of dishes, and the Instant Pot keeps all the cleanup to just one pot. Even if you are making yogurt, a chocolate pie, or a pot roast, you still have almost nothing to clean up.

Which brings us to the next great aspect of the Instant Pot: it combines several different kitchen gadgets into just one device. It is a rice cooker, slow cooker, pressure cooker, steamer, and much more.

You can cook an entire roast chicken in an Instant Pot—or make a chocolate cake. The versatility, ease of use, and speed of the Instant Pot are what has truly caught everyone's attention.

However, to a newbie, the Instant Pot can seem intimidating and daunting. The front of the pot can at first look confusing—even though it really could not be simpler. While there are a wide variety of features and buttons, I have simplified it all for you. Almost every recipe in this book uses the Manual mode. On some Instant Pot models this is called Pressure Cook mode.

While not true of all, just about every recipe in this book is to be cooked at high pressure, which is the default setting once you press the Manual (or Pressure Cook) button. From here, you simply adjust the time, and you are on your way! It is also important to properly close the Instant Pot and make sure it is sealed.

When opening the Instant Pot after cooking is complete, sometimes you will want to let the pressure release naturally, and sometimes you will want to perform a "quick release." But do not be intimidated. A quick release simply means that you carefully turn the pressure valve to Venting as soon as cooking is done, and this quickly releases the pressure that has built up during cooking.

INSTANT POT BUTTONS AND COOKING TERMS

Sauté: For this button, simply think of how your stove top cooks. This setting works on low, medium, or high heat, and is great for quickly warming, melting, searing, or browning your food. Many recipes begin by greasing the bottom of your Instant Pot with coconut oil (or other keto-friendly oil), then setting the Instant Pot to Sauté mode.

Manual/Pressure Cook: This is your go-to button. I have written this cookbook to be as easy to follow as possible, and this button allows you to set the Instant Pot in less than 15 seconds. Essentially, this mode defaults to cooking under high pressure, then allows you set the cooking time. While other buttons and modes can be useful, this is the most common way to cook with the Instant Pot.

Steam: I have not written many recipes in this cookbook to use the Steam function, but it can be useful. However, it should be clear that this is not really "steaming" food, per se—your food is still being pressure-cooked. The advantage to this mode is that the temperature of the pot rises very quickly (perfect for some vegetables and most fish). Note that you should always use a steamer basket or trivet when using this mode—otherwise you will burn your food.

Yogurt: This button stands out slightly, in that you can make yogurt (!) with the normal, default setting. However, since we are following a keto approach, most yogurts will be more like fermented cream, or Greek yogurt. Try making your own keto-friendly yogurt by using some heavy cream, with a tiny bit of coconut milk mixed in (bonus recipe!). In the More mode, this button also allows you to pasteurize milk.

Soup: Admittedly, I do not use this function very much. It can be used to keep some foods from separating and offers a very slow warm-up time. Some recipes could easily be made using this button, but I generally prefer Manual/Pressure Cook mode, as it cooks foods faster.

Keep Warm/Cancel: This button is pretty self-explanatory. When ending a program, the Cancel function is what to use, and the Keep Warm function comes on automatically after the cooking time is complete. This function allows your food to stay warm, even if you are not able to check on the Instant Pot right away. By default, the Keep Warm setting is always on (though it can be turned off, if desired).

Slow Cook: One of the features commonly spoken about when introducing the Instant Pot to someone is that it also works as a slow cooker. There are some slight differences in cooking temperatures when using an Instant Pot versus a traditional slow cooker, so make sure to pay attention to the following: Use the

The Essential Instant Pot® Keto Cookbook

medium or high setting for actual slow cooking, and the low setting for keeping your food warm.

[+] and [-]: These buttons adjust your cooking time. Simple as that!

Quick Release: This is simply immediately switching the valve to Venting, after the cooking time is complete. This is useful for vegetables and some meats, but also produces a large blast of steam, which you should be very careful to avoid getting into contact with. Carefully release the valve and keep your face far away from the steam's path.

Natural Release: A natural release means that you let the pressure naturally disperse from the Instant Pot once it is done cooking. This avoids the large release of steam that occurs when immediately releasing the pressure via the quick release technique.

INSTANT POT ACCESSORIES

The most affordable (and most Instant Pot–friendly) versions of these accessories are all categorized for you at InstantPotKetoCookbook.com. Note that there are even more ways to customize your Instant Pot experience, and many, many other tools out there. I have listed the ones I use most frequently.

Tongs: These are essential for removing anything from inside the Instant Pot that might be difficult to get a good grip on

(I'm looking at you, mason jars!). They can also be great for mixing and moving around ingredients.

Flexible Turner: Ever have something get stuck to the pot while you are cooking? Now imagine that that something is stuck inside a deep pot that might be very warm. This is where a flexible turner comes in.

Glass Lids: These are great for Sauté or Slow Cook modes. They are also great for minimizing the hot steam coming up into your face while using either of these functions.

Steamer Basket: This is a vital tool for steaming vegetables, cooking eggs, or cooking really any food that you do not want to have resting in liquid. A true must-have for any Instant Pot owner.

Kitchen Thermometer: This is a very versatile tool that will get a lot more use than with just your Instant Pot. A kitchen thermometer is vital for checking the temperature of meat and poultry, but can also be used in making yogurt.

7-inch Dishes and Pans: There is a wide variety of sizes of pans and dishes. If you have an 8-quart Instant Pot, use 8-inch round pans and dishes. If you own a 6-quart Instant Pot, be sure to buy 7-inch round versions. A springform pan is great for cheesecake, a round cake pan is vital for other desserts, and a Pyrex dish will cover just about everything else!

Gravy/Fat Separator: This can be used to separate liquids, fats, and juices. Depending on how you like to cook, this can be a great tool for completely changing the taste of certain dishes. If you want to remove fat from broth, this is also a good go-to.

Silicone Pans: Great for muffins, egg cups, loaves, cakes, and other dishes, these can also be used for separating cooking ingredients before they are used. Getting some of these pans can eliminate the need to make slings out of aluminum foil (see page xix) as well (which means you are far less likely to drop your favorite foods!).

Trivet: That's right—the simple stand that came with your Instant Pot. This has multiple uses, but an extra one allows you to do pot-in-pot (PIP) cooking. This is because it is usually taller than the one that comes with your Instant Pot, letting you save even more time by cooking two different foods at once.

Inner Pot: An extra inner pot is not *entirely* necessary, I will admit. But it definitely is nice to have one for meal prep, or when you are doing a lot of Instant Pot cooking in one day. Why? Because it saves you from having to immediately clean your original inner pot! Simple, but useful.

Immersion Blender: Blending right inside the Instant Pot is easy. Just grab an immersion blender and be careful if the inner pot is hot. Immersion blenders can also be used quickly and easily in bowls, or any other place where you're preparing something in which you might want a slightly smoother texture (like a frosting).

Electric Mixer: An electric mixer is more of a general, everyday kitchen appliance—but it is very useful for obtaining the best results for cakes, pies, cookies, or any other dish that requires the batter to have a perfectly even texture. I like to save lots of time (and hand-cramp pain), and just use the electric mixer with a large bowl compatible with the mixer. I'm done in 30 to 40 seconds, and can even do other things while the mixer does the heavy lifting for me.

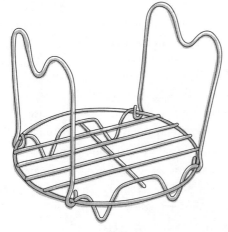

MAKING A SLING

To make a sling, simply fold a piece of aluminum foil in half lengthwise, twice, so you end up with a long, narrow piece of foil, which you can place under a dish, to make inserting it into and removing from the inner pot much easier. Make sure the folded sheet of foil is wide enough to balance the dish and long enough to use as handles (aluminum foil at 20 inches in length is usually ideal). Grab each end of the sling and lift the dish to lower it into the inner pot or to remove a warm one, carefully and easily.

INSTANT POT QUICK REFERENCE CHART

Food	Cooking Time (Minutes)	Release
Beef	25 to 30	Natural
Chicken	15 to 20	Quick
Eggs	5 to 10	Natural
Fish	2 to 5	Quick
Pork	20 to 25	Natural
Turkey	15 to 25	Quick
Vegetables	2 to 4	Quick

*These are general cooking times, intended only as a rough guide. Actual cooking times may sometimes range slightly outside of the minutes listed (especially if cooking foods in large quantities, or frozen foods).

KETO FOOD LIST

PROTEIN

Animal Protein
Pork
Beef
Wild Game
Duck
Chicken
Turkey
Wild-Caught Fish/
  Shellfish

Dairy
Cheese
Greek Yogurt
Cream

CARBS

Fruits
Dark Berries (blackberries,
  blueberries,
  raspberries,
  strawberries)
Lemons
Limes
Apples
Pears

Legumes
Beans
Green Peas

Vegetables
Bok Choy
Cucumber
Kale
Chives
Zucchini
Lettuce
Peppers
Tomatoes
Butternut Squash
Sweet Potatoes
Spaghetti Squash
Yams
Turnips
Carrots
Pumpkin
Dark Leafy Greens

FATS

Nuts and Seeds
Sunflower Seeds
Hemp Seeds
Chia Seeds
Sesame Seeds
Pumpkin Seeds
Hazelnuts
Cashews
Pecans
Pistachios

Walnuts
Macadamia Nuts
Almonds
Nut Butters
Macadamia Oil
Walnut Oil

Cooking Fats
Coconut Oil
Avocado Oil
Olive Oil

Animal Fats
Ghee
Tallow
Grass-fed Butter
Lard
Eggs
Organ Meats
Wild-Caught Fish/
  Shellfish

Other
Nut Milks
Coconut Flour
Almond Flour
MCT Oil
Dark Organic Chocolate
Sugar-Free Chocolate
  Chips

* This is a general list, not an exhaustive one.

** All food should be sourced as best as possible. Look for: organic, wild caught, grass fed, free range, sugar free/no sugar added, full fat.

The Essential Instant Pot® Keto Cookbook

KETO HERBS AND SPICES

Allspice
Anise Star
Annatto
Basil
Bay Leaf
Black Pepper
Black Peppercorns
Capsicums
Caraway
Cardamom
Cayenne Pepper
Celery
Chamomile
Chervil
Chili Powder
Chinese 5-Spice
Chipotle Powder
Chives
Cilantro
Cinnamon
Cloves
Cocoa Powder
Coriander

Cumin
Curry Powder
Dill
Fennel
Fenugreek
Garam Masala
Garlic Powder
Ginger
Green Peppercorns
Ground Cloves
Ground Ginger
Horseradish
Juniper
Lavender
Lemon Balm
Mace
Marjoram
Mustard Powder
Nutmeg
Onion Powder
Oregano
Paprika
Parsley

Peppercorn
Peppermint
Pink Peppercorns
Poultry Seasoning
Crushed Red Pepper
Rosemary
Saffron
Sage
Salt
Savory
Sea Salt
Sesame
Spearmint
Steak Seasoning
Tarragon
Thyme
Turmeric
Vanilla Bean
Wasabi Powder
White Pepper

* This is a general list, not an exhaustive one.

RECIPE FAQS AND NOTES

Instant Pot Size: All recipes were created in an 8-quart Instant Pot. I have done my absolute best to make sure that all recipes will work just as well with smaller Instant Pot models. However, there may be some occasions where you will need to slightly adjust ingredient amounts. There are even some recipes created specifically to work in your Instant Pot Mini! Look for the icon to easily and quickly identify these smaller-portioned recipes.

What Is the Best Type of Beef to Use?:

I personally enjoy the taste, texture, and superior nutrition of grass-fed beef. However, some may prefer to use well-sourced, leaner beef (96/4, 90/10, etc.) in some recipes. Leaner beef will help provide you with a slightly less "greasy" result. This is due to moisture and fat not escaping your Instant Pot during the cooking process.

Cooking Times:

Cooking times may vary slightly, due to altitude and other factors. I have done my best to make sure that all cooking times will provide you with a properly cooked dish. However, please make sure that everything is fully cooked before serving. On occasion, you may wish to cook your dish for a few minutes longer, or until your desired texture is reached. In all pressure cookers, it is always better to initially undercook foods, as this leaves open the ability to cook the food longer, until it is just as you desire. This is not the case when it comes to overcooking—there is no turning back from a recipe that has been cooked for too long.

Straining/Excess Water:

If you ever encounter excess water after a recipe is cooked, you will want to drain it from your dish before serving. Use a standard strainer to accomplish this.

What Type of Cookware Should I Use?:

As you look through the recipes in this book, you will see that I have listed " . . . in an Instant Pot–friendly dish . . ." as a common direction step. The great thing about the Instant Pot is that it is compatible with many different types of bowls, pans, and containers. A good rule of thumb is that any type of dish that is oven safe will generally be okay to use in the Instant Pot. Beyond that, it is up to you! You can experiment, test, modify, and use your preferred bowl, pan, glass dish—or any type of container you like (as long as it holds the food!). It should also be noted: Using different types of cookware may sometimes have a small impact on the required cooking time for the recipe.

What Size Cookware Should I Use?:

I am personally a big fan of using a 7-cup circular dish in the Instant Pot. This allows for a good-sized recipe (in terms of servings)—but also is small enough to easily transfer, store, and clean up. Stainless steel, aluminum, and metal cookware will provide the fastest cooking times. It should be noted that glass cookware usually adds a few minutes to the cook time of a recipe—so do not fret if your dish takes a few extra minutes to cook, when using glass cookware.

Can I Double or Halve Recipes?: Yes. This cookbook is designed for all models of the Instant Pot. But since there is such a wide range of sizes (from the Mini to the 8 quart), sometimes you will want to adjust recipes for your specific size (or if you want to make more or less of a dish).

Chocolate Chips: In the desserts section, you will frequently see "sugar-free chocolate chips" listed as an ingredient. I personally use Lily's brand of sugar-free chocolate chips for these recipes, as they contain no sugar, and are sweetened with stevia. For best results, I recommend you use this brand.

Swerve Sweetener: This unique sweetener is by far the best choice when it comes to making keto baked goods—it is very similar to sugar, and in fact measures at a 1:1 ratio with sugar. It is mostly erythritol, so if you are familiar with that sugar substitute, Swerve will taste very similar. Swerve is also non-GMO, non-glycemic, and natural, making it my favorite go-to keto sweetener.

Filtered Water: While technically any type of water will help bring the Instant Pot to pressure, I recommend that you use filtered water. This is to help ensure that you will not be consuming any bacterial and/or viral contaminants, as well as reducing exposure to chemicals like chlorine, which can negatively impact your health. It is also important to remember that water will never go into the Instant Pot directly—it will always be poured into the stainless steel inner pot.

Bacon/Turkey Bacon: Bacon is one of the most popular foods within the keto framework. However, for those looking to consume slightly fewer calories and a little bit less fat, you can easily substitute in turkey bacon, in any recipe of your choosing.

Sodium: Many dietary approaches suggest that you limit your sodium intake, to avoid health issues (like high blood pressure). Interestingly, a keto diet requires more sodium—not less. This is due to electrolyte imbalances that can occur, if electrolyte intake is not adequate. Low carbohydrate diets alter insulin and sodium levels inside the body—trust me, it's pretty complicated and well beyond the scope of this book! Many forget though—sodium is actually an essential nutrient—and those following a keto approach should generally aim for between 3,000mg–5,000mg (3–5 grams) of sodium, per day. I have accounted for this uptick in sodium intake with the recipes in this cookbook. So if something seems slightly more salty than you are used to – this is likely the reason why.

BREAKFAST

MINI BACON AND KALE FRITTATAS

Serves 4

Prep Time: 5 minutes, Cook Time: 20 minutes, Total Time: 25 minutes, Pressure: High, Release: Natural

Gluten Free, Dairy Free, Soy Free, 25 Minutes or Less, Kid Friendly

Mini breakfasts are always a big hit. These mini frittatas are no different. With quick prep and fast cooking times, they are a great example of how to easily make a keto breakfast in the Instant Pot.

6 eggs

4 slices no-sugar-added bacon, finely cut, cooked

1 cup kale, finely chopped

2 tablespoons coconut oil

½ teaspoon basil, dried

½ teaspoon chili powder (optional)

½ teaspoon cilantro, dried

½ teaspoon full-fat coconut milk

½ teaspoon freshly ground black pepper

½ teaspoon kosher salt

½ teaspoon parsley, dried

Nutrition Facts
Amount per Serving
Calories 276
Total Fat 21.5g
Total Carbohydrate 4.7g
Dietary Fiber 0.7g
Total Sugars 0.6g
Protein 16.4g

Pour 1 cup of filtered water into the inner pot of the Instant Pot, then insert the trivet. In a large bowl, thoroughly mix the eggs, bacon, kale, oil, basil, chili powder, cilantro, milk, pepper, salt, and parsley.

Once mixed, ladle mixture evenly inside four well-greased ramekins, or other small, heat-proof containers. Make sure to leave room on top of each for possible expansion during cooking. Place all ramekins or containers on the trivet.

Close the lid, set the pressure release to Sealing, and select Manual/Pressure Cook. Set the Instant Pot to 20 minutes on high pressure and let cook.

Once cooked, let the pressure naturally disperse from the Instant Pot for about 10 minutes, then carefully switch the pressure release to Venting. Open the Instant Pot, remove the ramekins with oven mitts, and let cool for 5–10 minutes. Serve, and enjoy!

PROTEIN SCRAMBLE

Serves 2

**Prep Time: 5 minutes, Cook Time: 20 minutes, Total Time: 25 minutes,
Pressure: High, Release: Natural**

Gluten Free, Soy Free, 25 Minutes or Less, Kid Friendly

The keto approach to eating is rewarding and healthy, in part because it promotes a healthy hormonal response in your body. This is largely due to the high amount of healthy fats consumed, as well as the good amount of bioavailable proteins you take in daily. This dish is infinitely customizable: Add a nutrient-dense vegetable to the scramble to see even better health results.

4 eggs
4 slices no-sugar-added bacon, cooked and finely cut
½ cup full-fat Cheddar cheese, shredded
1 cup spinach, chopped
2 tablespoons coconut oil
¼ cup full-fat coconut milk
½ teaspoon parsley, dried
½ teaspoon chili powder
½ teaspoon cumin, ground
½ teaspoon basil, dried
½ teaspoon kosher salt
½ teaspoon freshly ground black pepper

Grease the stainless steel inner pot of the Instant Pot, and pour in all ingredients. Mix thoroughly.

Add 1 cup of filtered water into the Instant Pot.

Close the lid, set the pressure release to Sealing, and select Manual/Pressure Cook. Set the Instant Pot to 20 minutes on high pressure.

Once cooked, let the pressure naturally disperse from the Instant Pot for about 10 minutes, then carefully switch the pressure release to Venting.

Open the Instant Pot, serve, and enjoy!

Nutrition Facts
Amount per Serving
Calories 767
Total Fat 65.7g
Total Carbohydrate 6.4g
Dietary Fiber 1.4g
Total Sugars 1.8g
Protein 38.5g

The Essential Instant Pot® Keto Cookbook

SPICY MORNING CHICKEN BOWL

Recipe courtesy of Thomas DeLauer

Serves 4

Prep Time: 5 minutes, Cook Time: 10 minutes, Total Time: 15 minutes, Pressure: High, Release: Quick

Gluten Free, Soy Free, 25 Minutes or Less

The Instant Pot is great at cooking meats quickly, and this breakfast bowl is a perfect example. Since eating chicken day after day can get a little tiresome, I spiced up this morning dish with some of my favorite hot spices. For a little less fire, omit the curry powder. Or, if you like living dangerously, double it!

2 tablespoons coconut oil

1 pound chicken, ground

2 tablespoons sugar-free or low-sugar salsa

1 cup full-fat Cheddar cheese, shredded

1 teaspoon curry powder

1/2 teaspoon parsley, dried

1/2 teaspoon basil, dried

1/2 cup spinach, chopped

1/2 teaspoon kosher salt

1/2 teaspoon freshly ground black pepper

1 tablespoon hot sauce

1/2 teaspoon cilantro, dried

Set the Instant Pot to Sauté and heat the oil, then add the chicken, salsa, cheese, curry powder, parsley, basil, spinach, salt, black pepper, hot sauce, and cilantro to the inner pot. Stir thoroughly.

Add in 1 cup of filtered water, then close the lid, set the pressure release to Sealing, and hit Cancel to stop the current program. Select Manual/Pressure Cook, set the Instant Pot to 10 minutes on high pressure, and let cook.

Once cooked, perform a quick release by carefully switching the pressure valve to Venting.

Open the Instant Pot, serve, and enjoy!

Nutrition Facts
Amount per Serving
Calories 350
Total Fat 19.7g
Total Carbohydrate 1.5g
Dietary Fiber 0.5g
Total Sugars 0.5g
Protein 40.2g

SIMPLE DECONSTRUCTED BREAKFAST PIZZA

Serves 4 to 5

**Prep Time: 5 minutes, Cook Time: 15 minutes, Total Time: 20 minutes,
Pressure: High, Release: Natural**

Gluten Free, Soy Free, 25 Minutes or Less, Kid Friendly

The chicken crust on this breakfast delicacy provides a nice punch of protein,
and you stay in fat-burning ketosis the whole time.

2 tablespoons avocado oil

1 pound chicken, ground

½ teaspoon basil, dried

½ teaspoon parsley, dried

**½ teaspoon crushed red pepper
(optional)**

½ teaspoon kosher salt

½ teaspoon freshly ground black pepper

**1 (14-ounce) small can sugar-free or low-
sugar crushed tomatoes, drained**

**1 cup full-fat Cheddar cheese, shredded
(or more, to taste)**

**2 to 4 slices no-sugar-added bacon,
cooked and finely cut (optional)**

Nutrition Facts
Amount per Serving
Calories 174
Total Fat 11.7g
Total Carbohydrate 8.8g
Dietary Fiber 2.3g
Total Sugars 3.9g
Protein 10.1g

Set the Instant Pot to Sauté, melt the oil, then add the chicken to the inner pot. Sauté the chicken until brown, and mix in ¼ cup of filtered water. Push the chicken down with a spatula or spoon to form a flat, even layer, covering the bottom of the pot.

In a small bowl, mix together the basil, parsley, red pepper (if using), salt, and black pepper.

Pour the tomatoes over the chicken, then add a layer of cheese, and finally, the bacon (if using). Sprinkle the spice and herb mixture evenly over top.

Close the lid, set the pressure release to Sealing, and hit Cancel to stop the current program. Select Manual/Pressure Cook, set the Instant Pot to 15 minutes on high pressure, and let cook.

Once cooked, let the pressure naturally disperse from the Instant Pot for about 10 minutes, then carefully switch the pressure release to Venting.

Open the Instant Pot, and carefully remove the pizza with a spatula. Serve, and enjoy!

HARD-BOILED EGGS

Serves 6 to 8

**Prep Time: 5 minutes, Cook Time: 5 minutes, Total Time: 10 minutes,
Pressure: High, Release: Quick**

Gluten Free, Dairy Free, Soy Free, 10 Minutes or Less, Kid Friendly

One of the amazing features of the Instant Pot is the ability to quickly and easily make keto-friendly meals. Hard-boiled eggs are a low-carb classic, and you can make a whole batch of hard-boiled eggs very efficiently with the Instant Pot. I like to prepare a large quantity and keep them stored for the next several days. This way I always have handy, on-the-go snacks available for the week. Little tricks like this will easily help you stay on the keto path.

6 to 8 eggs

Nutrition Facts
Amount per Serving
Calories 78
Total Fat 5g
Total Carbohydrate 0.5g
Dietary Fiber 0g
Total Sugars 0.5g
Protein 6.3g

Pour 1 cup filtered water into the inner pot of the Instant Pot, then insert the trivet, placing the eggs on top.

Close the lid, set the pressure release to Sealing, and hit Cancel to stop the current program. Select Manual/Pressure Cook, set the Instant Pot to 5 minutes on high pressure, and let cook.

Fill a small to medium bowl with ice and water and set aside.

Once cooked, perform a quick release by carefully switching the pressure valve to Venting.

Open the Instant Pot and, using tongs, place the eggs in the ice bath for 2 to 3 minutes. Peel, rinse, and enjoy! If making for later, wait to peel until serving, and store in refrigerator.

CLASSIC YOGURT

Serves 8

Prep Time: 5 minutes, Cook Time: 8 to 10 hours, Total Time: 8 to 10 hours, Pressure: High, Release: Natural

Gluten Free, Soy Free, Kid Friendly

This Instant Pot variation will have a slightly different texture than most yogurts you are probably used to eating, but it adds even more healthy nutrients.

6 (13-ounce) cans full-fat coconut milk

20 ounces full-fat, grass-fed Greek yogurt

1 cup dark berries, to serve (optional)

Nutrition Facts
Amount per Serving
Calories 446
Total Fat 50.5g
Total Carbohydrate 4.3g
Dietary Fiber 0.5g
Sugars 1.7g
Protein 10g

From each coconut milk can, scrape the cream layer off the top, then place the cream into the inner pot of the Instant Pot. Cover and reserve the remaining coconut milk in the refrigerator.

Close the lid of the Instant Pot, set the pressure release to Sealing, and press Yogurt and then press Adjust until the screen reads Boil. Once boiled, remove the inner pot and let cool. Use a food thermometer to check when the mixture reaches 100°F., then stir in Greek yogurt.

Return the inner pot to the Instant Pot, seal the lid, and press the Yogurt button, setting the time for 8 to 10 hours. A longer cook time will result in a yogurt that has a slightly more sour taste.

Once done, mix in desired amount of refrigerated coconut milk, to achieve preferred consistency. Place the yogurt in an airtight container and refrigerate until ready to serve. When ready to consume, stir in berries (if desired). The yogurt will keep for 5 days.

CHEDDAR-HERBED STRATA

Serves 4

Prep Time: 5 minutes, Cook Time: 40 minutes, Total Time: 45 minutes, Pressure:High, Release: Natural

Gluten Free, Soy Free, Kid Friendly

A strata is a great way to pack in some keto-friendly nutrition in just one dish, and it can be customized any number of ways. If I'm running particularly low on antioxidants, I'll add a few extra keto-friendly vegetables like broccoli, spinach, or kale. Try mixing in a few slices of bacon, or add some extra cheese to really make this pop.

6 eggs

1 cup full-fat Cheddar cheese, shredded

1 cup spinach, chopped

½ tablespoon salted grass-fed butter, softened

¼ (4-ounce) small onion, thinly sliced

½ teaspoon freshly ground black pepper

½ teaspoon kosher salt

½ teaspoon Dijon mustard

½ teaspoon paprika

½ teaspoon cayenne pepper

½ teaspoon cilantro, dried

½ teaspoon sage, dried

½ teaspoon parsley, dried

Nutrition Facts
Amount per Serving
Calories 179
Total Fat 14.5g
Total Carbohydrate 2g
Dietary Fiber 0.6g
Total Sugars 0.8g
Protein 10.3g

Pour 1 cup of filtered water into the inner pot of the Instant Pot, then insert the trivet. In a large bowl, combine the eggs, cheese, spinach, butter, onion, black pepper, salt, mustard, paprika, cayenne pepper, cilantro, sage, and parsley. Mix thoroughly. Transfer this mixture into a well-greased, Instant Pot–friendly dish.

Using a sling if desired, place the dish onto the trivet, and cover loosely with aluminum foil. Close the lid, set the pressure release to Sealing, and select Manual/Pressure Cook. Set the Instant Pot to 40 minutes on high pressure and let cook.

Once cooked, let the pressure naturally disperse from the Instant Pot for about 10 minutes, then carefully switch the pressure release to Venting.

Open the Instant Pot and remove the dish. Let cool, serve, and enjoy!

GRASS-FED BEEF BREAKFAST BOWL

Serves 4

**Prep Time: 5 minutes, Cook Time: 10 minutes, Total Time: 15 minutes,
Pressure: High, Release: Natural**

Gluten Free, Dairy Free, Soy Free, 25 Minutes or Less, Kid Friendly

Grass-fed beef is one of the best sources of bioavailable protein on the planet. By pairing it with nutrient-dense vegetables, and letting the Instant Pot do all the hard work, you get a perfect muscle-building and metabolism-revving breakfast. This fast and easy breakfast bowl will also easily keep you in fat-burning ketosis all day long.

2 tablespoons avocado oil

1 pound grass-fed beef, ground

½ teaspoon turmeric, ground

½ teaspoon crushed red pepper

½ teaspoon cayenne pepper

½ teaspoon cilantro, dried

½ teaspoon kosher salt

½ teaspoon freshly ground black pepper

Nutrition Facts
Amount per Serving
Calories 212
Total Fat 12g
Total Carbohydrate 0.9g
Dietary Fiber 0.5g
Total Sugars 0.1g
Protein 23.3g

Set the Instant Pot to Sauté and melt the oil. Place the grass-fed beef into the Instant Pot, breaking it up gently. Add the turmeric, red pepper, cayenne pepper, cilantro, salt, and black pepper. Mix thoroughly.

Pour in ½ cup of filtered water, close the lid, set the pressure release to Sealing, and hit Cancel to stop the current program. Select Manual/Pressure Cook, set the Instant Pot to 10 minutes on high pressure, and let cook.

Once cooked, let the pressure naturally disperse from the Instant Pot for about 10 minutes, then carefully switch the pressure release to Venting.

Open the Instant Pot, serve over vegetable of your choice, and enjoy!

CHOCOLATE CHIP MINI MUFFINS

Serves 7

Prep Time: 5 minutes, Cook Time: 20 minutes, Total Time: 25 minutes, Pressure: High, Release: Natural

Gluten Free, Soy Free, 25 Minutes or Less, Kid Friendly

These delectable chocolate chip mini muffins are an all-time favorite. Simple to make and delicious. Try sprinkling some cinnamon into the mix for a slightly different flavor profile.

1 cup blanched almond flour

2 eggs

¾ cup sugar-free chocolate chips

1 tablespoon vanilla extract

½ cup Swerve, confectioners (or more, to taste)

2 tablespoons salted grass-fed butter, softened

½ teaspoon salt

¼ teaspoon baking soda

Nutrition Facts
Amount per Serving
Calories 204
Total Fat 17.0g
Total Carbohydrate 10g
Dietary Fiber 1g
Total Sugars 7.4g
Protein 3.1g

Pour 1 cup of filtered water into the inner pot of the Instant Pot, then insert the trivet. Using an electric mixer, combine flour, eggs, chocolate chips, vanilla, Swerve, butter, salt, and baking soda. Mix thoroughly. Transfer this mixture into a well-greased Instant Pot–friendly muffin (or egg bites) mold.

Using a sling if desired, place the pan onto the trivet and cover loosely with aluminum foil. Close the lid, set the pressure release to Sealing, and select Manual/Pressure Cook. Set the Instant Pot to 20 minutes on high pressure and let cook.

Once cooked, let the pressure naturally disperse from the Instant Pot for about 10 minutes, then carefully switch the pressure release to Venting.

Open the Instant Pot and remove the pan. Let cool, serve, and enjoy!

DENVER OMELET

Serves 2

**Prep Time: 5 minutes, Cook Time: 20 minutes, Total Time: 25 minutes,
Pressure: High, Release: Natural**

Gluten Free, Soy Free, 25 Minutes or Less, Kid Friendly

The Denver omelet is an American classic, and this Instant Pot version is one of the easiest "set it and forget it" options. I like to use sharp Cheddar cheese to give this a little extra flavor, but you can experiment with any keto-friendly ingredient choices.

2 tablespoons avocado oil

¼ cup onion, chopped

¼ cup green bell pepper, finely chopped

¼ cup red bell pepper, finely chopped

6 eggs

2 slices no-sugar-added bacon, cooked and finely cut (optional)

½ cup full-fat Cheddar cheese, shredded

½ teaspoon basil, dried

½ teaspoon crushed red pepper

½ teaspoon parsley, dried

½ teaspoon kosher salt

½ teaspoon freshly ground black pepper

Nutrition Facts
Amount per Serving
Calories 439
Total Fat 32.3g
Total Carbohydrate 5.4g
Dietary Fiber 1.7g
Total Sugars 2.6g
Protein 31.4g

Set the Instant Pot to Sauté and heat the oil. Add the onion and peppers, and sauté for 4 minutes.

In a medium bowl, combine eggs, bacon, cheese, and spices. Pour mixture into a greased, Instant Pot–friendly dish. Add in the sautéed onion and peppers, thoroughly scraping out all the bits from the pot, and mix thoroughly.

Pour 1 cup of filtered water into the inner pot of the Instant Pot, then insert the trivet. Using a sling, place the glass dish inside the Instant Pot.

Close the lid, set the pressure release to Sealing, and hit Cancel to stop the current program. Select Manual/Pressure Cook, set the Instant Pot to 20 minutes on high pressure, and let cook.

Once cooked, let the pressure naturally disperse from the Instant Pot for about 10 minutes, then carefully switch the pressure release to Venting.

Open the Instant Pot, remove the dish, serve, and enjoy!

The Essential Instant Pot® Keto Cookbook

HOT CHOCOLATE BREAKFAST CEREAL

Serves 4

Prep Time: 5 minutes, Cook Time: 0 minutes, Total Time: 5 minutes, Pressure: High, Release: Quick

Gluten Free, Dairy Free, Soy Free, 10 Minutes or Less, Kid Friendly

Hot chocolate is a great way to warm up on a cold winter day, and this faux oatmeal makes it even better. If you do not like the taste of coconut milk, you can easily substitute in almond milk, or any other keto-friendly replacement. You can also add a tiny bit of pumpkin purée for a slightly different taste.

2 cups full-fat coconut milk

1 cup sugar-free chocolate chips

1 cup dried unsweetened coconut

1 cup macadamia nuts

⅓ cup Swerve, confectioners (or more, to taste)

¼ cup blanched almond flour

2 tablespoons unsweetened cocoa powder

½ teaspoon cinnamon, ground

½ teaspoon kosher salt

Nutrition Facts
Amount per Serving
Calories 453
Total Fat 44.1g
Total Carbohydrate 19.9g
Dietary Fiber 8.2g
Total Sugars 3.4g
Protein 6g

Set the Instant Pot to Sauté and add in 2 cups of filtered water, followed by the coconut milk.

Stir in chocolate chips, coconut, nuts, Swerve, flour, cocoa powder, cinnamon, and salt, thoroughly.

Close the lid and set the pressure release to Sealing. Select Manual/Pressure Cook with high pressure. The timer should be set to 0.

When the Instant Pot beeps, perform a quick release by carefully switching the pressure valve to Venting.

Serve and enjoy!

FAT BURNING COFFEE

Serves 2

**Prep Time: 5 minutes, Cook Time: 5 minutes, Total Time: 10 minutes,
Pressure: N/A, Release: N/A**

Gluten Free, Soy Free, 10 Minutes or Less

Mixing fat into coffee has become a huge trend. The nice cognitive kick that comes with the combination of healthy fats and caffeine is a perfect way to start a fast-paced day. If you want to sweeten the taste of your coffee a bit, try an all-natural creamer in addition to the Swerve already included in the recipe.

6 tablespoons salted grass-fed butter, softened

1 cup full-fat coconut milk

2 cups cold brew coffee

¼ cup Swerve, confectioners (or more, to taste)

3 tablespoons unflavored MCT oil

½ teaspoon cinnamon, ground (or more, to taste)

Set the Instant Pot to Sauté and begin to melt the butter.

Add in the milk, followed by the coffee, Swerve, oil, and cinnamon. Stir continuously until the ingredients are melted into a smooth consistency. Hit Cancel to stop the current program.

Serve and enjoy!

Nutrition Facts
Amount per Serving
Calories 760
Total Fat 85.7g
Total Carbohydrate 7.1g
Dietary Fiber 3g
Total Sugars 4g
Protein 3.1g

The Essential Instant Pot® Keto Cookbook

EGG BITES

Serves 2 to 4

Prep Time: 5 minutes, Cook Time: 10 minutes, Total Time: 15 minutes, Pressure: High, Release: Quick

Gluten Free, Soy Free, 25 Minutes or Less, Kid Friendly

These cute little delicacies make for a simple breakfast or a great snack. There are endless ways to customize them, as any keto-compliant topping will do. I personally like crushed red pepper, along with a touch of pepperoni—but feel free to get creative with any number of different flavor combinations.

6 eggs
½ cup spinach, finely chopped
½ cup bell peppers, finely chopped
½ cup full-fat Cheddar cheese, shredded
½ teaspoon kosher salt
½ teaspoon freshly ground black pepper
½ teaspoon cilantro, dried

Nutrition Facts
Amount per Serving
Calories 152
Total Fat 11.3g
Total Carbohydrate 2.1g
Dietary Fiber 0.4g
Total Sugars 1.4g
Protein 12.1g

Pour 1 cup of filtered water into the inner pot of the Instant Pot, then insert the trivet. In a large bowl, combine the eggs, spinach, bell peppers, cheese, salt, black pepper, and cilantro. Mix thoroughly. Transfer this mixture into a well-greased Instant Pot–friendly egg bites mold.

Using a sling if desired, place the pan onto the trivet, and cover loosely with aluminum foil. Close the lid, set the pressure release to Sealing, and select Manual/Pressure Cook. Set the Instant Pot to 10 minutes on high pressure and let cook.

Once cooked, perform a quick release by carefully switching the pressure valve to Venting. Open the Instant Pot and remove the pan. Let cool, serve, and enjoy! Store any leftovers in the refrigerator.

BREAKFAST CAKE

Serves 5 to 6

**Prep Time: 5 minutes, Cook Time: 40 minutes, Total Time: 45 minutes,
Pressure: High, Release: Natural**

Gluten Free, Soy Free, Kid Friendly

While cake for breakfast may sound unhealthy, the surprising truth is that this cake is a very healthy choice. I often like to add some extra nuts to the mix, as it gives the cake a little more crunch.

BASE

3 eggs

2 tablespoons salted grass-fed butter, softened

1 cup blanched almond flour

3/4 cup walnuts, chopped

1/2 cup organic pumpkin purée

1/4 cup heavy whipping cream

1/2 teaspoon salt

1/2 teaspoon baking powder

1/2 teaspoon cinnamon, ground

1/2 teaspoon nutmeg, ground

TOPPINGS

1/4 cup heavy whipping cream

1/2 cup Swerve, confectioners (or more, to taste)

1/2 cup unsweetened coconut flakes

Nutrition Facts
Amount per Serving
Calories 334
Total Fat 30.6g
Total Carbohydrate 8g
Dietary Fiber 4.7g
Total Sugars 0.9g
Protein 7.8g

Pour 1 cup of filtered water into the inner pot of the Instant Pot, then insert the trivet. Using an electric mixer, combine the eggs, butter, flour, walnuts, pumpkin, cream, salt, baking powder, cinnamon, and nutmeg. Mix thoroughly. Transfer this mixture into a well-greased, Instant Pot–friendly pan (or dish).

Using a sling if desired, place the pan onto the trivet, and cover loosely with aluminum foil. Close the lid, set the pressure release to Sealing, and select Manual/Pressure Cook. Set the Instant Pot to 40 minutes on high pressure, and let cook.

While cooking, mix all topping ingredients thoroughly in a large bowl.

Once cooked, let the pressure naturally disperse from the Instant Pot for about 10 minutes, then carefully switch the pressure release to Venting.

Open the Instant Pot and remove the pan. Sprinkle the topping mixture evenly over the cake. Let cool, serve, and enjoy!

The Essential Instant Pot® Keto Cookbook

MINI PANCAKE BITES

Serves 7

Prep Time: 5 minutes, Cook Time: 20 minutes, Total Time: 25 minutes, Pressure: High, Release: Natural

Gluten Free, Soy Free, 25 Minutes or Less, Kid Friendly

These keto mini pancake bites are very easy to make (as well as enjoy), and they truly feel like an indulgence. You can mix and match any number of flavors to make them, so truly let your imagination run wild. They also work great at parties or for family brunch gatherings. These are so good, you will forget they are low carb!

2 eggs

1 cup blanched almond flour

2/3 cup Swerve, confectioners (or more, to taste)

1/4 cup full-fat coconut milk

1 tablespoon salted grass-fed butter, softened

1/2 teaspoon kosher salt

1/4 teaspoon baking soda

Nutrition Facts
Amount per Serving
Calories 187
Total Fat 17.4g
Total Carbohydrate 4.3g
Dietary Fiber 1.9g
Total Sugars 1.5g
Protein 4.8g

Pour 1 cup of filtered water into the inner pot of the Instant Pot, then insert the trivet. In a large bowl, combine the eggs, flour, Swerve, milk, butter, salt and baking soda. Mix thoroughly. Transfer this mixture into a well-greased, Instant Pot–friendly egg bites mold, working in batches if need be. I prefer to stack two egg bites molds on top of each other, separating them with Mason jar lids (or similar dividers).

Using a sling if desired, place the pan onto the trivet and cover loosely with aluminum foil. Close the lid, set the pressure release to Sealing, and select Manual/Pressure Cook. Set the Instant Pot to 20 minutes on high pressure and let cook.

Once cooked, let the pressure naturally disperse from the Instant Pot for about 10 minutes, then carefully switch the pressure release to Venting.

Open the Instant Pot and remove the pan. Let cool, serve with your favorite toppings, and enjoy!

SIMPLE AND EASY BANANA BREAD

Serves 5 to 6

**Prep Time: 5 minutes, Cook Time: 40 minutes, Total Time: 45 minutes,
Pressure: High, Release: Natural**

Gluten Free, Dairy Free, Soy Free, Kid Friendly

Banana bread is a homemade classic, but is traditionally very high in carbohydrates.
This keto version keeps all the taste, but ditches all the carbs. Try mixing in a variety
of chopped nuts to add even more texture, once you have mastered this one.

3 eggs
1 cup blanched almond flour
1 banana, mashed
½ cup walnuts, chopped
¼ cup Swerve, confectioners (or more, to taste)
2 tablespoons coconut oil
1 teaspoon vanilla extract
1 teaspoon baking powder
½ teaspoon nutmeg, ground
½ teaspoon cinnamon, ground
½ teaspoon salt

Nutrition Facts
Amount per serving
Calories 187
Total Fat 15.5g
Total Carbohydrate 7.2g
Dietary Fiber 1.9g
Total Sugars 3g
Protein 5.5g

In a large bowl, combine the eggs, flour, banana, walnuts, Swerve, oil, vanilla, baking powder, nutmeg, cinnamon, and salt. Whisk thoroughly until a perfectly even mixture is obtained. Transfer the mixture from the bowl to a well-greased Instant Pot–friendly pan or dish.

Pour 2 cups filtered water into the inner pot of the Instant Pot and insert the trivet. Place the pan onto the trivet and cover loosely with aluminum foil. Close the lid, set the pressure release to Sealing, and select Manual/Pressure Cook. Set the Instant Pot to 40 minutes on high pressure, and let cook.

Once cooked, let the pressure naturally disperse from the Instant Pot for about 10 minutes, then carefully switch the pressure release to Venting.

Open the Instant Pot and remove the pan. Let cool, serve, and enjoy!

The Essential Instant Pot® Keto Cookbook

CINNAMON ROLL CAKES

Serves 7

Prep Time: 5 minutes, Cook Time: 20 minutes, Total Time: 25 minutes, Pressure: High, Release: Natural

Gluten Free, Soy Free, 25 Minutes or Less, Kid Friendly

These cakes work great for breakfast — or as a small treat at any time of the day.

BASE

2 cups blanched almond flour

2 eggs

½ cup Swerve, confectioners

2 tablespoons salted grass-fed butter, softened

1 tablespoon vanilla extract

½ teaspoon cinnamon, ground (or more, to taste)

½ teaspoon salt

¼ teaspoon baking soda

FROSTING

1 cup heavy whipping cream

½ cup Swerve, confectioners (or more, to taste)

Nutrition Facts
Amount per serving
Calories 225
Total Fat 21.5g
Total Carbohydrate 3.1g
Dietary Fiber 1.1g
Total Sugars 0.4g
Protein 4.3g

Pour 1 cup of filtered water into the inner pot of the Instant Pot, then insert the trivet. In a large bowl, combine the flour, eggs, Swerve, butter, vanilla, cinnamon, salt, and baking soda. Mix thoroughly. Transfer this mixture into a well-greased Instant Pot–friendly egg bites mold, working in batches if needed. I prefer to stack two egg bites molds on top of each other, separating them with Mason jar lids (or similar dividers).

Using a sling if desired, place the pan onto the trivet, and cover loosely with aluminum foil. Close the lid, set the pressure release to Sealing, and select Manual/Pressure Cook. Set the Instant Pot to 20 minutes on high pressure and let cook.

Once cooked, let the pressure release naturally for about 10 minutes.

Carefully switch the pressure release on the Instant Pot to Venting. Open the Instant Pot and remove the pan. While the food cools, mix frosting ingredients thoroughly in a small bowl, and set aside.

Once cooled, top each cake evenly with the frosting mixture.

CHOCOLATE BUTTER PECAN FAT BOMBS

Serves 5 to 6

Prep Time: 5 minutes, Cook Time: 5 minutes, Total Time: 10 minutes, Pressure: N/A, Release: N/A

Gluten Free, Soy Free, 10 Minutes or Less, Kid Friendly

Pecans are a true hidden weapon, as they are high in vitamin E, manganese, magnesium, and other nutrients. These buttery fat bombs will also keep you in fat-burning ketosis—though they sure do not taste like they will! These are great to keep on hand for emergencies, as they will fend off hunger for a few hours, keeping you away from sugar.

2 tablespoons salted grass-fed butter, softened

1 cup raw coconut butter

1 cup sugar-free chocolate chips

½ cup pecans, chopped (or more, to taste)

Nutrition Facts
Amount per serving
Calories 366
Total Fat 31.6g
Total Carbohydrate 15g
Dietary Fiber 6.9g
Total Sugars 0.3g
Protein 4.3g

Set the Instant Pot to Sauté and melt the butter.

Add the coconut butter, chocolate chips, and pecans to the Instant Pot, and mix thoroughly, until melted and smooth.

Pour mixture into a silicone mini-muffin mold. Freeze until firm. Remove from the muffin mold and store in an airtight container until ready to serve!

The Essential Instant Pot® Keto Cookbook

BACON AND SPINACH QUICHE

Serves 3

Prep Time: 5 minutes, Cook Time: 35 minutes, Total Time: 40 minutes, Pressure: High, Release: Natural

Gluten Free, Soy Free, Kid Friendly

Bacon is great at any time of day, but it really makes this crustless spinach breakfast quiche stand out. Sprinkle a little extra-crispy bacon on top of each serving to add even more mouthwatering texture to this morning delicacy. If you want to get an extra antioxidant boost, add in more kale or spinach.

½ cup full-fat coconut milk

½ cup full-fat Cheddar cheese, shredded

½ cup spinach, chopped

5 eggs

2 slices no-sugar-added bacon, cooked and finely chopped

½ teaspoon basil, dried

½ teaspoon parsley, dried

½ teaspoon freshly ground black pepper

¼ teaspoon kosher salt

Nutrition Facts
Amount per serving
Calories 343
Total Fat 28.4g
Total Carbohydrate 3.6g
Dietary Fiber 1.1g
Total Sugars 2g
Protein 19.7g

Pour 1 cup of filtered water into the inner pot of the Instant Pot, then insert the trivet.

Combine the coconut milk, cheese, spinach, eggs, bacon, basil, parsley, pepper, and salt, in an Instant Pot–safe dish. Mix thoroughly, then cover loosely with aluminum foil.

Using a sling if desired, gently place the covered dish on top of the trivet.

Close the lid, set the pressure release to Sealing, and hit Cancel to stop the current program. Select Manual/Pressure Cook, set the Instant Pot to 35 minutes on high pressure, and let cook.

Once cooked, let the pressure naturally disperse from the Instant Pot for about 10 minutes, then carefully switch the pressure release to Venting.

Open the Instant Pot, serve, and enjoy!

FAST AND EASY CHOCOLATE PUMPKIN BALLS

Serves 5 to 6

Prep Time: 5 minutes, Cook Time: 5 minutes, Total Time: 10 minutes, Pressure: High, Release: Natural

Gluten Free, Soy Free, 10 Minutes or Less, Kid Friendly

What do you get when you mix cinnamon, chocolate, and pumpkin? If your answer is "These incredibly easy keto pumpkin balls," you are correct! These are perfect for breakfast, Halloween, Thanksgiving, or at any time of day.

2 tablespoons salted grass-fed butter, softened

2 cups sugar-free chocolate chips

3/4 cup raw coconut butter

1/2 cup organic pumpkin purée (or more, to taste)

1/3 cup Swerve, confectioners (or more, to taste)

2 teaspoons coconut, shredded (optional)

1/8 teaspoon cinnamon, ground

Set the Instant Pot to Sauté and melt the grass-fed butter.

Add the chocolate chips, coconut butter, pumpkin, Swerve, coconut, and cinnamon to the Instant Pot. Mix thoroughly until melted.

Pour mixture into a silicone mini-muffin mold.

Freeze until firm. Serve and enjoy! For leftovers, store in an airtight container in the freezer for up to one month.

Nutrition Facts
Amount per serving
Calories 494
Total Fat 46.1g
Total Carbohydrate 22.3g
Dietary Fiber 10.3g
Total Sugars 4.4g
Protein 5.5g

The Essential Instant Pot® Keto Cookbook

DECONSTRUCTED CHICKEN BREAKFAST TACOS

Serves 4

**Prep Time: 5 minutes, Cook Time: 10 minutes, Total Time: 15 minutes,
Pressure: High, Release: Quick**

Gluten Free, Soy Free, 25 Minutes or Less, Kid Friendly

This is one of my favorite go-to breakfast recipes, as it adds some kick and spice to my morning routine. As anyone who has been eating keto for a while knows, it is nice to not have an egg-based breakfast every single day. Try serving these deconstructed breakfast tacos with a side of guacamole or with a glass of warm coconut milk.

2 tablespoons avocado oil

1 pound chicken, ground

½ cup full fat Cheddar cheese, shredded (optional)

1 jalapeño pepper, finely chopped

1 teaspoon lime juice

1 teaspoon hot sauce

½ teaspoon kosher salt

½ teaspoon freshly ground black pepper

1 cup avocado, mashed

¾ cup sugar-free or low-sugar salsa

1 tablespoon sour cream, at room temperature (optional)

Nutrition Facts
Amount per serving
Calories 334
Total Fat 16.9g
Total Carbohydrate 7.6g
Dietary Fiber 3.7g
Total Sugars 2g
Protein 38.1g

Set the Instant Pot to Sauté and heat the oil.

Add the chicken, cheese (if using), jalapeño, lime juice, hot sauce, salt, black pepper, and ½ cup of filtered water.

Close the lid, set the pressure release to Sealing, and hit Cancel to stop the current program. Select Manual/Pressure Cook, set the Instant Pot to 10 minutes on high pressure, and let cook.

Once cooked, perform a quick release by carefully switching the pressure valve to Venting.

Open the Instant Pot and serve, topped with the avocado, salsa, sour cream (if using).

PUMPKIN PORRIDGE

Serves 2 to 4

**Prep Time: 5 minutes, Cook Time: 10 minutes, Total Time: 15 minutes,
Pressure: High, Release: Quick**

Gluten Free, Dairy Free, Soy Free, 25 Minutes or Less, Kid Friendly

Porridge is a classic example of a carb-heavy food that I bet you thought you would be giving up forever once you went keto. The good news is that this keto porridge is warm, savory, and full of flavor. I sometimes like to stir in a small amount of grass-fed butter as well as add an extra pinch of cinnamon. This helps to add even more healthy fat and gives the dish an extra punch of flavor.

¼ cup unsweetened coconut flakes

2 cups full-fat coconut milk

1 cup pecans, chopped

1 cup organic pumpkin purée

¼ cup organic coconut flour

½ teaspoon ginger, finely grated

½ teaspoon cinnamon, ground

Swerve, confectioners to taste (optional)

½ cup dark berries, to serve (optional)

Nutrition Facts
Amount per serving
Calories 506
Total Fat 40.6g
Total Carbohydrate 33.5g
Dietary Fiber 16.9g
Total Sugars 7.5g
Protein 8.2g

Set the Instant Pot to Sauté, and toast the coconut flakes, stirring frequently so that they do not burn. Add in 2 cups of filtered water, as well as the milk.

Close the lid, set the pressure release to Sealing, and select Manual/Pressure Cook, with high pressure. The timer should be set to 0.

When the Instant Pot beeps, very carefully switch the pressure release to Venting. Stir in the pecans, pumpkin, flour, ginger, cinnamon, and Swerve (if using). Let sit for about 2 to 4 minutes (or until desired consistency is reached), stirring occasionally.

Serve with the dark berries (if desired), and enjoy!

The Essential Instant Pot® Keto Cookbook

TRADITIONAL COFFEE CAKE

Serves 5 to 6

Prep Time: 5 minutes, Cook Time: 40 minutes, Total Time: 45 minutes, Pressure: High, Release: Natural

Gluten Free, Soy Free, Kid Friendly

Commercially prepared coffee cake is usually very high in sugar, but this re-imagining contains virtually none.

BASE

2 eggs

2 tablespoons salted grass-fed butter, softened

1 cup blanched almond flour

1 cup pecans, chopped

¼ cup sour cream, at room temperature

¼ cup full-fat cream cheese, softened

½ teaspoon salt

½ teaspoon cinnamon, ground

½ teaspoon nutmeg, ground

¼ teaspoon baking soda

TOPPING

1 cup sugar-free chocolate chips

1 cup pecans, chopped

½ cup Swerve, confectioners (or more, to taste)

½ cup heavy whipping cream

Nutrition Facts
Amount per serving
Calories 267
Total Fat 22.7g
Total Carbohydrate 8.9g
Dietary Fiber 1.6g
Total Sugars 0.8g
Protein 7.3g

Pour 1 cup of filtered water into the inner pot of the Instant Pot, then insert the trivet. Using an electric mixer, combine the eggs, butter, flour, pecans, sour cream, cream cheese, salt, cinnamon, nutmeg, and baking soda. Mix thoroughly. Transfer this mixture into a well-greased, Instant Pot–friendly pan (or dish).

Using a sling if desired, place the pan onto the trivet, and cover loosely with aluminum foil. Close the lid, set the pressure release to Sealing, and select Manual/Pressure Cook. Set the Instant Pot to 40 minutes on high pressure and let cook.

While cooking, in a large bowl, mix the chocolate chips, pecans, Swerve, and whipping cream thoroughly. Set aside.

Once cooked, let the pressure naturally disperse from the Instant Pot for about 10 minutes, then carefully switch the pressure release to Venting.

Open the Instant Pot and remove the pan. Evenly sprinkle the topping mixture over the cake. Let cool, serve, and enjoy!

BACON AND EGG BAKE

Serves 2 to 3

**Prep Time: 5 minutes, Cook Time: 19 minutes, Total Time: 24 minutes,
Pressure: High, Release: Natural**

Gluten Free, Soy Free, 25 Minutes or Less, Kid Friendly

Bacon and eggs—truly a breakfast classic. This keto bacon and egg bake is a great example of the "set it and forget it" simplicity of the Instant Pot. Once you've mixed all of your ingredients in your baking dish, you can go do something else! This is much more convenient than tending over a hot skillet. I also like to crumble a little extra-crispy bacon on top of each serving from time to time.

5 eggs

3 slices no-sugar-added bacon, cooked and finely chopped

2 tablespoons avocado oil

½ cup kale, chopped

½ cup broccoli, chopped

½ cup heavy whipping cream

½ teaspoon cayenne pepper, ground

½ teaspoon basil, dried

½ teaspoon kosher salt

½ teaspoon freshly ground black pepper

Nutrition Facts
Amount per serving
Calories 302
Total Fat 23.9g
Total Carbohydrate 4.5g
Dietary Fiber 1.1g
Total Sugars 0.9g
Protein 17.6g

Pour in 1 cup of filtered water into the inner pot of the Instant Pot, then insert trivet. In a large bowl, combine the eggs, bacon, oil, kale, broccoli, whipping cream, cayenne pepper, basil, salt, and black pepper. Mix thoroughly.

Transfer mixture into a well-greased Instant Pot–friendly dish, and cover loosely with aluminum foil.

Close the lid, set the pressure release to Sealing, and hit Cancel to stop the current program. Select Manual/Pressure Cook, set the Instant Pot to 19 minutes on high pressure, and let cook.

Once cooked, let the pressure naturally disperse from the Instant Pot for about 10 minutes, then carefully switch the pressure release to Venting.

Open the Instant Pot, serve, and enjoy!

The Essential Instant Pot® Keto Cookbook

CHOCOLATE CINNAMON ROLL FAT BOMBS

Serves 5 to 6

**Prep Time: 5 minutes, Cook Time: 5 minutes, Total Time: 10 minutes,
Pressure: N/A, Release: N/A**

Gluten Free, Soy Free, 10 Minutes or Less, Kid Friendly

Traditional cinnamon rolls are very high in carbohydrates, but this modified keto version cuts down carbs drastically. These fat bombs also contain no sugar, and are infused with chocolate—along with metabolism-boosting coconut butter. They work great as a post-workout snack when you are craving something sugary—or even when you just need to prepare a quick treat for a party.

2 tablespoons coconut oil

2 cups raw coconut butter

1 cup sugar-free chocolate chips

1 cup heavy whipping cream

½ cup Swerve, confectioners (or more, to taste)

½ teaspoon cinnamon, ground (or more, to taste)

½ teaspoon vanilla extract

Set the Instant Pot to Sauté and melt the oil.

Add the butter, chocolate chips, whipping cream, Swerve, cinnamon, and vanilla to the Instant Pot and cook. Stir occasionally until the mixture reaches a smooth consistency.

Pour mixture into a silicone mini-muffin mold.

Freeze until firm. Serve, and enjoy!

Nutrition Facts
Amount per serving
Calories 372
Total Fat 32.2g
Total Carbohydrate 15.1g
Dietary Fiber 6.8g
Total Sugars 0.1g
Protein 4.2g

BREAKFAST BURRITOS

Serves 4

**Prep Time: 5 minutes, Cook Time: 15 minutes, Total Time: 20 minutes,
Pressure: High, Release: Quick**

Gluten Free, Soy Free, 25 Minutes or Less, Kid Friendly

Burritos are one of my favorite pre-keto foods. This Instant Pot keto adaptation
provides all the flavor and protein of traditional burritos, but still allows you to keep
burning fat. If you find yourself coming back to this recipe often, try mixing it up by
replacing the chicken with steak or turkey. I also like to sometimes add a touch of lime
or green chile to give the "burritos" some extra, authentic, Mexican flavor.

2 tablespoons avocado oil

¼ cup grass-fed bone broth

1 pound chicken, ground

½ teaspoon cumin, ground

½ teaspoon cayenne pepper, ground

½ teaspoon chili powder

½ teaspoon kosher salt

½ teaspoon freshly ground black pepper

**¼ cup full-fat Cheddar cheese, shredded
(optional)**

lettuce, to wrap

½ cup avocado, mashed

**½ cup sugar-free or low-sugar salsa,
(optional)**

**¼ cup sour cream, at room temperature
(optional)**

Set the Instant Pot to Sauté and heat
the oil.

Pour in bone broth and ¾ cup of
filtered water. Add the chicken, cumin,
cayenne pepper, chili powder, salt, black
pepper, and cheese to the Instant Pot, and
mix thoroughly.

Close the lid, set the pressure release
to Sealing, and hit Cancel to stop the
current program. Select Manual/Pressure
Cook, set the Instant Pot to 15 minutes on
high pressure, and let cook.

Once cooked, carefully switch the
pressure release to Venting. Drain the meat
of any excess liquid, spoon the chicken
mixture onto a lettuce wrap to make the
burrito. Top with avocado and, if using,
salsa and sour cream.

Nutrition Facts
Amount per serving
Calories 293
Total Fat 13.5g
Total Carbohydrate 5.8g
Dietary Fiber 2.4g
Total Sugars 1.4g
Protein 36.5g

The Essential Instant Pot® Keto Cookbook

BIG CHOCOLATE CHIP PANCAKE

Serves 5 to 6

**Prep Time: 5 minutes, Cook Time: 37 minutes, Total Time: 42 minutes,
Pressure: Low, Release: Quick**

Gluten Free, Soy Free, Kid Friendly

One of the biggest downsides of going keto is the perceived loss of some foods. But fear not—this recipe for making a delicious low-carb pancake in the Instant Pot will make you feel like you have not given up anything at all. Try substituting a different variety of nuts in place of the walnuts, if you are feeling adventurous.

Note: This is one of the trickier recipes to really get right; your cooking time may vary slightly. Be sure to liberally grease the inside of the Instant Pot so your giant pancake does not stick.

4 tablespoons salted grass-fed butter, softened

2 cups blanched almond flour

1/2 cup Swerve, confectioners (or more, to taste)

1 1/4 cups full-fat coconut milk

1/4 cup sugar-free chocolate chips

1/4 cup organic coconut flour

2 eggs

1 tablespoon walnuts, chopped

1/4 teaspoon baking soda

1/2 teaspoon salt

1/2 cup of dark berries, to serve (optional)

Nutrition Facts
Amount per serving
Calories 369
Total Fat 31g
Total Carbohydrate 16.4g
Dietary Fiber 6.7g
Total Sugars 3.7g
Protein 6.6g

Grease the bottom and sides of your Instant Pot with the butter. Make sure you coat it very liberally.

In a large bowl, mix together the almond flour, Swerve, milk, chocolate chips, coconut flour, eggs, walnuts, baking soda, and salt. Add this mixture to the Instant Pot. Close the lid, set the pressure release to Sealing, and select Multigrain. Set the Instant Pot to 37 minutes on low pressure, and let cook.

Switch the pressure release to Venting and open the Instant Pot. Confirm your pancake is cooked, then carefully remove it using a spatula. Serve with the berries (if desired), and enjoy!

Breakfast

FAST AND EASY HUEVOS RANCHEROS

Serves 4

Prep Time: 5 minutes, Cook Time: 20 minutes, Total Time: 25 minutes, Pressure: High, Release: Quick

Gluten Free, Soy Free, 25 Minutes or Less, Kid Friendly

Huevos rancheros are one of my all-time favorite breakfast meals. I oftentimes like to ramp up the flavor of this dish by adding a touch of lime juice and/or an extra variety of cheese. When I need a little extra kick, I will add a small sliver of Bhut jolokia—also known as "ghost pepper."

2 tablespoons coconut oil

6 eggs

1 (14-ounce) can sugar-free or low-sugar crushed tomatoes

1 cup full-fat Cheddar cheese, shredded

½ teaspoon cilantro, dried

½ teaspoon chili powder

½ jalapeño, finely chopped

½ teaspoon kosher salt

½ teaspoon freshly ground black pepper

Nutrition Facts
Amount per serving
Calories 278
Total Fat 22.8g
Total Carbohydrate 3.2g
Dietary Fiber 0.6g
Total Sugars 1.9g
Protein 15.4g

Pour ½ cup of filtered water into the Instant Pot and insert the trivet. In a large bowl, combine the coconut oil, eggs, tomatoes, cheese, cilantro, chili powder, jalapeño, salt, and black pepper. Mix thoroughly. Transfer this mixture into a well-greased, Instant Pot–friendly dish. Cover dish loosely with aluminum foil.

Using a sling, transfer the dish to the Instant Pot and place on top of the trivet.

Close the lid, set the pressure release to Sealing, and hit Cancel to stop the current program. Select Manual/Pressure Cook, set the Instant Pot to 20 minutes on high pressure, and let cook.

Once cooked, carefully switch the pressure release to Venting.

Open the Instant Pot, remove the dish, serve, and enjoy!

The Essential Instant Pot® Keto Cookbook

SIMPLE PUMPKIN MUG MUFFIN

Serves 1

**Prep Time: 5 minutes, Cook Time: 9 minutes, Total Time: 14 minutes,
Pressure: High, Release: Quick**

Gluten Free, Dairy Free, Soy Free, 25 Minutes or Less, Kid Friendly

Is there a more fun or satisfying way to make an entire meal than inside a mug?
This sweet start to your day is a real treat to have, while still adhering to a keto-
friendly diet. To round out a truly healthy breakfast, try pairing this with some
protein and nutrient-dense vegetables, as well as some warm coconut milk
(or butter-infused coffee).

½ cup Swerve, confectioners

½ cup blanched almond flour

2 tablespoons organic pumpkin purée

1 teaspoon sugar-free chocolate chips

1 tablespoon organic coconut flour

1 egg

1 tablespoon coconut oil

½ teaspoon pumpkin pie spice

½ teaspoon nutmeg, ground

½ teaspoon cinnamon, ground

⅛ teaspoon baking soda

Nutrition Facts
Amount per serving
Calories 297
Total Fat 22g
Total Carbohydrate 17.5g
Dietary Fiber 8.2g
Total Sugars 1.9g
Protein 8.5g

Mix the Swerve, almond flour, pumpkin purée, chocolate chips, coconut flour, egg, coconut oil, pumpkin pie spice, nutmeg, cinnamon, and baking soda in a large bowl. Transfer this mixture into a well-greased, Instant Pot–friendly mug.

Pour 1 cup of filtered water into the inner pot of the Instant Pot, and insert the trivet. Cover the mug in foil and place on top of the trivet.

Close the lid, set the pressure release to Sealing, and select Manual/Pressure Cook. Set the Instant Pot to 9 minutes on high pressure.

Once cooked, release the pressure immediately by switching the valve to Venting. Be sure your muffin is done by inserting a toothpick into the cake and making sure it comes out clean, as cook times may vary.

Remove mug and enjoy!

Breakfast

MEXICAN BREAKFAST CHILI

Serves 4

Prep Time: 5 minutes, Cook Time: 45 minutes, Total Time: 50 minutes, Pressure: High, Release: Natural

Gluten Free, Soy Free, Kid Friendly

I am a big fan of chili (in all forms), and making chili in the Instant Pot is a total breeze. I like to add some extra cheese (and even some bacon) when I make this particular chili. But feel free to experiment on your own with a wide variety of spices, as this preparation is very versatile. As a bonus, it works great for lunch or dinner, as well!

2 tablespoons coconut oil

1 pound grass-fed beef, ground

1 (14-ounce) can sugar-free or low-sugar diced tomatoes

½ cup full-fat Cheddar cheese, shredded (optional)

1 teaspoon hot sauce

½ teaspoon chili powder

½ teaspoon crushed red pepper

½ teaspoon cumin, ground

½ teaspoon kosher salt

½ teaspoon freshly ground black pepper

Nutrition Facts
Amount per serving
Calories 351
Total Fat 18.7g
Total Carbohydrate 5.9g
Dietary Fiber 2g
Total Sugars 3.5g
Protein 39g

Set the Instant Pot to Sauté and melt the oil.

Pour in ½ cup of filtered water, then add the beef, tomatoes, cheese, hot sauce, chili powder, red pepper, cumin, salt, and black pepper to the Instant Pot, stirring thoroughly.

Close the lid, set the pressure release to Sealing, and hit Cancel to stop the current program. Select Manual/Pressure Cook, set the Instant Pot to 45 minutes on high pressure and let cook.

Once cooked, let the pressure naturally disperse from the Instant Pot for about 10 minutes, then carefully switch the pressure release to Venting.

Open the Instant Pot, serve, and enjoy!

The Essential Instant Pot® Keto Cookbook

SUPER FAT CASSEROLE

Serves 5

**Prep Time: 5 minutes, Cook Time: 15 minutes, Total Time: 20 minutes,
Pressure: High, Release: Quick**

Gluten Free, Soy Free, 25 Minutes or Less, Kid Friendly

One of the key aspects of a successful keto-friendly approach is making sure you are getting enough healthy fats. As your body shifts into burning fat for fuel, you have to provide it with plenty of raw materials. This casserole is loaded with healthy fats, and also has a good amount of protein, as well as flavor. It can also work as a lunch or dinner choice, and is easy to store refrigerated, so you have it ready throughout the week.

1 tablespoon avocado oil

1 tablespoon coconut oil

1 tablespoon unflavored MCT oil

1 avocado, mashed

1/2 cup full-fat Cheddar cheese, shredded

1/2 cup spinach, chopped

1/2 teaspoon basil, dried

1/2 teaspoon kosher salt

1/2 teaspoon freshly ground black pepper

1/4 cup sugar-free or low-sugar salsa

1/4 cup heavy whipping cream

1 pound chicken, ground

Nutrition Facts
Amount per serving
Calories 405
Total Fat 30.4g
Total Carbohydrate 4.8g
Dietary Fiber 3g
Total Sugars 0.7g
Protein 30.3g

Pour 1 cup of filtered water inside the inner pot of the Instant Pot, then insert the trivet.

In a large bowl, combine and mix the avocado oil, coconut oil, MCT oil, avocado, cheese, spinach, basil, salt, black pepper, salsa, and whipping cream.

In a greased Instant Pot-safe dish, add the ground chicken in an even layer. Pour the casserole mixture over the chicken and cover with aluminum foil. Using a sling, place this dish on top of the trivet.

Close the lid, set the pressure release to Sealing, and select Manual/Pressure Cook. Set the Instant Pot to 15 minutes on high pressure, and let cook.

Once cooked, carefully switch the pressure release to Venting. Open the Instant Pot, serve, and enjoy!

CLASSIC "OATMEAL"

Serves 4

**Prep Time: 5 minutes, Cook Time: 4 minutes, Total Time: 9 minutes,
Pressure: High, Release: Quick**

Gluten Free, Soy Free, 10 Minutes or Less, Kid Friendly

Oatmeal is one of those carb-heavy favorites that I bet you thought you left behind for good, once you went keto. Fortunately, not only is it easy to make keto-friendly oatmeal, the Instant Pot makes it even easier! I like to make a big batch of this oatmeal for the week, and sometimes I'll even stir in some protein powder or nuts to give it even more nutrients.

2 tablespoons coconut oil

1 cup full-fat coconut milk

1 cup heavy whipping cream

½ cup macadamia nuts

½ cup pecans, chopped

⅓ cup Swerve, confectioners (or more, to taste)

¼ cup unsweetened coconut flakes

2 tablespoons hazelnuts, chopped

2 tablespoons chia seeds

½ teaspoon cinnamon, ground

Nutrition Facts
Amount per serving
Calories 506
Total Fat 53g
Total Carbohydrate 11.4g
Dietary Fiber 6.5g
Total Sugars 3.3g
Protein 5.7g

Before you get started, soak the chia seeds for about 5 to 10 minutes (can be up to 20, if desired) in 1 cup of filtered water. After soaking, set the Instant Pot to Sauté and add the coconut oil. Once melted, pour in the milk, whipping cream, and 1 cup of filtered water. Then add the macadamia nuts, pecans, Swerve, coconut flakes, hazelnuts, chia seeds, and cinnamon. Mix thoroughly inside the Instant Pot.

Close the lid, set the pressure release to Sealing, and hit Cancel to stop the current program. Select Manual/Pressure Cook, set the Instant Pot to 4 minutes on high pressure, and let cook.

Once cooked, carefully switch the pressure release to Venting.

Open the Instant Pot, serve, and enjoy!

DECONSTRUCTED BREAKFAST CASSEROLE

Serves 4 to 5

Prep Time: 5 minutes, Cook Time: 5 minutes, Total Time: 10 minutes, Pressure: N/A, Release: N/A

Gluten Free, Soy Free, 10 Minutes or Less, Kid Friendly

This fun and healthy breakfast dish allows you to make an entire meal on Sauté mode, all inside the Instant Pot. If you are looking for a little extra flavor, try adding a dash of jalapeño to the mix, or some curry powder. This dish also pairs well with some keto-friendly guacamole and some coffee infused with butter (or MCT oil).

2 tablespoons coconut oil

1 pound turkey, ground

1/2 cup heavy cream

3 slices no-sugar-added bacon, cooked and crumbled

1 teaspoon oregano, dried

1 cup bell peppers, chopped

1/2 teaspoon crushed red pepper (optional)

1/2 teaspoon kosher salt

1/2 teaspoon freshly ground black pepper

1/4 cup full-fat Cheddar cheese, shredded (optional)

1/2 cup spinach, chopped

Set the Instant Pot to Sauté and melt the coconut oil.

Add the turkey and cook thoroughly, mix in the cream, bacon, oregano, bell peppers, red pepper, salt, black pepper, cheese (if using), and spinach, as the turkey cooks. Once turkey is browned and cooked all the way through (about 5 to 10 minutes), remove all food from the inner pot.

Serve and enjoy!

Nutrition Facts
Amount per serving
Calories 374
Total Fat 25.1g
Total Carbohydrate 3.2g
Dietary Fiber 0.6g
Total Sugars 1.3g
Protein 33.1g

TRADITIONAL PORRIDGE

Serves 4

Prep Time: 5 minutes, Cook Time: 4 minutes, Total Time: 9 minutes, Pressure: High, Release: Quick

Gluten Free, Soy Free, 10 Minutes or Less, Kid Friendly

Porridge is a breakfast classic, but this keto porridge really takes it to the next level. It has an ultra-simple preparation process, which makes it one of my favorite ways to wake up on a weekend morning, as I can do other things while I prepare a breakfast that is warm, toasty, and nutritious. An extra dash of cinnamon or coconut flakes to the top of each bowl is a simple way to add even more flavor.

2 tablespoons coconut oil

1 cup full-fat coconut milk

2 tablespoons blanched almond flour

2 tablespoons sugar-free chocolate chips

1 cup heavy whipping cream

1/2 cup cashews, chopped

1/2 cup pecans, chopped

1/2 teaspoon cinnamon, ground

1/2 teaspoon erythritol, powder (or more, to taste)

1/4 cup unsweetened coconut flakes

Nutrition Facts
Amount per serving
Calories 533
Total Fat 51.1g
Total Carbohydrate 16.1g
Dietary Fiber 4.5g
Total Sugars 4g
Protein 6.7g

Set the Instant Pot to Sauté and melt the coconut oil.

Pour in the coconut milk, 1 cup of filtered water, then combine and mix the flour, chocolate chips, whipping cream, cashews, pecans, cinnamon, erythritol, and coconut flakes, inside the Instant Pot.

Close the lid, set the pressure release to Sealing, and hit Cancel to stop the current program. Select Manual/Pressure Cook, set the Instant Pot to 4 minutes on high pressure, and let cook.

Once cooked, perform a quick release by carefully switching the pressure valve to Venting.

Open the Instant Pot, serve, and enjoy!

EGG BAKE

Serves 4 to 5

Prep Time: 5 minutes, Cook Time: 30 minutes, Total Time: 35 minutes, Pressure: High, Release: Quick

Gluten Free, Soy Free, Kid Friendly

Eggs are one of the most perfect foods, in terms of nutrition. This easy-to-make egg bake will provide you with healthy protein, as well as plenty of other nutrients, like choline and B_{12}. The turmeric packs a nice punch of anti-inflammatory benefits, and you can mix and match any number of side dishes with it.

6 eggs

2 tablespoons coconut oil

1 avocado, mashed

1 cup full-fat Monterey Jack cheese, shredded

1 cup spinach, chopped

½ pound no-sugar-added bacon, sliced finely, cooked

½ teaspoon basil, dried

½ teaspoon turmeric, ground

½ teaspoon cayenne pepper, ground

½ teaspoon crushed red pepper

½ teaspoon freshly ground black pepper

½ teaspoon kosher salt

Nutrition Facts
Amount per serving
Calories 537
Total Fat 44.4g
Total Carbohydrate 5.3g
Dietary Fiber 3g
Total Sugars 0.8g
Protein 30g

Pour 1 cup of filtered water into the inner pot of the Instant Pot, and place the trivet inside. In a large bowl, combine the eggs, coconut oil, avocado, cheese, spinach, bacon, basil, turmeric, cayenne pepper, red pepper, black pepper, and salt. Mix thoroughly. Transfer this mixture into a well-greased, Instant Pot–friendly dish. Cover loosely with aluminum foil. Using a sling if desired, place this dish on top of the trivet.

Close the lid, set the pressure release to Sealing, and hit Cancel to stop the current program. Select Manual/Pressure Cook, set the Instant Pot to 30 minutes on high pressure, and let cook.

Once cooked, perform a quick release by carefully switching the pressure valve to Venting. Open the Instant Pot, serve, and enjoy!

Breakfast

SUNRISE PIZZA

Serves 4 to 5

**Prep Time: 5 minutes, Cook Time: 20 minutes, Total Time: 25 minutes,
Pressure: High, Release: Natural**

Gluten Free, Soy Free, 25 Minutes or Less, Kid Friendly

Typically, pizza for breakfast would not be a healthy choice, but each serving of this entrée meets one third of your daily protein requirement. The basil and tomatoes in this dish also add a nice zest, so you start your day on a fresh note. I like to sprinkle crushed red pepper on top of the finished pie to provide some extra kick.

CRUST

2 eggs

2 tablespoons salted grass-fed butter, softened

1 pound chicken, ground

1 cup full-fat Parmesan cheese, grated

⅓ cup blanched almond flour

TOPPING

1 (14-ounce) can fire roasted sugar-free or low-sugar tomatoes, drained

2 cups full-fat mozzarella cheese, shredded

1 cup spinach, chopped

½ teaspoon basil, dried

½ teaspoon crushed red pepper

½ teaspoon oregano, dried

½ teaspoon cilantro, dried

Nutrition Facts
Amount per serving
Calories 405
Total Fat 21.9g
Total Carbohydrate 5g
Dietary Fiber 0.9g
Total Sugars 1.5g
Protein 46.7g

Pour 1 cup of filtered water into the inner pot of the Instant Pot, then insert the trivet. In a large bowl, combine the eggs, butter, chicken, cheese, and flour. Mix thoroughly. Transfer this mixture into a greased, Instant Pot–friendly dish. Cover loosely with aluminum foil. Using a sling, place this dish on top of the trivet.

Close the lid, set the pressure release to Sealing, and select Manual/Pressure Cook. Set the Instant Pot to 10 minutes on high pressure and let cook.

Meanwhile, in a small bowl, mix together basil, red pepper, oregano, and cilantro, and set aside.

Once the crust is cooked, carefully switch the pressure release to Venting. Open the Instant Pot and add the tomatoes in an even layer, followed by the mozzarella cheese and the spinach. Sprinkle the spice and herb mixture over the top of the pizza. Loosely re-cover dish with aluminum foil.

The Essential Instant Pot® Keto Cookbook

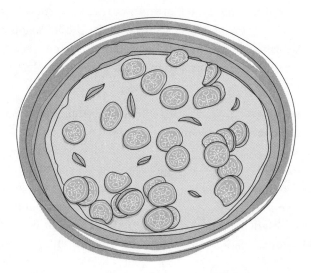

Close the lid to the Instant Pot, set the pressure release to Sealing, and select Manual/Pressure Cook. Set the Instant Pot to 10 minutes on high pressure and let cook again.

Once cooked, let the pressure naturally disperse from the Instant Pot for about 10 minutes, then carefully switch the pressure release to Venting.

Open the Instant Pot, serve, and enjoy!

FAST AND EASY SHAKSHUKA

Serves 2 to 4

**Prep Time: 5 minutes, Cook Time: 5 minutes, Total Time: 10 minutes,
Pressure: High, Release: Quick**

Gluten Free, Soy Free, 10 Minutes or Less, Kid Friendly

Shakshuka is a dish that originated in North Africa, but its taste appeals across many cultures. An easy way to think of it is as a similar flavor profile to a pizza, but without the crust. Making shakshuka in the Instant Pot could not be easier, as it is ready to eat after just 5 minutes of cooking. This also makes a great "breakfast for dinner" dish.

2 tablespoons coconut oil

2 cups full-fat Cheddar cheese, shredded

1 garlic clove, minced

½ teaspoon cilantro, dried

½ teaspoon cayenne pepper, ground

½ teaspoon cumin, ground

½ teaspoon oregano, dried

½ teaspoon freshly ground black pepper

½ teaspoon kosher salt

1 (14-ounce) can roasted sugar-free or low-sugar tomatoes

6 eggs

Nutrition Facts
Amount per serving
Calories 397
Total Fat 32.2g
Total Carbohydrate 4.5g
Dietary Fiber 0.8g
Total Sugars 2.4g
Protein 22.6g

Set the Instant Pot to Sauté and melt the coconut oil.

Add the cheese, garlic, cilantro, cayenne pepper, cumin, oregano, black pepper, salt, and tomatoes to the Instant Pot, and stir thoroughly.

Once combined, carefully crack the eggs into the mixture, maintaining the yolks. Make sure they are spaced evenly apart.

Close the lid, set the pressure release to Sealing, and hit Cancel to stop the current program. Select Manual/Pressure Cook, set the Instant Pot to 1 minute on high pressure, and let cook.

Once cooked, perform a quick release by carefully switching the pressure valve to Venting.

Open the Instant Pot, serve, and enjoy!

The Essential Instant Pot® Keto Cookbook

SIMPLE BREAKFAST CEREAL

Serves 4

**Prep Time: 5 minutes, Cook Time: 5 minutes, Total Time: 10 minutes,
Pressure: High, Release: Natural**

Gluten Free, Soy Free, 10 Minutes or Less, Kid Friendly

Cereal—the most traditional American breakfast food there is. Most followers of a paleo diet probably long ago gave up cereal—but there are always workarounds. More surprising, there are even keto-friendly cereal recipes—and this one is my personal favorite creations. The nuts provide a nice crispiness and satisfying texture, while the Instant Pot does the heavy lifting.

2 tablespoons coconut oil

1 cup full-fat coconut milk

½ cup cashews, chopped

½ cup heavy whipping cream

½ cup pecans, chopped

⅓ cup Swerve, confectioners (or more, to taste; optional)

¼ cup unsweetened coconut flakes

2 tablespoons flax seeds

2 tablespoons hazelnuts, chopped

2 tablespoons macadamia nuts, chopped

½ teaspoon cinnamon, ground

½ teaspoon nutmeg, ground

½ teaspoon turmeric, ground

Nutrition Facts
Amount per serving
Calories 455
Total Fat 44.6g
Total Carbohydrate 13.1g
Dietary Fiber 4.5g
Total Sugars 3.8g
Protein 6.2g

Set the Instant Pot to Sauté and melt the coconut oil. Pour in the coconut milk.

Add the cashews, whipping cream, pecans, Swerve, coconut flakes, flax seeds, hazelnuts, macadamia nuts, cinnamon, nutmeg, and turmeric to the Instant Pot. Stir thoroughly.

Close the lid, set the pressure release to Sealing, and hit Cancel to stop the current program. Select Manual/Pressure Cook, set the Instant Pot to 5 minutes on high pressure, and let cook.

Once cooked, let the pressure naturally disperse from the Instant Pot for about 10 minutes, then carefully switch the pressure release to Venting.

Open the Instant Pot, serve, and enjoy!

CAULIFLOWER BREAKFAST PUDDING

IPM

Serves 2

Prep Time: 5 minutes, Cook Time: 5 minutes, Total Time: 10 minutes, Pressure: High, Release: Natural

Gluten Free, Soy Free, 10 Minutes or Less, Kid Friendly

A classic breakfast choice, rice pudding is also very high in sugar and carbohydrates. This cauliflower keto adaptation cuts down drastically on the carbs, but packs in even more flavor. This small serving is also perfectly suited for the Instant Pot Mini.

2 tablespoons grass-fed butter

⅓ cup riced cauliflower

¼ cup Swerve confectioners (or more, to taste)

½ cup full-fat coconut milk

½ cup pecans, chopped

½ cup heavy whipping cream

Combine the butter, cauliflower, Swerve, and coconut milk into the inner pot of the Instant Pot, and stir thoroughly.

Close the lid, set the valve to Sealing, and select Manual/Pressure Cook. Set the Instant Pot to 5 minutes, on high pressure.

Once cooked, allow the pressure to naturally disperse, then stir in the pecans and heavy whipping cream.

Nutrition Facts
Amount per serving
Calories 354
Total Fat 36.4g
Total Carbohydrate 7.7g
Dietary Fiber 3.1g
Total Sugars 3.3g
Protein 3.7g

SPINACH FRITTATA

Serves 4 to 5

Prep Time: 5 minutes, Cook Time: 20 minutes, Total Time: 25 minutes, Pressure: High, Release: Natural

Gluten Free, Soy Free, 25 Minutes or Less, Kid Friendly

A delicious, easy, and versatile recipe. This frittata is one of my go-to recipes, as it does not require too much thought or effort (great for a busy weeknight). Nonetheless, it also works well for entertaining guests, as it ends up looking a lot more complicated than it actually is. This traditional Italian dish can also easily be customized to fit all your favorite inclinations, as well. Try adding different vegetables, herbs, or spices to create a whole new variation of a keto-friendly frittata

6 eggs

1 cup spinach, chopped

1 cup full-fat Cheddar cheese, shredded

1 cup full-fat Monterey Jack cheese, shredded (optional)

2 tablespoons coconut oil

1 cup bell peppers, chopped

½ teaspoon parsley, dried

½ teaspoon basil, dried

½ teaspoon turmeric, ground

½ teaspoon freshly ground black pepper

½ teaspoon kosher salt

Nutrition Facts

Amount per serving
Calories 310
Total Fat 25.2g
Total Carbohydrate 3.4g
Dietary Fiber 0.7g
Total Sugars 1.9g
Protein 18.4g

Pour 1 cup of filtered water into the inner pot of the Instant Pot, then insert the trivet.

In a large bowl, combine the eggs, spinach, Cheddar cheese, Monterey Jack cheese, coconut oil, bell peppers, parsley, basil, turmeric, black pepper, and salt, and stir thoroughly. Transfer this mixture into a well-greased Instant Pot–friendly dish.

Using a sling if desired, place the dish onto the trivet, and cover loosely with aluminum foil. Close the lid, set the pressure release to Sealing, and select Manual/Pressure Cook. Set the Instant Pot to 20 minutes on high pressure, and let cook.

Once cooked, let the pressure naturally disperse from the Instant Pot for about 10 minutes, then carefully switch the pressure release to Venting.

Open the Instant Pot, serve, and enjoy!

COCONUT YOGURT

Serves 4

Prep Time: 5 minutes, Cook Time: 8 hours, Total Time: 8 hours, 5 minutes
Pressure: High, Release: Natural

Gluten Free, Soy Free, Kid Friendly

This cool treat is great for your gut, providing many different
strains of beneficial bacteria.

6 (13-ounce) cans full-fat coconut milk

3 probiotic capsules

½ cup heavy whipping cream

½ cup dark berries, fresh (optional, to serve)

Nutrition Facts
Amount per Serving
Calories 476
Total Fat 50.5g
Total Carbohydrate 1.7g
Dietary Fiber 0.5g
Sugars 0.9g
Protein 10g

From each coconut milk can, scrape the cream layer off the top, then place the cream into the inner pot of the Instant Pot. Cover and reserve the remaining coconut milk layer in the refrigerator.

Close the lid, set the pressure release to Sealing, and select Yogurt. Hit Adjust until Boil is displayed.

Once cooked (the Instant Pot will beep to notify you), hit Cancel, open the lid, and remove the inner pot. Be careful where you place it, as it will be very hot.

Once the coconut cream is cooled to 100°F (use a meat thermometer to check), break open the probiotic capsules, and gently stir in their contents.

Return the inner pot to the Instant Pot, close the lid, set the pressure release to Sealing, and select Yogurt. Set the Instant Pot to 8 hours.

Once done, open the Instant Pot and thoroughly stir in the whipping cream. Scoop the yogurt into an airtight container (or simply keep it in the inner pot), and store in the refrigerator for up to 5 days.

The Essential Instant Pot® Keto Cookbook

ZUCCHINI FRIES WITH BACON AND EGGS

Serves 4

**Prep Time: 5 minutes, Cook Time: 20 minutes, Total Time: 25 minutes,
Pressure: High, Release: Quick**

Gluten Free, Soy Free, 25 Minutes or Less, Kid Friendly

In case you have never had zucchini fries, you are in for a treat.

ZUCCHINI FRIES
4 zucchinis, sliced into wedges

2 tablespoons blanched almond flour

1 cup full-fat Parmesan cheese

½ teaspoon kosher salt

½ teaspoon garlic powder

½ teaspoon crushed red pepper

BACON AND EGGS
2 tablespoons coconut oil

6 eggs

6 slices no-sugar-added bacon

Nutrition Facts
Amount per serving
Calories 522
Total Fat 37.8g
Total Carbohydrate 9.9g
Dietary Fiber 2.3g
Total Sugars 4g
Protein 39.4g

Pour 1 cup of filtered water into the inner pot of the Instant Pot, then insert the trivet. In a large bowl, thoroughly combine the zucchini fry ingredients and transfer this mixture to a well-greased, Instant Pot–friendly dish.

Using a sling if desired, place the dish onto the trivet, and cover loosely with aluminum foil. Close the lid, set the pressure release to Sealing, and select Manual/Pressure Cook. Set the Instant Pot to 20 minutes on high pressure and let cook.

Once cooked, carefully switch the pressure release to Venting. Open the lid and remove the dish. Set the zucchini fries aside, loosely covered with foil to keep them warm.

Pour out the remaining water and set the Instant Pot to Sauté. Melt the coconut oil.

Add in the eggs and bacon to the Instant Pot, and stir thoroughly, continuously.

Once bacon and eggs are both fully cooked (about 5 to 7 minutes) remove from the Instant Pot, and serve alongside the zucchini fries.

DONUT MUFFINS

Serves 7

Prep Time: 5 minutes, Cook Time: 20 minutes, Total Time: 25 minutes, Pressure: High, Release: Natural

Gluten Free, Soy Free, 25 Minutes or Less, Kid Friendly

Donuts and muffins. I doubt that I really need to explain the appeal of this one!

BASE

2 tablespoons grass-fed butter, softened

2 eggs

2 cups blanched almond flour

1/2 cup Swerve, confectioners (or more, to taste)

1/2 teaspoon nutmeg, ground

1/2 teaspoon cinnamon, ground

1/2 teaspoon salt

1/4 teaspoon baking soda

TOPPING

1 cup heavy whipping cream

1/2 cup Swerve, granular

Nutrition Facts
Amount per serving
Calories 153
Total Fat 15g
Total Carbohydrate 1.9g
Dietary Fiber 0.6g
Total Sugars 0.2g
Protein 3.3g

Pour 1 cup of filtered water into the inner pot of the Instant Pot, then insert the trivet. In a large bowl, combine the base ingredients, mixing thoroughly. Working in batches if needed, evenly distribute the mixture into a well-greased, Instant Pot–friendly egg bites mold. I prefer to stack two egg bites molds on top of each other, separating them with Mason jar lids (or similar dividers).

Using a sling if desired, place the pan onto the trivet, and cover loosely with aluminum foil. Close the lid, set the pressure release to Sealing, and select Manual/Pressure Cook. Set the Instant Pot to 20 minutes on high pressure and let cook.

Once cooked, let the pressure naturally disperse from the Instant Pot for about 10 minutes, then carefully switch the pressure release to Venting.

Open the Instant Pot and remove the dish. Let cool. While cooling, whisk together the whipping cream and Swerve (use a mixer, if desired). Once the muffins have completely cooled, drizzle icing over each, serve, and enjoy!

CRUSTLESS KALE QUICHE

Serves 4 to 5

Prep Time: 5 minutes, Cook Time: 20 minutes, Total Time: 25 minutes, Pressure: High, Release: Natural

Gluten Free, Soy Free, 25 Minutes or Less, Kid Friendly

Quiche was never one of my favorite foods growing up. But I have grown to love this version, as it packs some of my favorite foods all into one, easy-to-make dish. A fast, simple, and nutritious choice for any keto breakfast.

½ cup whole-milk ricotta cheese

½ cup full-fat Cheddar cheese, shredded

½ cup kale, chopped

6 eggs

6 slices no-sugar-added bacon, cooked and finely chopped

¼ cup full-fat coconut milk

2 tablespoons coconut oil

½ teaspoon freshly ground black pepper

½ teaspoon parsley, dried

½ teaspoon kosher salt

½ teaspoon basil, dried

¼ (4-ounce) small onion, thinly sliced

Nutrition Facts
Amount per serving
Calories 340
Total Fat 22.7g
Total Carbohydrate 3.4g
Dietary Fiber 0.5g
Total Sugars 1.3g
Protein 13.1g

Pour 1 cup of filtered water into the inner pot of the Instant Pot, then insert the trivet.

In a large bowl, combine the ricotta cheese, Cheddar cheese, kale, eggs, bacon, milk, oil, black pepper, parsley, salt, basil, coconut, and onion, and stir thoroughly. Then, transfer this mixture to a well-greased Instant Pot–friendly dish.

Place the dish onto the trivet, and cover loosely with aluminum foil. Close the lid, set the pressure release to Sealing, and select Manual/Pressure Cook. Set the Instant Pot to 20 minutes on high pressure and let cook.

Once cooked, let the pressure naturally disperse from the Instant Pot for about 10 minutes, then carefully switch the pressure release to Venting.

Open the Instant Pot, serve, and enjoy!

AVOCADO BREAKFAST BURGER

Serves 2

Prep Time: 5 minutes, Cook Time: 10 minutes, Total Time: 15 minutes, Pressure: N/A, Release: N/A

Gluten Free, Soy Free, 25 Minutes or Less, Kid Friendly

Packed with monounsaturated fatty acids, the avocado is a staple on any good keto meal plan. This breakfast burger starts your day off with the healthy fats of the avocado, as well as a generous portion of protein from the eggs. Try topping with a little hot sauce to wake up your taste buds.

2 tablespoons coconut oil

3 slices no-sugar-added bacon

2 eggs

½ cup full-fat Cheddar cheese, shredded

½ teaspoon freshly ground black pepper

½ teaspoon kosher salt

1 cup lettuce, shredded

1 avocado, halved and pitted

2 tablespoons sesame seeds

Set the Instant Pot to Sauté and melt the coconut oil.

Add bacon, eggs, cheese, pepper, and salt. Stir thoroughly and continuously.

Once fully cooked, remove from the Instant Pot. Use the avocado as your bun, placing the food on top, then add the lettuce. Complete the breakfast burger by adding the other half of the avocado on top, then sprinkling with the sesame seeds.

Nutrition Facts
Amount per serving
Calories 612
Total Fat 55.2g
Total Carbohydrate 12.6g
Dietary Fiber 8.1g
Total Sugars 1.3g
Protein 20.8g

CLASSIC HOT CHOCOLATE

Serves 2

Prep Time: 5 minutes, Cook Time: 2 minutes, Total Time: 7 minutes, Pressure: High, Release: Natural

Gluten Free, Soy Free, 10 Minutes or Less, Kid Friendly

Hot chocolate is a sugary treat usually reserved for the dead of winter. However, this keto version is sugar free and completely delicious. Try adding coconut creamer or a touch of grass-fed butter to add even more flavor and richness.

2 tablespoons coconut oil

2 cups full-fat coconut milk

6 tablespoons sugar-free chocolate chips

4 tablespoons raw cacao nibs

½ teaspoon cinnamon, ground

¼ cup heavy whipping cream

Nutrition Facts
Amount Per Serving
Calories 451
Total Fat 40.7g
Total Carbohydrate 24.3g
Dietary Fiber 8.0g
Total Sugars 6.9g
Protein 0g

Set the Instant Pot to Sauté and melt the coconut oil.

Pour in the coconut milk, and then add the chocolate chips, cacao nibs, cinnamon, and whipping cream. Stir thoroughly.

Close the lid, set the pressure release to Sealing, and hit Cancel to stop the current program. Select Manual/Pressure Cook, set the Instant Pot to 2 minutes on high pressure, and let cook.

Once cooked, let the pressure naturally disperse from the Instant Pot for about 10 minutes, then carefully switch the pressure release to Venting.

Open the Instant Pot, serve, and enjoy!

SIMPLE BACON AND EGGS

Serves 2

Prep Time: 5 minutes, Cook Time: 10 minutes, Total Time: 15 minutes, Pressure: N/A, Release: N/A

Gluten Free, Soy Free, 25 Minutes or Less, Kid Friendly

A true American combination, this classic breakfast pairing works well with any low-carb approach. One trick to getting the best tasting bacon and eggs is to never overcook the eggs, but to slightly overcook the bacon.

6 eggs

2 tablespoons grass-fed butter, softened

6 slices no-sugar-added bacon

½ teaspoon freshly ground black pepper

½ teaspoon kosher salt

Nutrition Facts
Amount per serving
Calories 608
Total Fat 49g
Total Carbohydrate 2.2g
Dietary Fiber 0.1g
Total Sugars 1g
Protein 37.8g

Whisk the eggs and set aside. Set the Instant Pot to Sauté and melt the butter. Add the bacon and let cook until it begins to crisp.

Add the eggs, pepper, and salt to the Instant Pot, and stir thoroughly and continuously.

Once bacon and eggs are both fully cooked, remove from the Instant Pot, serve, and enjoy!

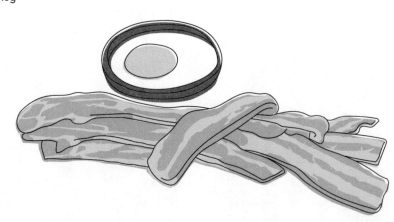

The Essential Instant Pot® Keto Cookbook

CAULIFLOWER HASH

Serves 4

Prep Time: 5 minutes, Cook Time: 10 minutes, Total Time: 15 minutes, Pressure: N/A, Release: N/A

Gluten Free, Soy Free, 25 Minutes or Less, Kid Friendly

Hash browns are a traditional breakfast side, but they are a bit high in carbohydrates to truly fit a keto approach. This is where cauliflower comes in. Browning nicely, but still keeping our net carbs low, this is the perfect keto-friendly side for any breakfast recipe.

2 tablespoons grass-fed butter, softened

1 pound cauliflower, chopped into small pieces

½ teaspoon paprika, fresh

½ teaspoon freshly ground black pepper

½ teaspoon garlic

½ teaspoon kosher salt

Nutrition Facts
Amount per serving
Calories 85
Total Fat 6.2g
Total Carbohydrate 6.4g
Dietary Fiber 3g
Total Sugars 2.8g
Protein 2.3g

Set the Instant Pot to Sauté and melt the butter.

Add the cauliflower to the Instant Pot, then mix in paprika, ground pepper, garlic, and salt. Continue to stir until fully cooked (hash will be cooked when browned).

Remove from the Instant Pot, serve, and enjoy!

PUMPKIN PIE FAT BOMBS

IPM

Serves 12

Prep Time: 5 minutes, Cook Time: 5 minutes, Total Time: 10 minutes, Pressure: N/A, Release: N/A

Gluten Free, Soy Free, 10 Minutes or Less, Kid Friendly

Pumpkin pie is one of my all-time favorite holiday treats. These fat bombs—made perfectly in your Instant Pot Mini—bring back all the fond memories of holiday gatherings, but don't have any of the downsides of consuming too much sugar.

3 tablespoons grass-fed butter, softened

1 cup raw coconut butter

½ cup pecans, chopped

1 cup organic pumpkin purée

½ teaspoon pumpkin pie spice (or more, to taste)

Nutrition Facts
Amount per serving (2)
Calories 199
Total Fat 22.1g
Total Carbohydrate 1.9g
Dietary Fiber 0.7g
Total Sugars 0.7g
Protein 0.4g

Set the Instant Pot to Sauté and melt the grass-fed butter.

Add the coconut butter, pecans, pumpkin purée, and pumpkin pie spice to the Instant Pot. Mix thoroughly, until smooth and melted.

Pour mixture evenly into a silicone mini-muffin mold.

Refrigerate (or freeze) until firm. Serve and enjoy! Store any leftovers in the freezer.

The Essential Instant Pot® Keto Cookbook

FAST AND EASY CANJA DE GALINHA

Serves 4

Prep Time: 5 minutes, Cook Time: 5 minutes, Total Time: 10 minutes, Pressure: High, Release: Quick

Gluten Free, Soy Free, 10 Minutes or Less, Kid Friendly

This traditional Portuguese soup makes for a unique breakfast. Our keto-friendly adaptation replaces the potatoes and rice, and brings down the overall amount of carbohydrates. Canja de Galinha is also an immune-friendly soup, and works just as well at lunchtime or dinnertime. Sprinkle in your favorite immune-boosting herbs and spices (like turmeric) to add even more beneficial nutrients.

4 cups grass-fed bone broth

1 pound chicken breasts, cooked and shredded

1 cup cauliflower, chopped

2 tablespoons grass-fed butter, softened

1/2 teaspoon parsley, dried

1/2 teaspoon garlic

1/4 (4-ounce) small onion, thinly sliced

2 bay leaves

Nutrition Facts
Amount per serving
Calories 217
Total Fat 8.7g
Total Carbohydrate 2.3g
Dietary Fiber 0.9g
Total Sugars 0.9g
Protein 31.3g

Add the bone broth, chicken, cauliflower, butter, parsley, garlic, onion, and bay leaves to the Instant Pot. Stir thoroughly.

Close the lid, set the pressure release to Sealing, and hit Cancel to stop the current program. Select Manual/Pressure Cook, set the Instant Pot to 5 minutes on high pressure, and let cook.

Once cooked, perform a quick release by carefully switching the pressure valve to Venting. Open the Instant Pot, serve, and enjoy!

TRADITIONAL SCONES

Serves 7

Prep Time: 5 minutes, Cook Time: 40 minutes, Total Time: 45 minutes, Pressure: High, Release: Natural

Gluten Free, Soy Free, Kid Friendly

Scones are a traditional treat from the United Kingdom, and it is relatively easy to adapt them for a keto diet. By using a more favorable keto-friendly flour, we avoid the pitfalls of traditional pastries. Try adding some nuts or shredded coconut to ramp up the flavor of the finished scones, or use a small amount of dark berries instead of the chocolate chips.

BASE
2 tablespoons grass-fed butter, softened

2 eggs

1 cup blanched almond flour

1/2 cup Swerve, confectioners (or more, to taste)

1/2 teaspoon vanilla extract

1/4 teaspoon baking soda

TOPPING
1/4 cup sugar-free chocolate chips

1/4 cup heavy whipping cream

1/2 cup Swerve, confectioners (or more, to taste)

Nutrition Facts
Amount per serving
Calories 133
Total Fat 11.7g
Total Carbohydrate 2.8g
Dietary Fiber 0.5g
Total Sugars 0.2g
Protein 3.8g

Pour 1 cup of filtered water into the inner pot of the Instant Pot, then insert the trivet. In a large bowl, combine the butter, eggs, almond flour, Swerve, vanilla, and baking soda, and mix thoroughly. Then, transfer this mixture to a well-greased Instant Pot–friendly pan (or dish).

Using a sling if desired, place the pan onto the trivet, and cover loosely with aluminum foil. Close the lid, set the pressure release to Sealing, and select Manual/Pressure Cook. Set the Instant Pot to 40 minutes on high pressure, and let cook.

Once cooked, let the pressure naturally disperse from the Instant Pot for about 10 minutes, then carefully switch the pressure release to Venting.

Open the Instant Pot and remove the dish. Let the scones cool for 15 minutes in the pan. Turn the uncut scone out onto a cookie sheet or serving dish and cut

into triangle-shaped wedges to form the individual scones.

Meanwhile, in a small bowl, mix together the chocolate chips, whipping cream, and Swerve, then microwave the mixture for 30 seconds (or until melted and smooth). Drizzle or spread the topping evenly over the scones. Allow the scones to finish cooling, then serve and enjoy!

BACON AND EGG CASSEROLE

Serves 4 to 5

**Prep Time: 5 minutes, Cook Time: 20 minutes, Total Time: 25 minutes,
Pressure: High, Release: Natural**

Gluten Free, Soy Free, 25 Minutes or Less, Kid Friendly

This filling and flavorful breakfast dish gets even easier in the Instant Pot. Once you have your ingredients assembled, it's as easy as closing the lid and walking away. If you want to mix things up a bit, you can substitute the bacon with ham. Simple, easy, and delicious!

6 eggs

6 slices no-sugar-added bacon, cooked and crumbled

2 tablespoons coconut oil

1 cup full-fat Cheddar cheese, shredded

1 cup full-fat Monterey Jack cheese, shredded

1 cup broccoli, chopped

½ teaspoon cayenne pepper, ground

½ teaspoon crushed red pepper

½ teaspoon paprika, fresh

½ teaspoon freshly ground black pepper

½ teaspoon kosher salt

Nutrition Facts
Amount per serving
Calories 429
Total Fat 34.7g
Total Carbohydrate 2.8g
Dietary Fiber 0.7g
Total Sugars 1g
Protein 26.8g

Pour 1 cup of filtered water into the inner pot of the Instant Pot, then insert the trivet. In a large bowl, mix the eggs, bacon, coconut oil, Cheddar, Monterey Jack, broccoli, cayenne pepper, red pepper, paprika, black pepper, and salt. Then, transfer this mixture to a well-greased Instant Pot–friendly dish.

Using a sling if desired, place the dish onto the trivet, and cover loosely with aluminum foil. Close the lid, set the pressure release to Sealing, and select Manual/Pressure Cook. Set the Instant Pot to 20 minutes on high pressure, and let cook.

Once cooked, let the pressure naturally disperse from the Instant Pot for about 10 minutes, then carefully switch the pressure release to Venting.

Open the Instant Pot, serve, and enjoy!

CAULIFLOWER EGG MUFFINS

Serves 4

**Prep Time: 5 minutes, Cook Time: 20 minutes, Total Time: 25 minutes,
Pressure: High, Release: Natural**

Gluten Free, Soy Free, 25 Minutes or Less, Kid Friendly

Do you remember mini pizza bagels? If so, these low-carb egg muffins may seem very familiar to you. The Instant Pot makes cooking these even easier, and they work just as well for breakfast as they do as an appetizer at dinner parties. Try different varieties of keto-friendly cheese to spice things up, or add in some jalapeño.

6 eggs
2 tablespoons grass-fed butter, softened
1 tablespoon coconut milk
1 cup mozzarella cheese, shredded
½ cup full-fat Cheddar cheese, shredded
16 uncured pepperoni slices (optional)
½ cup riced cauliflower, cooked
½ cup spinach, chopped
½ cup bell peppers, chopped
½ teaspoon basil, dried
½ teaspoon oregano, dried
½ teaspoon parsley, dried
½ teaspoon freshly ground black pepper
½ teaspoon kosher salt

Nutrition Facts
Amount per serving
Calories 354
Total Fat 29.2g
Total Carbohydrate 3.4g
Dietary Fiber 0.8g
Total Sugars 1.8g
Protein 19.5g

Pour 1 cup of filtered water into the inner pot of the Instant Pot, then insert the trivet. In a large bowl, mix the eggs, butter, milk, mozzarella, Cheddar, pepperoni, cauliflower, spinach, bell peppers, basil, oregano, parsley, black pepper, and salt.

Once mixed, transfer into a well-greased Instant Pot–friendly muffin pan, filling evenly.

Place the pan onto the trivet, and cover loosely with aluminum foil. Close the lid, set the pressure release to Sealing, and select Manual/Pressure Cook. Set the Instant Pot to 20 minutes on high pressure, and let cook.

Once cooked, let the pressure naturally disperse from the Instant Pot for about 10 minutes, then carefully switch the pressure release to Venting.

Open the Instant Pot, serve, and enjoy!

GLUTEN-FREE ZUCCHINI BREAD

Serves 5 to 6

**Prep Time: 5 minutes, Cook Time: 40 minutes, Total Time: 45 minutes,
Pressure: High, Release: Natural**

Gluten Free, Dairy Free, Soy Free, Kid Friendly

This holiday favorite is a little bit on the higher end of the acceptable
carbohydrate range, so watch your portion sizes.

3 eggs

1 cup blanched almond flour

¾ cup zucchini, grated

1 teaspoon vanilla extract

¼ teaspoon baking soda

**½ cup Swerve, confectioners (or more,
to taste)**

½ teaspoon nutmeg, ground

½ teaspoon cinnamon, ground

½ teaspoon salt

Nutrition Facts
Calories 207
Total Fat 19.4g
Total Carbohydrate 3.6g
Dietary Fiber 1.2g
Total Sugars 0.8g
Protein 5.9g

In a large bowl, mix the eggs, flour, zucchini, vanilla, baking soda, Swerve, nutmeg, cinnamon, and salt. Stir thoroughly.

Pour 1 cup of filtered water into the Instant Pot, and insert the trivet. Transfer the mixture from the bowl into a well-greased Instant Pot–friendly pan (or dish).

Using a sling if desired, place the pan onto the trivet, and cover loosely with aluminum foil. Close the lid, set the pressure release to Sealing, and select Manual/Pressure Cook. Set the Instant Pot to 40 minutes on high pressure, and let cook.

Once cooked, let the pressure naturally leave the Instant Pot, for about 10 minutes, then switch the pressure release to Venting.

Open the Instant Pot and remove the pan. If desired, finish bread by removing foil and placing pan on a baking sheet. Place the baking sheet in a 350°F oven for 2 to 3 minutes (or until desired texture is reached).

Let cool, and enjoy!

The Essential Instant Pot® Keto Cookbook

CLASSIC STEAK AND EGGS

Serves 2 to 3

**Prep Time: 5 minutes, Cook Time: 20 minutes, Total Time: 25 minutes,
Pressure: High, Release: Quick**

Gluten Free, Dairy Free, Soy Free, 25 Minutes or Less, Kid Friendly

Steak and eggs is a high-protein classic, and it is by far one of the most delicious keto breakfasts to choose from. Cooking this in the Instant Pot only makes things easier. Try pairing this with a side of avocado, guacamole, or even bacon.

2 tablespoons avocado oil

½ pound sirloin steak

6 eggs

½ teaspoon parsley, dried

½ teaspoon freshly ground black pepper

½ teaspoon kosher salt

Nutrition Facts
Amount per serving
Calories 280
Total Fat 14.7g
Total Carbohydrate 1.4g
Dietary Fiber 0.5g
Total Sugars 0.7g
Protein 34.2g

Set the Instant Pot to Sauté and heat the oil. Sear the steak for 2 to 5 minutes on each side, until reaching desired texture.

Add the eggs, parsley, black pepper, and salt to the Instant Pot. Stir thoroughly.

Close the lid, set the pressure release to Sealing, and hit Cancel to stop the current program. Select Manual/Pressure Cook, set the Instant Pot to 20 minutes on high pressure, and let cook.

Once cooked, carefully switch the pressure release to Venting. Open the Instant Pot, serve, and enjoy!

LUNCH

LOBSTER BISQUE

Serves 5

Prep Time: 5 minutes, Cook Time: 4 minutes, Total Time: 9 minutes, Pressure: High, Release: Quick

Gluten Free, Soy Free, 10 Minutes or Less, Kid Friendly

Creamy, full of flavor, and downright indulgent—this keto-friendly delicacy is hands-down my absolute favorite lunchtime treat. I like to impart a creamy, buttery flavor to the bisque, which helps the other accents come out. Pair this with your favorite nutrient-dense vegetables—like spinach, broccoli, or kale—for a well-rounded meal.

3 lobster tails

3 cups grass-fed bone broth

3 cups canned, sugar-free, or low-sugar diced tomatoes

2 tablespoons Old Bay seasoning

1 garlic clove, crushed

1 teaspoon thyme, ground

1 teaspoon hot sauce (or to taste)

½ teaspoon paprika, fresh

½ teaspoon kosher salt

½ teaspoon freshly ground black pepper

2 cups heavy whipping cream

Nutrition Facts
Amount per serving
Calories 366
Total Fat 18.1g
Total Carbohydrate 10.6g
Dietary Fiber 0.2g
Total Sugars 7.5g
Protein 30.1g

Remove lobster meat from shells, roughly chop, and refrigerate (covered). Place the shells in the Instant Pot, then add the bone broth, tomatoes, Old Bay, garlic, thyme, hot sauce, paprika, salt, and pepper.

Close the lid, set the pressure release to Sealing, and select Manual/Pressure Cook. Set the Instant Pot to 4 minutes on high pressure and let cook.

Once cooked, perform a quick release. Using tongs, remove and throw away the shells. Switch the Instant Pot to Keep Warm mode. Mix in whipping cream, then purée with an immersion blender, until obtaining a smooth consistency.

Once done, stir in lobster tails, return lid, and seal the valve. Cook on Manual/Pressure Cook again for 3 minutes (or until desired tenderness and consistency). Perform a quick release by carefully switching the pressure valve to Venting.

HIGH-PROTEIN CHILI

Serves 5

**Prep Time: 5 minutes, Cook Time: 18 minutes, Total Time: 23 minutes,
Pressure: High, Release: Natural**

Gluten Free, Soy Free, 25 Minutes or Less, Kid Friendly

This chili is simple, easy, and full of flavor. Topping it with a little avocado packs even more healthy fat into your day. And if you like your chili to be a little less greasy, use a very lean cut of ground beef.

2 tablespoons avocado oil

2 garlic cloves, minced

1 pound grass-fed beef, ground

1/2 teaspoon crushed red pepper

1/2 teaspoon chili powder

1/2 cup full-fat Cheddar cheese, shredded

1/2 teaspoon basil, dried

1/2 teaspoon kosher salt

1/2 teaspoon freshly ground black pepper

1 (14-ounce) can crushed sugar-free or low-sugar tomatoes

Nutrition Facts
Amount per serving
Calories 233
Total Fat 10.2g
Total Carbohydrate 2.7g
Dietary Fiber 0.8g
Total Sugars 1g
Protein 30.6g

Set the Instant Pot to Sauté and heat the oil. Then add the garlic, sautéing for 2 to 3 minutes.

Pour in 1/2 cup of filtered water, then add the beef, red pepper, chili powder, cheese, basil, salt, black pepper, and tomatoes to the Instant Pot.

Close the lid, set the pressure release to Sealing, and hit Cancel to stop the current program. Select Manual/Pressure Cook, set the Instant Pot to 18 minutes on high pressure, and let cook.

Once cooked, let the pressure naturally disperse from the Instant Pot for about 10 minutes, then carefully switch the pressure release to Venting. Open the Instant Pot, serve, and enjoy!

CREAMY BACON SOUP

Serves 4

**Prep Time: 5 minutes, Cook Time: 10 minutes, Total Time: 15 minutes,
Pressure: High, Release: Quick**

Gluten Free, Soy Free, 25 Minutes or Less, Kid Friendly

Perfect for a cold winter day, this bacon soup is rich with flavor and very low on carbs. This is definitely a crowd-pleasing recipe, and it will likely remind you of the flavor of a bacon cheeseburger. Pair with a side of broccoli or spinach, to round out your healthy nutrient intake.

10 slices no-sugar-added bacon

6 cups grass-fed bone broth

6 ounces full-fat cream cheese, softened

5 tablespoons sugar-free or low-sugar tomato paste

4 tablespoons grass-fed butter, softened

2 teaspoons cumin, ground

2 teaspoons chili powder

1 garlic clove, chopped

½ teaspoon basil, dried

½ teaspoon parsley, dried

½ teaspoon cayenne pepper, ground

½ teaspoon freshly ground black pepper

1 cup heavy whipping cream

1 cup full-fat Cheddar cheese, shredded

Nutrition Facts
Calories 804
Total Fat 67.7g
Total Carbohydrate 11.5g
Dietary Fiber 1.5g
Total Sugars 2.9g
Protein 37.2g

Set the Instant Pot to Sauté. Add the bacon, and let cook until it is slightly crispy. Using tongs, place the bacon onto paper towels.

Add the bone broth, cream cheese, tomato paste, butter, cumin, chili powder, garlic, basil, parsley, cayenne pepper, and black pepper to the Instant Pot. Stir thoroughly. Close the lid, set the pressure release to Sealing, and select Manual/Pressure Cook. Set the Instant Pot to 10 minutes on high pressure, and let cook.

Once cooked, perform a quick release by switching the valve to Venting. You may want to cover the valve with a towel, to avoid spilling the soup. Turn off the heat, remove the lid, stir in whipping cream, and let soup sit for 10 minutes.

Serve soup into bowls and crumble bacon on top. Sprinkle in Cheddar cheese, as desired.

CLASSIC BEEF STEW

Serves 5

**Prep Time: 5 minutes, Cook Time: 15 minutes, Total Time: 20 minutes,
Pressure: High, Release: Natural**

Gluten Free, Dairy Free, Soy Free, 25 Minutes or Less, Kid Friendly

There is nothing quite like a hearty beef stew, and this recipe comes straight from
my grandmother to you. The Instant Pot allows us to make this recipe quite quickly,
but you may want to experiment with the slow cooker function, to really bring
out all the flavor here. Try pairing this keto-friendly stew with a side of spinach
and some cauliflower rice.

2 tablespoons avocado oil

1 pound beef stew meat, cubed

1 clove garlic, minced

3 cups grass-fed bone broth

2 ounces wild mushrooms

2 carrots, cut up

1 bay leaf

½ teaspoon parsley, dried

½ teaspoon kosher salt

½ teaspoon freshly ground black pepper

Nutrition Facts
Amount per serving
Calories 208
Total Fat 6.4g
Total Carbohydrate 4.7g
Dietary Fiber 1.1g
Total Sugars 1.4g
Protein 31.2g

Set the Instant Pot to Sauté and heat the
oil. Add the beef and cook until browned,
stirring occasionally. Add the garlic and
cook for an additional 1 minute.

Add the bone broth, mushrooms,
carrots, bay leaf, parsley, salt, and black
pepper to the Instant Pot.

Close the lid, set the pressure release
to Sealing, and hit Cancel to stop the
current program. Select Manual/Pressure
Cook, set the Instant Pot to 15 minutes on
high pressure, and let cook.

Once cooked, let the pressure
naturally disperse from the Instant Pot for
about 10 minutes, then carefully switch the
pressure release to Venting.

Open the Instant Pot, remove bay leaf,
serve, and enjoy!

FAST AND EASY ITALIAN CHICKEN SOUP

Serves 6

**Prep Time: 5 minutes, Cook Time: 10 minutes, Total Time: 15 minutes,
Pressure: High, Release: Quick**

Gluten Free, Dairy Free, Soy Free, 25 Minutes or Less, Kid Friendly

There is nothing like a hearty, comforting soup, and this one really takes the cake. While the Instant Pot makes this recipe much faster to prepare, it is definitely worth trying a longer and slower version of this soup by letting it simmer for 1 to 2 hours. You might be surprised at how much it changes the flavor.

4 cups grass-fed bone broth

1 pound chicken, ground

½ teaspoon hot peppers, chopped

½ teaspoon rosemary, ground

½ teaspoon oregano, dried

½ teaspoon basil, dried

½ teaspoon kosher salt

½ teaspoon freshly ground black pepper

2 tablespoons coconut oil

1 (14-ounce) can sugar-free or low-sugar fire roasted tomatoes

Add the bone broth, chicken, hot peppers, rosemary, oregano, basil, salt, black pepper, oil, and tomatoes to the Instant Pot.

Close the lid, set the pressure release to Sealing, and select Manual/Pressure Cook. Set the Instant Pot to 10 minutes on high pressure, and let cook.

Once cooked, immediately switch the pressure release to Venting. Do this carefully, as hot steam may rise up.

Open the Instant Pot, pour soup evenly into bowls, and enjoy!

Nutrition Facts
Amount per serving
Calories 183
Total Fat 6.9g
Total Carbohydrate 3.3g
Dietary Fiber 0.5g
Total Sugars 1g
Protein 25.3g

SIMPLE SLOPPY JOES

Serves 4

**Prep Time: 5 minutes, Cook Time: 15 minutes, Total Time: 20 minutes,
Pressure: High, Release: Natural**

Gluten Free, Soy Free, 25 Minutes or Less, Kid Friendly

Sloppy joes likely remind you of your school cafeteria. In those memories, I am willing to bet the quality of those meals was not quite up to par (to say the least). These sloppy joes, however, are extremely flavorful, and store very well for later in the week. The best part—they are high in protein and low in carbs, so you will stay in fat-burning ketosis.

2 tablespoons avocado oil

2 garlic cloves, minced

¼ (4-ounce) small onion, thinly sliced

1 pound grass-fed beef, ground

1 stalk celery, chopped

1 teaspoon sugar-free or low-sugar tomato paste

1 tablespoon Worcestershire sauce

1 teaspoon chili powder

1 teaspoon hot sauce

½ teaspoon cayenne pepper, ground

½ teaspoon coriander

½ teaspoon kosher salt

½ teaspoon freshly ground black pepper

¼ cup sugar-free or low-sugar ketchup

Set the Instant Pot to Sauté and heat the oil. Then sauté the garlic and onion, for 1 to 2 minutes.

Pour in 1 cup of filtered water, then add the beef, celery, tomato paste, Worcestershire sauce, chili powder, hot sauce, cayenne pepper, coriander, salt, black pepper, and ketchup to the Instant Pot.

Close the lid, set the pressure release to Sealing, and hit Cancel to stop the current program. Select Manual/Pressure Cook, set the Instant Pot to 15 minutes on high pressure, and let cook.

Once cooked, let the pressure naturally disperse from the Instant Pot for about 10 minutes, then carefully switch the pressure release to Venting.

Open the Instant Pot, carefully drain any excess liquid, serve in bowls (or on your favorite keto-friendly buns), and enjoy!

Nutrition Facts
Amount per serving
Calories 249
Total Fat 8.2g
Total Carbohydrate 7.1g
Dietary Fiber 1g
Total Sugars 4.8g
Protein 35.2g

The Essential Instant Pot® Keto Cookbook

TRADITIONAL GOULASH

Serves 5

**Prep Time: 5 minutes, Cook Time: 18 minutes, Total Time: 23 minutes,
Pressure: Low, Release: Natural**

Gluten Free, Dairy Free, Soy Free, 25 Minutes or Less

Goulash is a dish handed down from Hungary—all the way back from medieval times,
no less. But my modern take on this classic recipe brings the carb count way down.
Try mixing in an extra variety of keto-friendly cheese to add even more flavor.

2 tablespoons coconut oil

1 pound beef stew meat, cubed

2 tablespoons avocado oil

2 tablespoons paprika

1 teaspoon garlic, minced

½ teaspoon cumin, ground

½ teaspoon coriander

½ onion, chopped

½ teaspoon cayenne pepper, ground

½ teaspoon kosher salt

½ teaspoon freshly ground black pepper

1 (14-ounce) can sugar-free or low-sugar diced tomatoes

Nutrition Facts
Amount per serving
Calories 255
Total Fat 12.3g
Total Carbohydrate 7.5g
Dietary Fiber 3g
Total Sugars 3.5g
Protein 29g

Set the Instant Pot to Sauté and melt the coconut oil. Brown the beef, then set aside. Wipe out the inner pot, then return it to the Instant Pot.

Add the avocado oil, and sauté the paprika, garlic, cumin, coriander, onion, cayenne pepper, salt, black pepper, and tomatoes together, for 3 minutes. Next, pour in 4 cups of filtered water, and stir.

Close the lid, set the pressure release to Sealing, and hit Cancel to stop the current program. Select Manual/Pressure Cook, set the Instant Pot to 18 minutes on low pressure, and let cook.

Once cooked, let the pressure naturally disperse from the Instant Pot for about 10 minutes, then carefully switch the pressure release to Venting.

Open the Instant Pot, serve, and enjoy!

CLASSIC CHICKEN "NOODLE" SOUP

Serves 6

Prep Time: 5 minutes, Cook Time: 12 minutes, Total Time: 17 minutes, Pressure: High, Release: Quick

Gluten Free, Dairy Free, Soy Free, 25 Minutes or Less, Kid Friendly

Chicken noodle soup is undeniably a comfort food favorite. However, it is traditionally loaded with carbohydrates. This keto-friendly variation replaces the noodles with zucchinis, so you keep burning fat. This dish is perfect for when you are feeling under the weather—or when you just want a hearty bowl of something soothing and nutritious.

7 cups grass-fed chicken bone broth

1 pound chicken breasts, cubed, cooked

2 tablespoons avocado oil

1 teaspoon oregano, dried

1 carrot, chopped

½ teaspoon basil, dried

½ teaspoon parsley, dried

½ teaspoon kosher salt

½ teaspoon freshly ground black pepper

2 zucchinis, spiralized

Nutrition Facts
Amount per serving
Calories 200
Total Fat 6.4g
Total Carbohydrate 6.1g
Dietary Fiber 1.3g
Total Sugars 1.7g
Protein 28.6g

Pour the chicken broth into the inner pot of the Instant Pot. Add in the chicken, avocado oil, oregano, carrot, basil, parsley, salt, black pepper, and zucchinis. Stir to combine.

Close the lid, set the pressure release to Sealing, and hit Cancel to stop the current program. Select Manual/Pressure Cook, set the Instant Pot to 5 minutes on high pressure, and let cook.

Once cooked, immediately switch the pressure release to Venting (do this carefully).

Remove the lid, stir in the zucchini noodles, and enjoy!

COCONUT BUTTERNUT SQUASH SOUP

Serves 5 to 6

Prep Time: 5 minutes, Cook Time: 10 minutes, Total Time: 15 minutes, Pressure: High, Release: Quick

Gluten Free, Dairy Free, Soy Free, 25 Minutes or Less, Kid Friendly

Coconut and butternut squash are two of my favorite flavors. This soup combines them both to make a rich, creamy delicacy. Adding an extra tablespoon of grass-fed butter will add some more flavor, if desired. Pair with a side of protein, and a green leafy vegetable.

2 tablespoons coconut oil

4 cloves garlic, minced

6 cups grass-fed bone broth

2 cups butternut squash, cubed

½ teaspoon curry powder

½ teaspoon ginger, finely grated

½ teaspoon kosher salt

½ teaspoon freshly ground black pepper

2 cups full-fat coconut milk

Nutrition Facts
Amount per serving
Calories 278
Total Fat 23.7g
Total Carbohydrate 12.9g
Dietary Fiber 2.9g
Total Sugars 3.7g
Protein 7.4g

Set the Instant Pot to Sauté and melt the oil, then add the garlic. Sauté for 2 minutes.

Pour in the bone broth, then add the butternut squash, curry powder, ginger, salt, and pepper to the Instant Pot. Close the lid, set the pressure release to Sealing, and hit Cancel to stop the current program. Select Manual/Pressure Cook, set the Instant Pot to 10 minutes on high pressure, and let cook.

Once cooked, perform a quick release by carefully switching the pressure valve to Venting.

Open the lid and purée the coconut milk directly in the Instant Pot, using an immersion blender, until desired consistency is achieved.

EASY HEALING BONE BROTH

Recipe courtesy of Dr. Kellyann Petrucci

Serves 4

Prep Time: 5 minutes, Cook Time: 140 minutes, Total Time: 145 minutes, Pressure: High, Release: Natural

Gluten Free, Dairy Free, Soy Free

Bone broth is one of the hottest foods around right now. This gut-healing food cooks great in the Instant Pot, and works as an accompaniment to a meal, or all on its own. I frequently like to have a warm mug of bone broth with my breakfast or as part of a modified intermittent fast.

3 cloves garlic, mashed

1 tablespoon apple cider vinegar

1 carrot, chopped

½ teaspoon basil, dried

½ teaspoon kosher salt

½ teaspoon freshly ground black pepper

bones from your preferred animal

Nutrition Facts
Amount per serving
Calories 11
Total Fat 0g
Total Carbohydrate 2.4g ·
Dietary Fiber 0.5g
Total Sugars 0.8g
Protein 0.3g

Add garlic, vinegar, carrot, basil, kosher salt, black pepper, and bones to the inner pot of the Instant Pot and cover with water.

Close the lid, set the pressure release to Sealing, and select Manual/Pressure Cook. Set the Instant Pot to 140 minutes on high pressure, and let cook.

Once cooked, let the pressure naturally disperse from the Instant Pot for about 15 minutes, then carefully switch the pressure release to Venting. Open the Instant Pot, serve, and enjoy! Store leftover bone broth in the refrigerator or freezer.

10-MINUTE SALMON AND VEGETABLES

Recipe courtesy of Paleo Magazine

Serves 4

Prep Time: 5 minutes, Cook Time: 5 minutes, Total Time: 10 minutes, Pressure: High, Release: Quick

Gluten Free, Dairy Free, Soy Free, 10 Minutes or Less, Kid Friendly

Salmon is rich with bioavailable protein and brain-friendly nutrients. The Instant Pot makes cooking any seafood a breeze.

1/2 bunch fresh parsley, plus more for garnish

2 to 3 sprigs fresh tarragon

1 1/2 pounds wild salmon fillets

1 tablespoon olive oil

Sea salt and black pepper to taste

1 medium lemon, thinly sliced

2 medium zucchinis, julienned

2 medium bell peppers (any color), seeded and julienned

2 medium carrots, julienned

Nutrition Facts
Amount per serving
Calories 188
Total Fat 8.9g
Total Carbohydrate 10.7g
Dietary Fiber 2.4g
Total Sugars 6g
Protein 17.7g

Place ¾ cup of filtered water, the parsley, and tarragon into the Instant Pot. Insert the steamer rack with the handles extending up.

Place the salmon on the rack, skin-side down. Drizzle with the olive oil. Season generously with salt and pepper. Top with the lemon slices.

Close the lid, set the pressure release to Sealing, press Steam, and set the time to 3 minutes.

Once done, perform a quick release, being careful to avoid the released steam. Remove the lid and the rack with the salmon. Set fillets aside and keep them warm.

Discard the herbs, but keep the liquid in the pot. Add the zucchinis, peppers, and carrots to the pot and close the lid.

Press Sauté and allow the vegetables to cook until tender, 2 to 3 minutes. When vegetables are cooked to desired tenderness, remove and season to taste with salt and pepper. Serve with the salmon and a garnish of parsley.

CRISPY BACON CHILI

Recipe courtesy of Brandon Routh

Serves 4

**Prep Time: 5 minutes, Cook Time: 35 minutes, Total Time: 40 minutes,
Pressure: High, Release: Natural**

Gluten Free, Dairy Free, Soy Free, Kid Friendly

Does it get any more satisfying than this chili? Loaded with protein, flavor, and bacon, this keto-friendly recipe will satisfy your every craving. Generously sprinkle on more cheese before serving to add even more protein and taste to this already loaded dish. Or get a little friendly with your curry powder and crushed red pepper to make this chili with an extra kick.

2 tablespoons coconut oil

2 garlic cloves, minced

5 slices of bacon, cooked, finely chopped

1 teaspoon cumin, ground

1 teaspoon crushed red pepper

1 pound grass-fed beef, ground

½ tablespoon garlic powder

½ teaspoon chili powder

½ teaspoon oregano, dried

½ teaspoon kosher salt

½ teaspoon freshly ground black pepper

1 (14-ounce) can sugar-free or low-sugar crushed tomatoes

Nutrition Facts
Amount per serving
Calories 394
Total Fat 31.6g
Total Carbohydrate 8g
Dietary Fiber 2.1g
Total Sugars 3g
Protein 20.6g

Set the Instant Pot to Sauté and melt the oil. Sauté the garlic for 2 to 3 minutes, then pour in ½ cup of filtered water.

Add the bacon, cumin, red pepper, beef, garlic powder, chili powder, oregano, salt, black pepper, and tomatoes to the Instant Pot.

Close the lid, set the pressure release to Sealing, and hit Cancel to stop the current program. Select Manual/Pressure Cook, set the Instant Pot to 35 minutes on high pressure, and let cook.

Once cooked, let the pressure naturally disperse from the Instant Pot for about 10 minutes, then carefully switch the pressure release to Venting.

Open the Instant Pot, serve, and enjoy!

The Essential Instant Pot® Keto Cookbook

CLASSIC PUMPKIN SOUP

Serves 8

Prep Time: 5 minutes, Cook Time: 8 minutes, Total Time: 13 minutes, Pressure: High, Release: Natural

Gluten Free, Soy Free, 25 Minutes or Less, Kid Friendly

There is just something about pumpkin soup on a fall day. This nostalgic recipe has a hint of cinnamon and a dash of spice. Add a small touch of butter to give it an even creamier texture.

1 sugar pumpkin
4 cups chicken broth
1/2 cup heavy whipping cream
1/2 teaspoon cinnamon, ground
1/2 cup full-fat coconut milk
1/2 teaspoon kosher salt
1/2 teaspoon freshly ground black pepper
1 teaspoon parsley, dried

Nutrition Facts
Amount per serving
Calories 100
Total Fat 7.4g
Total Carbohydrate 7.3g
Dietary Fiber 2.1g
Total Sugars 2.7g
Protein 1.1g

Place the pumpkin on a stable work surface. Cut off the stem, slice pumpkin in half, and scoop out any seeds. Pour 1 cup of filtered water into the inner pot of the Instant Pot, then insert the trivet. Place the pumpkin on top of the trivet.

Close the lid, set the pressure release to Sealing, and select Manual/Pressure Cook. Set the Instant Pot to 8 minutes on high pressure, and let cook.

Once cooked, let the pressure naturally disperse from the Instant Pot for about 10 minutes, then carefully switch the pressure release to Venting. Remove pumpkin.

In a blender, add the pumpkin, along with the chicken broth, whipping cream, cinnamon, milk, salt, and pepper. Blend until desired consistency. Set the Instant Pot to Sauté and return soup to the inner pot.

When warm enough (usually after 2 to 5 minutes), serve with the parsley, and enjoy!

HEARTY HAMBURGER SOUP

Serves 4

Prep Time: 5 minutes, Cook Time: 25 minutes, Total Time: 30 minutes, Pressure: High, Release: Natural

Gluten Free, Soy Free, Kid Friendly

This uniquely protein-rich soup is great for now, and storing for later. Crumble some extra bacon in each bowl to add a crisp texture. And for a slightly thicker soup, use one less cup of bone broth.

2 tablespoons coconut oil

1 pound grass-fed beef, ground

4 cups grass-fed bone broth

3 slices no-sugar-added bacon, cooked and finely chopped (optional)

1 cup full-fat Cheddar cheese, shredded (optional)

1 carrot, chopped

1 celery stalk, chopped

1/2 teaspoon parsley, dried

1/2 teaspoon crushed red pepper

1/2 teaspoon basil, dried

1/2 teaspoon kosher salt

1/2 teaspoon freshly ground black pepper

1 (14-ounce) can sugar-free or low-sugar diced tomatoes

Nutrition Facts
Amount per serving
Calories 514
Total Fat 30.2g
Total Carbohydrate 9.5g
Dietary Fiber 2.3g
Total Sugars 4.4g
Protein 49.4g

Set the Instant Pot to Sauté and melt the oil. Add the beef and brown for 2 to 5 minutes.

Pour in bone broth, then add the bacon, cheese, carrot, celery, parsley, red pepper, basil, salt, black pepper, and tomatoes to the Instant Pot.

Close the lid, set the pressure release to Sealing and hit Cancel to stop the current program. Select Manual/Pressure Cook, set the Instant Pot to 25 minutes on high pressure, and let cook.

Once cooked, let the pressure naturally disperse from the Instant Pot for about 10 minutes, then carefully switch the pressure release to Venting.

Open the Instant Pot, serve, and enjoy!

BASIL-LIME CARNITAS

Serves 4

Prep Time: 5 minutes, Cook Time: 30 minutes, Total Time: 35 minutes, Pressure: High, Release: Natural

Gluten Free, Dairy Free, Soy Free, Kid Friendly

Did you know that carnitas translates directly as "little meats"? Carnitas can traditionally take a long time to cook to reach that fork-tender consistency, but the Instant Pot shows its strength here and brings down the cooking time significantly. Once you try cooking carnitas this way, it is unlikely you will go back to the more time-consuming process. I also sometimes like to make my carnitas a little spicier by adding some curry powder, chili powder, or ghost pepper.

2 tablespoons avocado oil

1 pound pork shoulder, chopped

½ jalapeño, finely chopped

½ teaspoon oregano, dried

½ teaspoon chili powder

½ teaspoon cumin, ground

½ teaspoon basil, dried

½ teaspoon kosher salt

½ teaspoon freshly ground black pepper

½ teaspoon lime juice

Nutrition Facts
Amount per serving
Calories 344
Total Fat 25.3g
Total Carbohydrate 1.1g
Dietary Fiber 0.7g
Total Sugars 0.1g
Protein 26.7g

Set the Instant Pot to Sauté and heat the oil. Brown pork shoulder (takes about 10 minutes).

Pour in 1 cup of filtered water, then add the jalapeño, oregano, chili powder, cumin, basil, salt, and black pepper to the Instant Pot.

Close the lid, set the pressure release to Sealing, and hit Cancel to stop the current program. Select Manual/Pressure Cook, set the Instant Pot to 30 minutes on high pressure, and let cook.

Once cooked, let the pressure naturally disperse from the Instant Pot for about 10 minutes, then carefully switch the pressure release to Venting.

Open the Instant Pot, stir in lime juice, serve, and enjoy!

KUNG PAO CHICKEN

Serves 5

**Prep Time: 5 minutes, Cook Time: 17 minutes, Total Time: 22 minutes,
Pressure: High, Release: Quick**

Gluten Free, Dairy Free, Soy Free, 25 Minutes or Less

My absolute favorite Chinese food delivery meal, Kung Pao chicken, is usually very spicy—and very salty. The Instant Pot allows you to re-create this takeout favorite at home, and it is easy to add other keto-friendly flavors to the mix. I have left out the sugar that is traditionally in Kung Pao, and opted instead for a spicier version to keep this dish maximally low-carb.

2 tablespoons coconut oil

1 pound boneless, skinless chicken breasts, cubed

6 tablespoons hot sauce

1 cup cashews, chopped

½ teaspoon ginger, finely grated

½ teaspoon chili powder

½ teaspoon kosher salt

½ teaspoon freshly ground black pepper

Set the Instant Pot to Sauté and melt the oil. Add the chicken, hot sauce, cashews, ginger, chili powder, salt, and pepper to the Instant Pot.

Close the lid, set the pressure release to Sealing, and hit Cancel to stop the current program. Select Manual/Pressure Cook, set the Instant Pot to 17 minutes on high pressure, and let cook.

Once cooked, carefully switch the pressure release to Venting.

Open the Instant Pot, serve, and enjoy!

Nutrition Facts
Amount per serving
Calories 380
Total Fat 25g
Total Carbohydrate 9.7g
Dietary Fiber 1g
Total Sugars 1.6g
Protein 30.6g

The Essential Instant Pot® Keto Cookbook

HOT 'N' SPICY TURKEY MEATBALLS

Recipe courtesy of Robb Wolf

Serves 5

Prep Time: 5 minutes, Cook Time: 25 minutes, Total Time: 30 minutes, Pressure: High, Release: Natural

Gluten Free, Dairy Free, Soy Free, Kid Friendly

Meatballs are another American classic, and luckily for us, they are also keto-friendly. I have added some extra spice to this traditional dish to bring out some more flavor. Pair these meatballs with some dark leafy greens like spinach, kale, or steamed broccoli.

1 pound turkey, ground
¼ cup hot sauce (or more, to taste)
2 tablespoons coconut oil
1 teaspoon ginger, finely grated
½ teaspoon chili powder
½ teaspoon basil, dried
½ teaspoon kosher salt
½ teaspoon freshly ground black pepper

Nutrition Facts
Amount per serving
Calories 205
Total Fat 10.1g
Total Carbohydrate 0.7g
Dietary Fiber 0.2g
Total Sugars 0.2g
Protein 26.7g

Form ground turkey into 1½ inch meatballs and place in a single layer into a greased Instant Pot–friendly dish. In a small bowl, stir together the hot sauce, oil, ginger, chili powder, basil, salt, and pepper. When mixed, sprinkle evenly over the meatballs.

Pour 1 cup of filtered water into the inner pot of the Instant Pot and insert the trivet. Using a sling, place the dish with the meatballs onto the trivet.

Close the lid, set the pressure release to Sealing, and select Manual/Pressure Cook. Set the Instant Pot to 25 minutes on high pressure and let cook.

Once cooked, let the pressure naturally disperse from the Instant Pot for about 10 minutes, then carefully switch the pressure release to Venting. Open the Instant Pot, serve, and enjoy!

SPICY BUFFALO CHICKEN SOUP

Serves 4

Prep Time: 5 minutes, Cook Time: 10 minutes, Total Time: 15 minutes, Pressure: High, Release: Quick

Gluten Free, Soy Free, 25 Minutes or Less, Kid Friendly

When most people think of "buffalo chicken," they likely imagine some kind of buffalo wings, traditionally enjoyed at a Super Bowl party. However, I have distilled this memorable and addictive flavor down into a spicy, keto-friendly soup. Add some extra spice to give this dish even more of a kick, and be sure to pair it with some nutrient-dense vegetables (and likely a big glass of water!).

3 cups grass-fed bone broth

2 tablespoons avocado oil

2 tablespoons hot sauce (or more, to taste)

2 tablespoons buffalo sauce

1 pound chicken breasts, cooked, shredded

1 cup full-fat Cheddar cheese, shredded (optional)

½ teaspoon chili powder

½ teaspoon cayenne powder

½ teaspoon kosher salt

½ teaspoon freshly ground black pepper

1 (14-ounce) can sugar-free or low-sugar fire roasted tomatoes

Add all ingredients to the Instant Pot. Stir and mix thoroughly.

Close the lid, set the pressure release to Sealing, and select Manual/Pressure Cook. Set the Instant Pot to 10 minutes on high pressure and let cook.

Once cooked, carefully switch the pressure release to Venting. Open the Instant Pot, strain to your desired consistency, and enjoy!

Nutrition Facts
Amount per serving
Calories 383
Total Fat 18.8g
Total Carbohydrate 6.4g
Dietary Fiber 1.6g
Total Sugars 1.8g
Protein 43.8g

The Essential Instant Pot® Keto Cookbook

SAVORY PUMPKIN AND BACON SOUP

Serves 4

**Prep Time: 5 minutes, Cook Time: 10 minutes, Total Time: 15 minutes,
Pressure: Low, Release: Natural**

Gluten Free, Soy Free, 25 Minutes or Less, Kid Friendly

The sweet and crisp flavors of pumpkin and bacon match up perfectly in this soup.
Great for a fall day or a cold winter night, this dish pairs well with just about anything.
Try adding slightly more cream or a small serving of butter for even more richness.

2 tablespoons coconut oil

4 slices no-sugar-added bacon, finely chopped and cooked

2 cups grass-fed bone broth

2 cups organic pumpkin purée

2 cups full-fat coconut milk

1/2 cup full-fat Cheddar cheese, shredded (optional)

1/2 teaspoon crushed red pepper

1/2 teaspoon kosher salt

1/2 teaspoon freshly ground black pepper

1/4 cup heavy whipping cream

Add all ingredients to the Instant Pot. Stir and mix thoroughly.

Close the lid, set the pressure release to Sealing, and hit Cancel to stop the current program. Select Manual/Pressure Cook, set the Instant Pot to 10 minutes on low pressure, and let cook.

Once cooked, let the pressure naturally disperse from the Instant Pot for about 10 minutes, then carefully switch the pressure release to Venting. Open the Instant Pot, serve, and enjoy!

Nutrition Facts
Amount per serving
Calories 578
Total Fat 51.2g
Total Carbohydrate 18.5g
Dietary Fiber 6.3g
Total Sugars 8.2g
Protein 17.4g

BUNLESS BACON CHEESEBURGER

Serves 4

Prep Time: 5 minutes, Cook Time: 15 minutes, Total Time: 20 minutes, Pressure: High, Release: Natural

Gluten Free, Soy Free, 25 Minutes or Less, Kid Friendly

Forget fast food—make this instead!

6 slices no-sugar-added bacon

2 tablespoons grass-fed butter, softened

1 pound grass-fed beef, ground

1/2 teaspoon cayenne pepper, ground

1/2 teaspoon crushed red pepper

1/2 teaspoon paprika, fresh

1/2 teaspoon freshly ground black pepper

1/2 teaspoon kosher salt

1/2 cup full-fat Cheddar cheese, shredded

1/2 cup full-fat Monterey Jack cheese, shredded

Nutrition Facts
Amount per serving
Calories 591
Total Fat 48.7g
Total Carbohydrate 4.1g
Dietary Fiber 1g
Total Sugars 0.2g
Protein 33.4g

Place the bacon slices on aluminum foil, laid out evenly.

Set the Instant Pot to Sauté. Add the grass-fed butter to the Instant Pot, melting it gently.

In a large bowl, mix the beef, cayenne pepper, red pepper, paprika, black pepper, and salt. Form 2 large, thin patties with the beef.

Add 1/2 cup of filtered water to the Instant Pot, then add the patties. Add the trivet to create a second cooking layer, and place the aluminum foil with the bacon on top. Be sure to fold the edges of the aluminum foil upward.

Close the lid, set the pressure release to Sealing, and select Manual/Pressure Cook. Set the Instant Pot to 15 minutes on high pressure and let cook.

Once cooked, let the pressure naturally disperse from the Instant Pot for about 10 minutes, then carefully switch the pressure release to Venting.

Open the lid and remove the food. Top the burgers with the Cheddar, Monterey Jack, bacon, and serve.

15-MINUTE FAJITAS

Serves 4

**Prep Time: 5 minutes, Cook Time: 10 minutes, Total Time: 15 minutes,
Pressure: High, Release: Natural**

Gluten Free, Soy Free, 25 Minutes or Less, Kid Friendly

Fajitas are a favorite Mexican dish, and this Instant Pot version is particularly fun.
Simple, flavorful, and easy—these are great to make on a busy day. Pair with a bowl of
dark leafy greens and some guacamole for a fantastic lunch or dinner.

2 tablespoons avocado oil

2 bell peppers, chopped

2 garlic cloves, minced

**1 pound chicken breasts, cut into thin
strips**

1 teaspoon chili powder

1 teaspoon oregano, dried

1/2 teaspoon freshly ground black pepper

1/2 teaspoon cumin, ground

1/2 teaspoon kosher salt

1 avocado, mashed

1 cup full-fat Cheddar cheese, shredded

3/4 cup sour cream, at room temperature

Nutrition Facts
Amount per serving
Calories 610
Total Fat 43.9g
Total Carbohydrate 12.4g
Dietary Fiber 4.7g
Total Sugars 3.6g
Protein 43.1g

Set the Instant Pot to Sauté and heat
the avocado oil. Add in the bell peppers,
garlic, chicken, chili powder, oregano,
black pepper, cumin, salt, and ½ cup of
filtered water.

Close the lid, set the pressure release
to Sealing, and select Manual/Pressure
Cook. Set the Instant Pot to 10 minutes on
high pressure and let cook.

Once cooked, let the pressure
naturally disperse from the Instant Pot for
about 10 minutes, then carefully switch the
pressure release to Venting.

Open the lid and remove the food.
Serve inside of your favorite keto-friendly
wraps, and top with the avocado, cheese,
and sour cream.

5-INGREDIENT MINESTRONE SOUP

IPM

Serves 2

**Prep Time: 5 minutes, Cook Time: 5 minutes, Total Time: 10 minutes,
Pressure: High, Release: Quick**

Gluten Free, Soy Free, 10 Minutes or Less, Kid Friendly

A good mix of vegetables and Parmesan cheese make this soup truly unique. Try making this in your Instant Pot Mini, as it's perfectly proportioned for small gatherings.

2 cups grass-fed bone broth

½ stalk celery, chopped

1 (14-ounce) can sugar-free or low-sugar fire roasted tomatoes

½ cup green beans, cut up into pieces

¼ cup full-fat Parmesan cheese, grated

Nutrition Facts
Amount per serving
Calories 154
Total Fat 6g
Total Carbohydrate 10.1g
Dietary Fiber 2g
Total Sugars 3.5g
Protein 14.5g

Pour bone broth into the inner pot, then add the celery, tomatoes, and green beans.

Close the lid, set the pressure release to Sealing, and select Manual/Pressure Cook. Set the Instant Pot to 5 minutes on high pressure and let cook.

Once cooked, perform a quick release by carefully switching the pressure valve to Venting. Stir in the Parmesan cheese and serve.

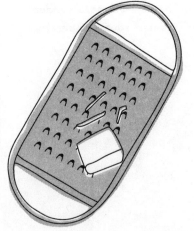

The Essential Instant Pot® Keto Cookbook

AVOCADO-CILANTRO TACOS

Serves 4

**Prep Time: 5 minutes, Cook Time: 15 minutes, Total Time: 20 minutes,
Pressure: High, Release: Natural**

Gluten Free, Soy Free, 25 Minutes or Less, Kid Friendly

These tacos are tasty, quick, and easy to make. The Instant Pot makes Taco Tuesday
a breeze and you can swap out flavors. Try adding a sprinkle of lime juice
to the mixture—or some jalapeño, curry powder, or crushed red pepper—to
keep things interesting.

2 tablespoons coconut oil

1 pound grass-fed beef, ground

1 teaspoon cilantro, dried

1/2 teaspoon chili powder

1 avocado, mashed

2 cups full-fat Cheddar cheese, shredded

1/2 cup sour cream, at room temperature

1 cup lettuce, shredded

Nutrition Facts
Amount per serving
Calories 664
Total Fat 48.5g
Total Carbohydrate 6.9g
Dietary Fiber 3.6g
Total Sugars 0.8g
Protein 50.4g

Set the Instant Pot to Sauté, and melt the
oil gently. Add the beef, cilantro, chili
powder, and avocado. Stir in 1/2 cup of
filtered water. Close the lid, set the pressure
release to Sealing, and select Manual/
Pressure Cook. Set the Instant Pot to 15
minutes on high pressure and let cook.

Once cooked, let the pressure
naturally disperse from the Instant Pot for
about 10 minutes, then carefully switch the
pressure release to Venting.

Open the lid and remove the food.
Serve inside your favorite keto-friendly
tacos shells, and top with the cheese, sour
cream, and lettuce.

15-MINUTE VEGETABLE SOUP

Recipe courtesy of Paleo Magazine

Serves 4

**Prep Time: 5 minutes, Cook Time: 10 minutes, Total Time: 15 minutes,
Pressure: High, Release: Natural**

Gluten Free, Dairy Free, Soy Free, 25 Minutes or Less, Kid Friendly

This vegetable soup from my friends at *Paleo Magazine* is loaded with nutrients.

½ cup dried porcini mushrooms

1 tablespoon coconut or avocado oil

1 medium yellow onion, diced

2 medium stalks celery, diced

2 medium carrots, diced

1 cup white mushrooms, sliced

4 cloves garlic, minced or finely grated

1 tablespoon fresh rosemary, finely chopped

1 teaspoon Italian seasoning

½ teaspoon smoked paprika

2 cups bite-size broccoli florets

3 cups kale, chopped

1 medium zucchini, diced

1 (14-ounce) can sugar-free or low-sugar diced tomatoes

4 cups chicken or vegetable broth

Nutrition Facts
Amount per serving
Calories 342
Total Fat 5.6g
Total Carbohydrate 22.1g
Dietary Fiber 6.7g
Total Sugars 7.8g
Protein 46.3g

Place the porcini mushrooms in a bowl and cover with boiling water. Soak for 15 to 30 minutes. Drain and chop.

Meanwhile, set the Instant Pot to Sauté. Add the oil. When hot, add the onion, celery, and carrots. Cook, stirring often, for 2 to 3 minutes.

Add the rehydrated porcini mushrooms and white mushrooms. Sauté for 1 to 2 minutes.

Add the garlic, rosemary, Italian seasoning, and paprika. Sauté for 1 minute.

Add the broccoli, kale, and zucchini. Stir to combine.

Add the tomatoes and broth. Close the lid, set the pressure release to Sealing, and select Manual/Pressure Cook. Set the Instant Pot to 10 minutes on high pressure and let cook.

Once cooked, let the pressure naturally disperse from the Instant Pot for 2 to 3 minutes, then carefully switch the pressure release to Venting.
Remove the lid. Season to taste with salt and pepper.

TURKEY BURGER WITH BACON-WRAPPED AVOCADO FRIES

Serves 4

Prep Time: 5 minutes, Cook Time: 10 minutes, Total Time: 15 minutes, Pressure: High, Release: Natural

Gluten Free, Dairy Free, Soy Free, 25 Minutes or Less, Kid Friendly

These bacon-wrapped avocado fries are one of my favorite indulgences.

2 tablespoons coconut oil

6 slices no-sugar-added bacon

1 avocado, sliced into thin strips

1/2 pound turkey, ground

1/2 teaspoon freshly ground black pepper

1/2 teaspoon parsley, dried

1/2 teaspoon turmeric, ground

1/2 teaspoon basil, dried

1/2 teaspoon kosher salt

2 cups broccoli, chopped

Nutrition Facts
Amount per serving
Calories 429
Total Fat 31.5g
Total Carbohydrate 8.1g
Dietary Fiber 4.7g
Total Sugars 1g
Protein 29.4g

On a piece of aluminum foil, wrap the bacon around the avocado slices. If any bacon remains, wrap slices a second time, until no bacon is left. In a separate bowl, mix the turkey, black pepper, parsley, turmeric, basil, and salt. Once combined, form one large, thin patty with the seasoned turkey.

Saute oil in Instant Pot, then pour in 1/4 cup of filtered water, and place the turkey patty in the middle. Then add the broccoli.

Insert the trivet, then place the aluminum foil with the avocado fries on top. Be sure to fold the edges of the aluminum foil upward. Close the lid, set the pressure release to Sealing, and select Manual/Pressure Cook. Set the Instant Pot to 10 minutes on high pressure and let cook.

Once cooked, let the pressure naturally disperse from the Instant Pot for about 10 minutes, then carefully switch the pressure release to Venting.

Open the lid and remove the food. Cut the patty into 4 equal parts and serve alongside the avocado fries.

SHRIMP AND AVOCADO SALAD

Serves 4

**Prep Time: 5 minutes, Cook Time: 3 minutes, Total Time: 8 minutes,
Pressure: Low, Release: Natural**

Gluten Free, Dairy Free, Soy Free, 10 Minutes or Less, Kid Friendly

Shrimp is a nutritional powerhouse and is loaded with protein, vitamin B_{12}, selenium, and much more. Paired with the healthy monounsaturated fats found in avocado, this makes for a very healthy salad. Add an extra dab of butter to the shrimp to get an even more flavorful salad.

2 tablespoons coconut oil

1 pound shrimp, thawed and deveined

1 cup bell peppers, chopped

1/2 cup spinach, chopped

1/2 cup kale, chopped

1/2 cup bok choy, chopped

1 avocado, mashed

2 tablespoons walnuts, chopped

1/2 teaspoon turmeric, ground

1/2 teaspoon parsley, dried

1/2 teaspoon ginger, finely grated

1/2 teaspoon freshly ground black pepper

1/2 teaspoon basil, dried

Nutrition Facts
Amount per serving
Calories 338
Total Fat 21g
Total Carbohydrate 10.4g
Dietary Fiber 4.5g
Total Sugars 1.9g
Protein 28.6g

Set the Instant Pot to Sauté. Add the oil, melting it gently.

Pour 1 cup filtered water into the Instant Pot, then add the shrimp. Close the lid, set the pressure release to Sealing, and select Manual/Pressure Cook. Set the Instant Pot to 3 minutes on low pressure and let cook.

In the meantime, make a salad by tossing together the bell peppers, spinach, kale, bok choy, mashed avocado, and walnuts.

When the shrimp is cooked, carefully switch the pressure release to Venting.

Open the lid and remove the shrimp. Add it atop the tossed salad. Sprinkle the turmeric, parsley, ginger, black pepper, and basil on top, evenly. Enjoy!

MUSHROOM BURGERS

Serves 2

**Prep Time: 5 minutes, Cook Time: 20 minutes, Total Time: 25 minutes,
Pressure: High, Release: Natural**

Gluten Free, Soy Free, 25 Minutes or Less, Kid Friendly

Did you know a mushroom works as a perfect bun substitute?

1 pound grass-fed beef, ground

½ teaspoon cayenne pepper, ground

½ teaspoon oregano, dried

½ teaspoon freshly ground black pepper

½ teaspoon kosher salt

4 portobello mushroom caps

1 cup lettuce, shredded

1 cup tomatoes, diced

1 teaspoon Dijon mustard

¼ (4-ounce) small onion, thinly sliced

½ cup full-fat Cheddar cheese, shredded

Nutrition Facts
Amount per serving
Calories 510
Total Fat 33.5g
Total Carbohydrate 7.6g
Dietary Fiber 2.1g
Total Sugars 2.1g
Protein 40.5g

Preheat your oven to 350°F. Place the mushroom caps on a lightly greased baking sheet.

Add ½ cup of filtered water to the Instant Pot, then insert the trivet. In a large bowl, mix the beef with the cayenne pepper, oregano, black pepper, and salt. Form two well-crafted patties, and place these patties on top of the trivet.

Close the lid, set the pressure release to Sealing, and select Manual/Pressure Cook. Set the Instant Pot to 20 minutes on high pressure and let cook.

While cooking, heat the mushroom caps in the oven for 5 minutes per side. When done, remove and let cool.

Once cooked, let the pressure naturally disperse from the Instant Pot for about 10 minutes, then carefully switch the pressure release to Venting. Open the lid and remove the meat. Place burgers on top of two of the mushroom caps. Top the burgers with the remaining ingredients, and complete each burger with the remaining mushroom caps.

20-MINUTE PEPPERONI PIZZA

Serves 5 to 6

**Prep Time: 5 minutes, Cook Time: 15 minutes, Total Time: 20 minutes,
Pressure: High, Release: Natural**

Gluten Free, Soy Free, 25 Minutes or Less, Kid Friendly

Pizza is one of the highest carbohydrate foods out there. However, this clever keto adaptation cuts down the carbs to almost nothing. It also cooks very easily inside the Instant Pot, and comes loaded with protein. Add some extra varieties of cheese and some extra toppings, like japaleño, to make the reusability of this recipe truly endless.

CRUST

2 tablespoons full-fat cream cheese, softened

1 egg

¾ cup blanched almond flour

½ cup full-fat Parmesan cheese, grated

TOPPING

½ teaspoon oregano, dried

½ teaspoon basil, dried

½ teaspoon crushed red pepper

1 (14-ounce) can sugar-free or low-sugar diced tomatoes, drained

1 cup mozzarella cheese, shredded

1 cup full-fat Cheddar cheese, shredded

16 pepperoni slices, uncured

½ cup bell peppers, chopped

Nutrition Facts
Amount per serving
Calories 366
Total Fat 28.7g
Total Carbohydrate 5.5g
Dietary Fiber 0.9g
Total Sugars 1.5g
Protein 20.8g

Pour 1 cup of filtered water into the inner pot of the Instant Pot, then insert the trivet.

Mix the cream cheese, egg, almond flour, and Parmesan together thoroughly, in a large bowl. Then transfer the mixture in a well-greased, Instant Pot–friendly pan (or dish). Cover loosely with aluminum foil, and then place this pan on top of the trivet.

Close the lid, set the pressure release to Sealing, and select Manual/Pressure Cook. Set the Instant Pot to 10 minutes on high pressure, and let cook.

Meanwhile, in a small bowl, mix together oregano, basil, and red pepper flakes, and set aside. Once the crust is cooked, carefully switch the pressure release to Venting. Open the Instant Pot, and very carefully remove the aluminum foil. Construct pizza by adding an even layer of diced tomatoes, mozzarella and Cheddar cheese, pepperoni, and bell

The Essential Instant Pot® Keto Cookbook

peppers. Sprinkle spice mixture over top. Loosely re-cover dish with aluminum foil.

Close the lid to the Instant Pot, set the pressure release to Sealing, and select Manual/Pressure Cook. Set the Instant Pot to 5 minutes on high pressure and let cook again.

Once cooked, let the pressure naturally disperse from the Instant Pot for about 10 minutes, then carefully switch the pressure release to Venting. Open the Instant Pot, serve, and enjoy!

TRADITIONAL EGG DROP SOUP

Serves 5 to 6

**Prep Time: 5 minutes, Cook Time: 5 minutes, Total Time: 10 minutes,
Pressure: High, Release: Natural**

Gluten Free, Soy Free, 10 Minutes or Less, Kid Friendly

Egg drop soup is a traditional Chinese dish, and this version has been modified to lower the carbohydrate content. The eggs found in this soup are a great source of many nutrients, including protein, choline, and vitamin B_{12}. Serve this soup with a side salad to maximize your nutrient intake.

8 cups grass-fed bone broth

4 tablespoons grass-fed butter, softened

1 scallion, thinly sliced

½ teaspoon basil, dried

½ teaspoon cayenne pepper, ground

½ teaspoon parsley, dried

½ teaspoon kosher salt

6 eggs, whisked

Nutrition Facts
Amount per serving
Calories 177
Total Fat 12.4g
Total Carbohydrate 3.3g
Dietary Fiber 0.1g
Total Sugars 0.4g
Protein 12.2g

Pour the bone broth, butter, scallion, basil, cayenne pepper, parsley, and salt into the Instant Pot.

Close the lid, set the pressure release to Sealing, and select Manual/Pressure Cook. Set the Instant Pot to 5 minutes on high pressure and let cook.

Once cooked, let the pressure naturally disperse from the Instant Pot for about 10 minutes, then carefully switch the pressure release to Venting.

Gently pour in the eggs, and let sit for 1 minute, until they form ribbon-like strands.

Stir, serve, and enjoy!

CLAM CHOWDER

Serves 5 to 6

Prep Time: 5 minutes, Cook Time: 5 minutes, Total Time: 10 minutes, Pressure: High, Release: Natural

Gluten Free, Soy Free, 10 Minutes or Less, Kid Friendly

Clams are one of the healthiest foods in the world, as they are loaded with protein, iron, selenium, vitamin C, and so much more. Yet clams are also often criminally underutilized in everyday meal plans. This take on classic clam chowder cuts down drastically on the sugar and carbohydrates by substituting in cauliflower—but it still retains all the flavor of the classic preparation.

2 cups full-fat coconut milk

2 bay leaves

1 cup grass-fed bone broth

1 pound cauliflower, chopped

1 cup celery, finely chopped

½ teaspoon freshly ground black pepper

½ teaspoon kosher salt

¼ (4-ounce) small onion, thinly sliced

2 (7-ounce) cans clams, chopped, drained

1 cup heavy whipping cream

Nutrition Facts
Amount per serving
Calories 314
Total Fat 26.7g
Total Carbohydrate 17.8g
Dietary Fiber 4.4g
Total Sugars 7.1g
Protein 5.2g

Add the coconut milk, bay leaves, bone broth, cauliflower, celery, black pepper, salt, and onion to the Instant Pot. Stir thoroughly.

Close the lid, set the pressure release to Sealing, and select Manual/Pressure Cook. Set the Instant Pot to 5 minutes on high pressure and let cook.

Once cooked, let the pressure naturally disperse from the Instant Pot for about 3 minutes, then carefully switch the pressure release to Venting. Open the Instant Pot, remove bay leaves with tongs, and then stir in the clams and whipping cream.

Turn on Sauté mode, and let cook for 2 to 3 minutes (or until desired consistency). Serve, and enjoy!

BROCCOLI AND CHEDDAR SOUP

Serves 4

Prep Time: 5 minutes, Cook Time: 10 minutes, Total Time: 15 minutes, Pressure: High, Release: Quick

Gluten Free, Soy Free, 25 Minutes or Less, Kid Friendly

Broccoli is loaded with vitamin C, vitamin K, chromium, and many phytonutrients. This nutritious and delectable soup is a perfect keto lunch, and the Cheddar will have you forgetting all about how healthy this soup really is. Try adding some crumbled bacon on top of each bowl before serving for some extra decadence.

4 tablespoons grass-fed butter, softened

4 cups grass-fed bone broth

2 cups broccoli, chopped

1 cup celery, chopped

1/2 teaspoon garlic

1/2 teaspoon parsley, dried

1/2 teaspoon freshly ground black pepper

1/2 teaspoon kosher salt

1/4 (4-ounce) small onion, thinly sliced

2 cups full-fat Cheddar cheese, shredded

Nutrition Facts
Amount per serving
Calories 391
Total Fat 30.9g
Total Carbohydrate 7.4g
Dietary Fiber 1.8g
Total Sugars 1.7g
Protein 20.6g

Set the Instant Pot to Sauté. Add the butter, melting it gently .

Pour in the bone broth, then add the broccoli, celery, garlic, parsley, black pepper, salt, and onion to the Instant Pot. Close the lid, set the pressure release to Sealing, and select Manual/Pressure Cook. Set the Instant Pot to 10 minutes on high pressure and let cook.

Once cooked, perform a quick release. Open the lid and stir in the cheese until melted. Serve, and enjoy!

PARMESAN-OREGANO MEATBALLS

Serves 4 to 5

Prep Time: 5 minutes, Cook Time: 20 minutes, Total Time: 25 minutes, Pressure: High, Release: Natural

Gluten Free, Soy Free, 25 Minutes or Less, Kid Friendly

Meatballs are one of the best ways to quickly get some protein and healthy fats, and these keto meatballs always get rave reviews. These are great to freeze or refrigerate, so you have food for the whole week. Whip up a fresh salad or some dark leafy greens while these cook, and you will have a perfect meal in no time.

2 tablespoons coconut oil

1 pound grass-fed beef, ground

1 cup full-fat Parmesan cheese, grated

½ cup blanched almond flour

½ teaspoon oregano, dried

½ teaspoon cumin, ground

½ teaspoon kosher salt

½ teaspoon freshly ground black pepper

½ teaspoon garlic powder

½ teaspoon parsley, dried

1 (14-ounce) can sugar-free or low-sugar diced tomatoes

Nutrition Facts
Calories 424
Total Fat 28.5g
Total Carbohydrate 6.8g
Dietary Fiber 1.8g
Total Sugars 2.8g
Protein 36.8g

Set the Instant Pot to Sauté. Add the oil, melting it gently. Meanwhile, in a large bowl, combine the beef, Parmesan cheese, flour, oregano, cumin, salt, black pepper, garlic powder, parsley, and tomatoes. Once well-combined, form 1½ inch meatballs.

Place the meatballs inside the Instant Pot, then gently pour in any remaining tomatoes and liquid from the bowl. Close the lid, set the pressure release to Sealing, and select Manual/Pressure Cook. Set the Instant Pot to 20 minutes on high pressure and let cook.

Once cooked, let the pressure naturally disperse from the Instant Pot for about 10 minutes, then carefully switch the pressure release to Venting.

Open the lid and remove the food. Serve, and enjoy! Store any leftovers in the refrigerator or freezer.

FAST AND EASY GUMBO

(IPM)

Serves 2

**Prep Time: 5 minutes, Cook Time: 15 minutes, Total Time: 20 minutes,
Pressure: High, Release: Quick**

Gluten Free, Dairy Free, Soy Free, 25 Minutes or Less

The official state cuisine of Louisiana, gumbo is one of my favorite stews. It's thick, full
of flavor, and always easy to make. This version is perfect for your Instant Pot Mini,
and cooks up in just 20 minutes. A great weeknight choice.

2 cups grass-fed bone broth

½ pound grass-fed beef

¼ teaspoon arrowroot powder

½ stalk celery, chopped

¼ cup bell peppers, chopped

¼ (4-ounce) small onion, finely chopped

Nutrition Facts
Amount per serving
Calories 239
Total Fat 12.1g
Total Carbohydrate 4.9g
Dietary Fiber 0.6g
Total Sugars 1.8g
Protein 26.3g

Pour bone broth into the inner pot of the
Instant Pot, then add the grass-fed beef,
breaking it up thoroughly.

Close the lid, set the pressure release
to Sealing, and select Manual/Pressure
Cook. Set the Instant Pot to 15 minutes on
high pressure and let cook.

Once cooked, perform a quick release
by carefully switching the pressure valve
to Venting. Stir in the arrowroot powder,
celery, bell peppers, and onion. Serve and
enjoy!

CLASSIC GRILLED CHEESE

Serves 2

Prep Time: 5 minutes, Cook Time: 10 minutes, Total Time: 15 minutes, Pressure: High, Release: Natural

Gluten Free, Soy Free, 15 Minutes or Less, Kid Friendly

A perfectly cooked grilled cheese is one of my all-time favorite comfort foods. I know that I am not alone on this one, and luckily there is a great way to convert the carb-heavy favorite into a keto standard. Pair this with Garlic Tomato-Basil Soup (page 98) or enjoy it with a big salad.

CRUST
2 tablespoons grass-fed butter, softened
1 egg
2 tablespoons psyllium husks
½ cup blanched almond flour
¼ teaspoon baking soda

FILLING
¼ cup full-fat Cheddar cheese, shredded
¼ cup full-fat Monterey Jack cheese, shredded
¼ cup mozzarella cheese, full-fat, shredded

Nutrition Facts
Amount per serving
Calories 309
Total Fat 28.3g
Total Carbohydrate 3.5g
Dietary Fiber 1.1g
Total Sugars 0g
Protein 10.3g

In a large bowl, mix the egg, butter, psyllium, almond flour, and baking soda. In a well-greased, Instant Pot–friendly dish, evenly spread out this crust mixture. In the middle of the crust mixture, pour in the Cheddar, Monterey Jack, and mozzarella cheese.

Pour 1 cup of filtered water into the inner pot of the Instant Pot, then insert the trivet. Place the dish containing your sandwich on top of the trivet, covering it loosely with aluminum foil. Close the lid, set the pressure release to Sealing, and select Manual/Pressure Cook. Set the Instant Pot to 10 minutes on high pressure and let cook.

Once cooked, let the pressure naturally disperse from the Instant Pot for about 10 minutes, then carefully switch the pressure release to Venting. Open the lid and remove the food. Let cool a little bit, and carefully fold in half to form a sandwich, with the cheese in the center.

10-MINUTE PIZZA SOUP

(IPM)

Serves 2

Prep Time: 5 minutes, Cook Time: 5 minutes, Total Time: 10 minutes, Pressure: N/A, Release: N/A

Gluten Free, Soy Free, 10 Minutes or Less, Kid Friendly

Like the always-delicious pizza fries, this pizza soup folds up all the flavor of your favorite slice into one Instant Pot–friendly bowl. This flavor-packed dish works great in an Instant Pot Mini, and it is also one of my favorite kid friendly recipes out there.

2 cups full-fat Cheddar cheese, shredded

1 (14-ounce) can sugar-free or low-sugar fire roasted tomatoes

1/2 cup heavy whipping cream

1/2 teaspoon basil, dried

1/2 teaspoon oregano, dried

Nutrition Facts
Amount per serving
Calories 585
Total Fat 48.6g
Total Carbohydrate 7.5g
Dietary Fiber 1.2g
Total Sugars 3.7g
Protein 28.8g

Start by pouring 2 cups of filtered water into the inner pot of the Instant Pot, then add cheese, tomatoes, whipping cream, basil, and oregano, mixing together thoroughly.

Set the Instant Pot to Sauté and let cook for 5 minutes (or until cheese is melted), stirring occasionally. Ladle soup into bowls and enjoy!

CHICKEN SALAD WITH SUPER GREENS

Serves 4

Prep Time: 5 minutes, Cook Time: 20 minutes, Total Time: 25 minutes, Pressure: High, Release: Quick

Gluten Free, Dairy Free, Soy Free, 25 Minutes or Less, Kid Friendly

This chicken salad is a veritably perfect representation of good nutrition. It is packed with healthy protein, vegetables, and healthy fats. Sprinkle a small amount of ground turmeric over your bowl to add even more antioxidants to this nutritional powerhouse.

2 tablespoons avocado oil
1 pound chicken breast, cubed
½ teaspoon basil, dried
½ teaspoon parsley, dried
½ teaspoon turmeric, ground
½ teaspoon freshly ground black pepper
½ teaspoon kosher salt
2 tablespoons pine nuts, toasted
1 avocado, mashed
1 cup kale, chopped
1 cup arugula, chopped
1 cup Swiss chard, chopped
½ cup spinach, chopped

Nutrition Facts
Amount per serving
Calories 377
Total Fat 23.2g
Total Carbohydrate 7.7g
Dietary Fiber 4.2g
Total Sugars 0.6g
Protein 35.4g

Pour the avocado oil into the Instant Pot, then add the chicken, basil, parsley, turmeric, black pepper, salt, and ½ cup of filtered water. Close the lid, set the pressure release to Sealing, and select Manual/Pressure Cook. Set the Instant Pot to 20 minutes on high pressure and let cook.

Toss the pine nuts, avocado, kale, arugula, Swiss chard, and spinach, into a salad.

When cooking is complete, quickly turn the pressure valve to Venting. Open the lid, and remove the food.

Add the chicken to the salad, serve, and enjoy!

GARLIC TOMATO-BASIL SOUP

Serves 4

**Prep Time: 5 minutes, Cook Time: 20 minutes, Total Time: 25 minutes,
Pressure: High, Release: Natural**

Gluten Free, Soy Free, 25 Minutes or Less, Kid Friendly

Tomato soup is a great pick me up for a rainy day. On top of that, it pairs perfectly
with the Classic Grilled Cheese (page 95). Try adding one extra tablespoon of butter
to add even more flavor and richness to this hearty favorite.

2 tablespoons coconut oil

2 cloves garlic, minced

**1 cup full-fat Cheddar cheese, shredded
(optional)**

1 teaspoon basil, dried

1/2 teaspoon kosher salt

1/4 (4-ounce) small onion, thinly sliced

**2 (14-ounce) cans sugar-free or low-sugar
diced tomatoes**

1/2 cup heavy whipping cream

Nutrition Facts
Amount per serving
Calories 264
Total Fat 22.1g
Total Carbohydrate 9.4g
Dietary Fiber 2.5g
Total Sugars 5.7g
Protein 9.3g

Set the Instant Pot to Sauté mode. Add the
oil, melting it gently.

Mix in the garlic, cheese, basil, salt,
onion, and tomatoes. Close the lid, set
the pressure release to Sealing, and select
Manual/Pressure Cook. Set the Instant
Pot to 20 minutes on high pressure and
let cook.

Once cooked, let the pressure
naturally disperse from the Instant Pot for
about 10 minutes, then carefully switch the
pressure release to Venting.

Open the lid and stir in the heavy
whipping cream. Blend with an immersion
blender to achieve a smooth texture, if
desired.

Serve, and enjoy!

The Essential Instant Pot® Keto Cookbook

COCONUT CURRY MUSSELS

Serves 4

Prep Time: 5 minutes, Cook Time: 2 minutes, Total Time: 7 minutes, Pressure: High, Release: Quick

Gluten Free, Soy Free, 10 Minutes or Less

Did you know that mussels are one of the most nutritionally beneficial shellfish? They have vitamins, minerals, healthy fatty acids, and even have a good amount of iron. This recipe is a brilliant way to include them in your regular diet, and the coconut adds just the perfect accent.

2 tablespoons grass-fed butter, softened

1 (14-ounce) can full-fat coconut milk

1 pound mussels, cleaned

¼ (4-ounce) small onion, thinly sliced

2 teaspoons curry powder

½ teaspoon kosher salt

½ teaspoon ginger, finely grated

½ teaspoon cilantro, dried

½ teaspoon cayenne pepper, ground

Nutrition Facts
Amount per serving
Calories 388
Total Fat 32.4g
Total Carbohydrate 11.2g
Dietary Fiber 2.8g
Total Sugars 3.7g
Protein 16g

Set the Instant Pot to Sauté mode. Add the butter, melting it gently.

Pour in the coconut milk, then mix in the mussels, onion, curry powder, salt, ginger, cilantro, and cayenne pepper. Close the lid, set the pressure release to Sealing, and select Manual/Pressure Cook. Set the Instant Pot to 2 minutes on high pressure and let cook.

Once cooked, perform a quick release by carefully switching the pressure valve to Venting, and remove the mussels. Discard any mussels whose shells have not opened. Serve, and enjoy!

EASY POKE BOWL

Serves 2 to 4

**Prep Time: 5 minutes, Cook Time: 3 minutes, Total Time: 8 minutes,
Pressure: High, Release: Natural**

Gluten Free, Dairy Free, Soy Free, 25 Minutes or Less, Kid Friendly

Poke bowls have exploded in popularity over the last few years. This poke bowl combines the brain-enriching benefits of salmon, with the beneficial healthy monounsaturated fats found in avocados. Sprinkle with a bit of turmeric, to add even more anti-inflammatory health benefits.

1 cup coconut aminos

1 pound wild-caught salmon

1 tablespoon lime juice

2 cups cauliflower rice, cooked

1 drop stevia, liquid

1 avocado, peeled and sliced

1 seaweed sheet

½ teaspoon ginger, finely grated

Nutrition Facts
Amount per serving
Calories 332
Total Fat 16.9g
Total Carbohydrate 19.2g
Dietary Fiber 4.4g
Total Sugars 1.3g
Protein 24.2g

Pour the coconut aminos into the Instant Pot. Insert the trivet. Place the salmon on the trivet, skin-side down, and slowly pour lime juice over it.

Close the lid, set the pressure release to Sealing, and select Manual/Pressure Cook. Set the Instant Pot to 3 minutes on high pressure and let cook.

Once cooked, perform a quick release by carefully switching the pressure valve to Venting.

Open the lid and remove the salmon. In a large bowl, combine the cauliflower rice, stevia, avocado, seaweed, and ginger. Then add the salmon.

Serve, and enjoy!

The Essential Instant Pot® Keto Cookbook

5-INGREDIENT ALBONDIGAS SOUP

Recipe courtesy of True Fare

(IPM)

Serves 2

**Prep Time: 5 minutes, Cook Time: 15 minutes, Total Time: 20 minutes,
Pressure: High, Release: Quick**

Gluten Free, Dairy Free, Soy Free, 25 Minutes or Less, Kid Friendly

If you like meatballs and you like a little bit of spice—this is the perfect dish for you.
Made perfectly in an Instant Pot Mini, this soup is also ready in just 15 minutes—and
only requires 5 ingredients.

2 cups grass-fed bone broth

**1 (14-ounce) can sugar-free or low-sugar
fire roasted tomatoes**

1/2 teaspoon paprika, fresh

1/2 teaspoon chili powder, dried

1/2 pound grass-fed beef, ground

Nutrition Facts
Amount per serving
Calories 298
Total Fat 17.2g
Total Carbohydrate 7.6g
Dietary Fiber 1.5g
Total Sugars 3.1g
Protein 26.1g

Pour bone broth into the inner pot of
the Instant Pot, then add the tomatoes,
paprika, and chili powder.

Form 6 meatballs with the grass-fed
beef, then add them in with the other
ingredients.

Close the lid, set the pressure release
to Sealing, and select Manual/Pressure
Cook. Set the Instant Pot to 15 minutes on
high pressure and let cook.

Once cooked, perform a quick release
by carefully switching the pressure valve to
Venting, and serve.

CRISPY BACON BOMB

Serves 4

**Prep Time: 10 minutes, Cook Time: 20 minutes, Total Time: 30 minutes,
Pressure: High, Release: Natural**

Gluten Free, Soy Free

Bacon is definitely one of the flavorful perks of the keto diet. This unique dish is absolutely loaded with taste and feels like a treat, yet it is still packed with antioxidants and plenty of healthy nutrients. I like to use bacon that is on the thinner side, so it ends up being a little crispier, once cooked. Serve with a salad, or soup.

1 pound no-sugar-added bacon

¼ cup full-fat Cheddar cheese, shredded

6 slices full-fat provolone cheese

¼ cup full-fat Monterey Jack cheese, shredded

½ cup spinach, chopped

½ teaspoon chili powder

½ teaspoon cayenne pepper, ground

½ teaspoon freshly ground black pepper

Nutrition Facts
Amount per serving
Calories 395
Total Fat 30.7g
Total Carbohydrate 1.8g
Dietary Fiber 0.3g
Total Sugars 0.3g
Protein 27g

On a large cookie sheet covered with aluminum foil, tightly weave the bacon, forming a bottom layer. Go over and then under, making it as tight as possible. If you are having trouble visualizing how to proceed, form a T shape with two pieces of bacon, and then continue to interlink.

Add the Cheddar, provolone, and Monterey Jack on top, followed by the spinach. Sprinkle on the chili powder, cayenne pepper, and black pepper. Push down gently on the top of the food, and then roll it into a ball. You want this to be done as tightly as possible. Transfer this ball into a well-greased, Instant Pot–friendly dish.

Pour 1 cup of filtered water into the inner pot of the Instant Pot, then insert the trivet. Using a sling if desired, place the dish on top of the trivet.

Close the lid, set the pressure release to Sealing, and select Manual/Pressure Cook. Set the Instant Pot to 20 minutes on

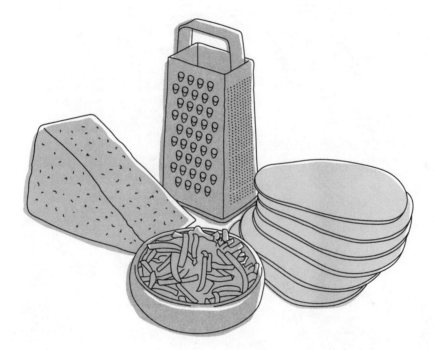

high pressure and let cook. While cooking, preheat the oven to 350°F, if you'd like to have a crispier dish.

Once cooked, let the pressure naturally disperse from the Instant Pot for about 10 minutes, then carefully switch the pressure release to Venting.

Open the lid and remove the food.

If desired, finish the bomb in the oven by returning it to the cookie sheet and cooking for 5 to 10 minutes (or until desired crispness is reached). Serve and enjoy!

HOW TO MAKE A BACON WEAVE

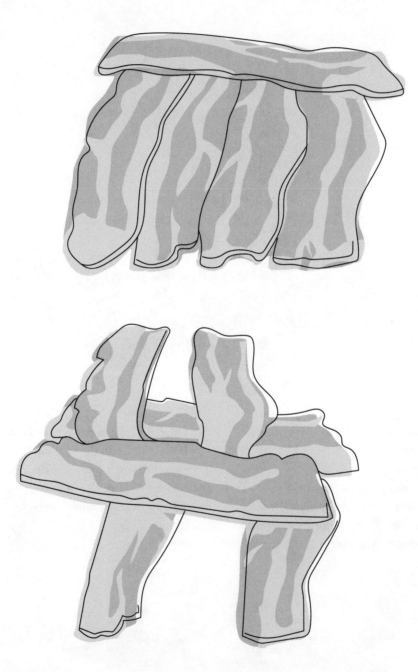

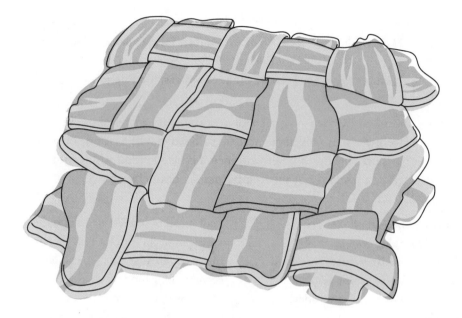

HAM AND CHEESE BAKE

Serves 2 to 4

**Prep Time: 5 minutes, Cook Time: 20 minutes, Total Time: 25 minutes,
Pressure: High, Release: Natural**

Gluten Free, Soy Free, 25 Minutes or Less, Kid Friendly

Ham and cheese sandwiches were a childhood staple for many of us. Since a keto approach will nix any bread, this ham and cheese bake makes a good substitute. The best part? It is actually much healthier, since it is also loaded with vegetables, and leaves out the empty calories of the bread.

2 tablespoons coconut oil

1 cup heavy whipping cream

1 cup full-fat Cheddar cheese, shredded

½ pound cauliflower, chopped

½ cup mozzarella cheese, shredded

½ pound ham, sliced

½ cup bell peppers, chopped

½ teaspoon freshly ground black pepper

½ teaspoon basil, dried

½ teaspoon oregano, dried

½ teaspoon rosemary, ground

½ teaspoon kosher salt

Nutrition Facts
Amount per serving (4)
Calories 492
Total Fat 39.3g
Total Carbohydrate 10.4g
Dietary Fiber 3.3g
Total Sugars 3.1g
Protein 25.8g

Pour 1 cup of filtered water into the inner pot of the Instant Pot, then insert the trivet. In a large bowl, combine the coconut oil, whipping cream, Cheddar, cauliflower, mozzarella, ham, bell peppers, black pepper, basil, oregano, rosemary, and salt, mixing thoroughly. Transfer this mixture into a well-greased, Instant Pot–friendly dish.

Using a sling if desired, place the dish onto the trivet, and cover loosely with aluminum foil. Close the lid, set the pressure release to Sealing, and select Manual/Pressure Cook. Set the Instant Pot to 20 minutes on high pressure and let cook.

Once cooked, let the pressure naturally disperse from the Instant Pot for about 10 minutes, then carefully switch the pressure release to Venting.

Open the Instant Pot and remove the dish. Let cool, serve, and enjoy!

MUG LASAGNA

Serves 2 to 3

**Prep Time: 5 minutes, Cook Time: 5 minutes, Total Time: 10 minutes,
Pressure: High, Release: Natural**

Gluten Free, Soy Free, 10 Minutes or Less, Kid Friendly

Lasagna is a great meal—but it can be time-consuming and complicated to cook. This innovative keto mug variety is still rich with flavor—but is much faster and easier to make. It works great for a solo night in, or for a quick meal on the weekend. Try adding a little extra cheese on top, when serving, to make this dish even more palatable.

2 tablespoons whole milk ricotta cheese

2 tablespoons full-fat Cheddar cheese, shredded

½ cup full-fat Parmesan cheese, grated

½ zucchini, thinly sliced

½ teaspoon basil, dried

½ teaspoon oregano, dried

½ teaspoon freshly ground black pepper

½ teaspoon kosher salt

⅓ cup full-fat mozzarella cheese, shredded

½ (14-ounce) can sugar-free or low-sugar roasted tomatoes, drained

Nutrition Facts
Amount per serving
Calories 177
Total Fat 11g
Total Carbohydrate 5.2g
Dietary Fiber 0.9g
Total Sugars 1.6g
Protein 15.7g

Pour 1 cup filtered water into the Instant Pot, then insert the trivet. In a large bowl, combine the ricotta, Cheddar, Parmesan, zucchini, basil, oregano, black pepper, salt, mozzarella, and tomatoes. Mix thoroughly. Transfer this mixture into a well-greased, Instant Pot–friendly mug (or multiple, smaller mugs, if desired).

Place the mug onto the trivet, and cover loosely with aluminum foil. Close the lid, set the pressure release to Sealing, and select Manual/Pressure Cook. Set the Instant Pot to 5 minutes on high pressure and let cook.

Once cooked, let the pressure naturally disperse from the Instant Pot for about 10 minutes, then carefully switch the pressure release to Venting.

Open the Instant Pot, and remove the mug. Let cool, serve, and enjoy!

DINNER

BABY BACK RIBS

Serves 4 to 6

Prep Time: 5 minutes, Cook Time: 45 minutes, Total Time: 50 minutes, Pressure: High, Release: Natural

Gluten Free, Dairy Free, Soy Free, Kid Friendly

This delicious entrée provides protein, iron, B$_{12}$, and much more. The ribs are also a breeze to make, and are definitely one of my favorite Instant Pot recipes. Pair with cauliflower rice or a bowl full of dark leafy greens for a perfect dinner.

1 cup grass-fed bone broth

1 tablespoon crushed red pepper

1 tablespoon chili powder

¼ cup yellow mustard

1 teaspoon hot sauce

½ teaspoon oregano, dried

½ teaspoon kosher salt

½ teaspoon freshly ground black pepper

¼ teaspoon cumin, ground

2 racks baby back ribs (about 2 to 3 pounds)

Barbecue sauce (Tessemae's, or other keto-approved brand) to serve

Nutrition Facts
Amount per serving
Calories 762
Total Fat 57g
Total Carbohydrates 5g
Dietary Fiber 0.5g
Sugars 2g
Protein 39g

Pour bone broth into the Instant Pot.

In a large bowl, mix the red pepper, chili powder, mustard, hot sauce, oregano, salt, black pepper, and cumin together thoroughly.

Rub mixture over ribs, then place the ribs in the Instant Pot, on a rack, with the meatier part of the ribs facing outward.

Secure lid, and cook in Meat/Stew mode for 45 minutes (or until desired tenderness), with valve sealed.

Switch the pressure release to Venting, remove ribs, and brush lightly with barbecue sauce.

NOTE: You can also place the ribs on a baking sheet, and perform the additional step of finishing them in the oven. They should take about 5 minutes, per side.

POACHED SALMON

Recipe courtesy of Nom Nom Paleo

Serves 4

**Prep Time: 5 minutes, Cook Time: 3 minutes, Total Time: 8 minutes,
Pressure: High, Release: Natural**

Gluten Free, Dairy Free, Soy Free, 10 Minutes or Less, Kid Friendly

This simple, delicious, and nutritious salmon recipe is a great use of the Instant Pot. The key to cooking fish in the Instant Pot is simple: Have a very short cooking time. Try smearing some extra butter and a touch of garlic over the cooked fish to enhance its delicate flavor.

2 lemons, sliced

4 salmon fillets

8 tablespoons grass-fed butter, softened

2 teaspoons Dijon mustard

1 garlic clove, chopped

1 teaspoon thyme, ground

1/2 teaspoon parsley, dried

1/2 teaspoon kosher salt

1/2 teaspoon freshly ground black pepper

Nutrition Facts
Amount per serving
Calories 472
Total Fat 35.3g
Total Carbohydrate 4.6g
Dietary Fiber 1.5g
Total Sugars 1.1g
Protein 35.2g

Inside the Instant Pot, place a layer of aluminum foil, then line with a single layer of lemon slices.

Pour 1 inch of filtered water into the inner pot. Add in salmon, with the skin facing down. Put on the lid, and seal the valve. Cook on Steam for 3 minutes. While cooking, in a medium bowl, melt the butter in the microwave (45 seconds), then add in the mustard, garlic, thyme, parsley, salt, and pepper; stirring thoroughly.

Once salmon is cooked, perform a quick release by carefully switching the pressure valve to Venting. Do not let the salmon cook for longer than 3 minutes; remove it immediately after the quick release.

Discard lemon slices and place salmon fillets on plates. Serve with the prepared sauce.

WHOLE ROAST CHICKEN

Serves 6

**Prep Time: 5 minutes, Cook Time: 25 minutes, Total Time: 30 minutes,
Pressure: High, Release: Natural**

Gluten Free, Soy Free, Kid Friendly

This is undoubtedly the first recipe you should show your friends when you purchase your Instant Pot. They may (understandably) be skeptical that you can cook an entire chicken inside a fairly small cooking appliance. The chicken goes best with a plate of greens or cauliflower rice. It's a complete gourmet meal—all done in under an hour.

4 tablespoons grass-fed butter, softened

1 teaspoon basil, dried

1 teaspoon cilantro, dried

1/2 teaspoon kosher salt

1/2 teaspoon freshly ground black pepper

1/2 cup grass-fed bone broth

1 whole chicken

Nutrition Facts
Amount per serving
Calories 215
Total Fat 13.4g
Total Carbohydrate 0.3g
Dietary Fiber 0.1g
Total Sugars 0g
Protein 21.6g

In a large bowl, thoroughly mix the butter, basil, cilantro, salt, and pepper.

Pour bone broth into the Instant Pot. Add the chicken (with the breast facing down). Baste lightly with the buttery mixture.

Seal the valve and secure the lid of the Instant Pot. Cook for 25 minutes on the Meat setting. Once cooked, let the pressure naturally disperse from the Instant Pot for about 15 minutes, then carefully switch the pressure release to Venting.

Remove chicken, carve, and enjoy!

PORK CHOPS

Serves 4 to 6

**Prep Time: 5 minutes, Cook Time: 30 minutes, Total Time: 35 minutes,
Pressure: High, Release: Natural**

Gluten Free, Soy Free, Kid Friendly

Pork chops are another comfort food favorite, but you may be surprised to learn they are both keto and able to be cooked easily in the Instant Pot. These chops will provide you with a healthy dose of protein, as well as a good amount of vitamin B_6. Pair with some buttered green beans or some of your other favorite low-carb vegetables.

2 tablespoons coconut oil

4 pork chops, boneless

1 tablespoon grass-fed butter

1 teaspoon crushed red pepper

1/2 teaspoon parsley, dried

1/2 teaspoon garlic powder

1/2 teaspoon chili powder

1/2 teaspoon basil, dried

1/2 teaspoon kosher salt

1/2 teaspoon freshly ground black pepper

1/4 cup hot sauce (or other preferred sauce)

Nutrition Facts
Amount per serving
Calories   232
Total Fat 19.9g
Total Carbohydrate 0.8g
Dietary Fiber 0.3g
Total Sugars 0.2g
Protein 12.2g

Set the Instant Pot to Sauté and melt the oil. Brown the sides of the pork chops; this should take about 5 minutes per side.

Add 1 cup of filtered water, butter, red pepper, parsley, garlic powder, chili powder, basil, salt, and black pepper to the Instant Pot. Close the lid, set the pressure release to Sealing, and hit Cancel to stop the current program. Select Manual/Pressure Cook, set the Instant Pot to 30 minutes on high pressure, and let cook.

Once cooked, let the pressure naturally disperse from the Instant Pot for about 10 minutes, then carefully switch the pressure release to Venting. Remove the pork chops, and rub with the hot sauce (or other preferred sauce). Serve, and enjoy!

The Essential Instant Pot® Keto Cookbook

SIMPLE CRAB LEGS

Serves 5

Prep Time: 5 minutes, Cook Time: 3 minutes, Total Time: 8 minutes, Pressure: High, Release: Quick

Gluten Free, Dairy Free, Soy Free, 10 Minutes or Less, Kid Friendly

This recipe is as simple as I could make it—but you should not stop there. Crab legs go great with any number of foods, including (but not limited to): artichokes, Brussels sprouts, zucchini, broccoli, spinach, green beans, cauliflower rice—and many more. Try also pairing these crab legs with my recipes for lobster and crab bisque (pages 61 & 122), for even more protein.

2 pounds crab legs, thawed

Nutrition Facts
Amount per serving
Calories 152
Total Fat 4.8g
Total Carbohydrate 0g
Dietary Fiber 0g
Total Sugars 0g
Protein 18.8g

Pour 1 cup of water into the Instant Pot and insert trivet.

Place the crab legs on top of the trivet.

Select Manual/Pressure Cook, set the Instant Pot to 3 minutes on high pressure, and let cook.

Immediately after cook time completes, carefully switch the pressure release to Venting.

Set crab legs on a plate, and serve with whatever desired!

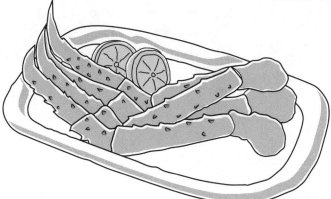

HOT 'N' SPICY MEATLOAF

Serves 4

Prep Time: 5 minutes, Cook Time: 35 minutes, Total Time: 40 minutes, Pressure: High, Release: Natural

Gluten Free, Dairy Free, Soy Free

This meatloaf might not be the prettiest thing you ever make in the Instant Pot, but it might be the tastiest. It also provides a huge amount of protein, B vitamins, minerals, and more. Try pairing it with mashed cauliflower, carrots, or any dark leafy green (spinach, kale, broccoli, bok choy, Swiss chard).

1 pound grass-fed beef, ground

1 teaspoon curry powder

½ teaspoon parsley, dried

½ teaspoon turmeric, ground

½ teaspoon paprika, fresh

½ teaspoon chili powder

½ teaspoon basil, dried

½ teaspoon crushed red pepper

½ teaspoon coconut aminos

½ teaspoon kosher salt

½ teaspoon freshly ground black pepper

Nutrition Facts
Amount per serving
Calories 253
Total Fat 15.2g
Total Carbohydrate 1.2g
Dietary Fiber 0.6g
Total Sugars 0.1g
Protein 26.5g

Pour 1 cup of filtered water into the inner pot of the Instant Pot, and insert the trivet.

On a piece of aluminum foil, mix together the beef, curry powder, parsley, turmeric, paprika, chili powder, basil, red pepper, coconut aminos, salt, and black pepper. Form into one large loaf. Move this (and the aluminum foil) to rest on top of the trivet.

Close the lid, set the pressure release to Sealing, and select Manual/Pressure Cook. Set the Instant Pot to 35 minutes on high pressure and let cook.

Once cooked, let the pressure naturally disperse from the Instant Pot for about 10 minutes, then carefully switch the pressure release to Venting. Open the Instant Pot, serve, and enjoy!

CLAMBAKE

Serves 4 to 5

**Prep Time: 5 minutes, Cook Time: 6 minutes, Total Time: 11 minutes,
Pressure: High, Release: Quick**

Gluten Free, Dairy Free, Soy Free, 25 Minutes or Less

A clambake is not only a great time; this recipe will provide you with almost an entire day's worth of nutrients! It might be personal preference, but the taste of just-cooked lobster is one of my favorite things in the world. This can pair with any number of foods, like mashed cauliflower, asparagus, broccoli, spinach, kale, or a big bowl of dark leafy greens. Smear a little butter on the seafood, and watch it melt into heavenly perfection.

2 tablespoons avocado oil

1 cup grass-fed bone broth

20 clams, scrubbed

2 lobster tails, thawed if frozen

½ teaspoon kosher salt

½ teaspoon freshly ground black pepper

Nutrition Facts
Amount per serving
Calories 137
Total Fat 1.7g
Total Carbohydrate 3g
Dietary Fiber 0.3g
Total Sugars 0g
Protein 26.1g

Set the Instant Pot to Sauté and heat the oil.

Pour in the bone broth. Working in batches (if needed), add the clams, lobster tails, salt, and pepper to the Instant Pot. Close the lid, set the pressure release to Sealing and hit Cancel to stop the current program. Select Manual/Pressure Cook, set the Instant Pot to 6 minutes on high pressure, and let cook.

Immediately upon completion, carefully switch the pressure release to Venting.

Remove clams and lobster tails, and serve with whatever is desired!

DECONSTRUCTED BACON PIZZA

Serves 4

Prep Time: 5 minutes, Cook Time: 10 minutes, Total Time: 15 minutes, Pressure: High, Release: Natural

Gluten Free, Soy Free, 25 Minutes or Less, Kid Friendly

Bacon pizza truly feels like a cheat, but it's not. This genius Instant Pot recipe provides a surprisingly large amount of protein, in addition to the truly mouthwatering taste. Sprinkle your finished pizza with some crushed red pepper to provide some extra heat.

2 tablespoons coconut oil

1 pound turkey, ground

½ teaspoon kosher salt

½ teaspoon freshly ground black pepper

1 (14-ounce) can sugar-free or low-sugar crushed tomatoes

2 cups full-fat Cheddar cheese, shredded

4 slices no-sugar-added bacon, cut finely, cooked

Nutrition Facts
Amount per serving
Calories 595
Total Fat 39.1g
Total Carbohydrate 3.7g
Dietary Fiber 0.6g
Total Sugars 1.8g
Protein 54.4g

Set the Instant Pot to Sauté and melt the oil. Add ground turkey, salt, and pepper. Cook until browned, stirring occasionally. Arrange the turkey so that it's in a single layer, acting as the "crust." In order, add the salt, black pepper, tomatoes, Cheddar, and bacon. Do not mix.

Close the lid, set the pressure release to Sealing and hit Cancel to stop the current program. Select Manual/Pressure Cook, set the Instant Pot to 10 minutes on high pressure, and let cook.

Once cooked, let the pressure naturally disperse from the Instant Pot for about 10 minutes, then carefully switch the pressure release to Venting.

Open the Instant Pot, serve, and enjoy!

FAST AND EASY CHICKEN CACCIATORE

Serves 4 to 5

Prep Time: 5 minutes, Cook Time: 18 minutes, Total Time: 23 minutes, Pressure: High, Release: Quick

Gluten Free, Dairy Free, Soy Free, 25 Minutes or Less, Kid Friendly

This chicken cacciatore recipe is a great weeknight fix for dinner, and it will also leave leftovers for a few more nights thereafter. I recommend pairing this with a salad, preferably loaded up with some healthy fats (like avocado). You can also drink a warm mug of bone broth (page 70), which goes perfectly with this dish.

6 tablespoons coconut oil

5 chicken legs

1 bell pepper, diced

1/2 teaspoon basil, dried

1/2 onion, chopped

1/2 teaspoon parsley, dried

1/2 teaspoon kosher salt

1/2 teaspoon freshly ground black pepper

1 (14-ounce) can sugar-free or low-sugar diced tomatoes

Nutrition Facts
Amount per serving
Calories 344
Total Fat 24.3g
Total Carbohydrate 5.1g
Dietary Fiber 1.6g
Total Sugars 3.2g
Protein 26.5g

Set the Instant Pot to Sauté and melt the oil. Add the chicken and sauté until the outside is browned. Remove chicken and set aside.

Sauté pepper, basil, onion, parsley, salt, black pepper, and tomatoes together in the Instant Pot.

Pour in 1/2 cup of filtered water, then return the chicken to the pot, on top of all other ingredients. Close the lid, set the pressure release to Sealing, and hit Cancel to stop the current program. Select Manual/Pressure Cook, set the Instant Pot to 18 minutes on high pressure, and let cook.

Immediately upon cooking, carefully switch the pressure release to Venting. Open the Instant Pot, serve, and enjoy!

SPICY MEXICAN CHICKEN

Serves 4

Prep Time: 5 minutes, Cook Time: 17 minutes, Total Time: 22 minutes, Pressure: High, Release: Quick

Gluten Free, Dairy Free, Soy Free, 25 Minutes or Less, Kid Friendly

I am big fan of spices, as I have had chicken more times than I can possibly count. Spices and hot flavors keep things interesting, and this Mexican chicken is no different. Try a blend of different cheeses melted over the finished chicken for even more flavor. Or try adding a small bit of cilantro or green chile.

2 tablespoons avocado oil

1 pound chicken, ground,

½ jalapeño, finely chopped

½ teaspoon coriander

½ teaspoon crushed red pepper

½ teaspoon curry powder

½ teaspoon chili powder

½ teaspoon kosher salt

½ teaspoon freshly ground black pepper

¼ poblano chili pepper, finely chopped

1 (14-ounce) can sugar-free or low-sugar fire roasted tomatoes

Set the Instant Pot to Sauté and heat the oil. Pour in ½ cup water, then add the chicken, jalapeño, coriander, red pepper, curry powder, chili powder, salt, black pepper, chili pepper, and tomatoes.

Close the lid, set the pressure release to Sealing and hit Cancel to stop the current program. Select Manual/Pressure Cook, set the Instant Pot to 17 minutes on high pressure, and let cook.

Immediately upon cooking, carefully switch the pressure release to Venting. Open the Instant Pot, serve, and enjoy!

Nutrition Facts
Amount per serving
Calories 269
Total Fat 14.7g
Total Carbohydrate 4.2g
Dietary Fiber 1.2g
Total Sugars 2.2g
Protein 30g

The Essential Instant Pot® Keto Cookbook

CLASSIC POT ROAST

Serves 5 to 6

**Prep Time: 5 minutes, Cook Time: 55 minutes, Total Time: 60 minutes,
Pressure: High, Release: Natural**

Gluten Free, Soy Free, Kid Friendly

The Instant Pot is truly capable of wonders, and this pot roast is undoubtedly one of them. Cooking the pot roast in the Instant Pot brings down the cooking time from many hours to just one, and the meat will still be tender and taste great. This pot roast also goes perfectly with a small amount of carrots, a side salad, or mashed cauliflower.

2 tablespoons coconut oil

3 pounds beef chuck roast

1 cup grass-fed butter

½ teaspoon paprika, fresh

½ teaspoon parsley, dried

½ teaspoon basil, dried

½ teaspoon chili powder

½ teaspoon kosher salt

½ teaspoon freshly ground black pepper

Nutrition Facts
Amount per serving
Calories 486
Total Fat 40g
Total Carbohydrate 0.4g
Dietary Fiber 0.2g
Total Sugars 0g
Protein 29.8g

Set the Instant Pot to Sauté and melt the oil. Sauté the pot roast briefly to sear the outside of the meat, then remove.

Pour 1 cup of filtered water into the inner pot of the Instant Pot, then add the butter, paprika, parsley, basil, chili powder, salt, and black pepper. Last, return the beef to the pot.

Once all ingredients are in the Instant Pot, close the lid, set the pressure release to Sealing, and hit Cancel to stop the current program. Select Manual/Pressure Cook, set the Instant Pot to 55 minutes on high pressure, and let cook.

Once cooked, let the pressure naturally disperse from the Instant Pot for about 10 minutes, then carefully switch the pressure release to Venting. Open the Instant Pot, serve, and enjoy!

GRANDMA'S CLASSIC MEATBALLS

Serves 4

Prep Time: 5 minutes, Cook Time: 16 minutes, Total Time: 21 minutes, Pressure: High, Release: Quick

Gluten Free, Dairy Free, Soy Free, 25 Minutes or Less, Kid Friendly

These super meatballs are packed with healthy fats, protein, vitamins, and minerals. The included mozzarella makes them absolutely delectable, and the basil adds just the right amount of flavor. Pair these with any number of healthy greens like broccoli, asparagus, Swiss chard, spinach, kale, Brussels sprouts, or bok choy.

2 tablespoons avocado oil

2 tablespoons coconut oil

1 pound grass-fed beef, ground

1/2 teaspoon cayenne pepper, ground

1/2 teaspoon crushed red pepper

1/2 teaspoon basil, dried

1/2 teaspoon kosher salt

1/2 teaspoon freshly ground black pepper

2 (14-ounce) cans sugar-free or low-sugar fire roasted tomatoes

Nutrition Facts
Amount per serving
Calories 343
Total Fat 22.7g
Total Carbohydrate 6.2g
Dietary Fiber 1.5g
Total Sugars 3.5g
Protein 26.4g

Set the Instant Pot to Sauté and heat the avocado oil. In a large bowl, mix together the coconut oil, beef, cayenne pepper, red pepper, basil, salt, and black pepper. Form the mixture into 1½ inch meatballs and place them into the Instant Pot. Then, pour the tomatoes evenly over the meatballs.

Close the lid, set the pressure release to Sealing, and hit Cancel to stop the current program. Select Manual/Pressure Cook, set the Instant Pot to 16 minutes on high pressure, and let cook.

Once cooked, carefully switch the pressure release to Venting. Open the Instant Pot, serve by sprinkling your favorite shredded cheese over the meatballs (if desired), and enjoy!

BONE BROTH BRISKET

Serves 4 to 5

Prep Time: 5 minutes, Cook Time: 75 minutes, Total Time: 80 minutes, Pressure: High, Release: Quick

Gluten Free, Dairy Free, Soy Free

This bone broth-based dish is packed with a large amount of nutrients. Not only does bone broth assist in healing your gut, but the brisket is very high in vitamin B_{12} and protein. Complete this delicious dinner with a healthy salad, full of fresh greens, and some healthy fats (like extra-virgin olive oil, or avocado).

2 tablespoons coconut oil

½ teaspoon garlic salt

½ teaspoon crushed red pepper

½ teaspoon basil, dried

½ teaspoon kosher salt

½ teaspoon freshly ground black pepper

1 (14-ounce) can sugar-free or low-sugar diced tomatoes

1 cup grass-fed bone broth

1 pound beef brisket, chopped, thawed

Nutrition Facts
Amount per serving
Calories 240
Total Fat 11.1g
Total Carbohydrate 4.9g
Dietary Fiber 1.5g
Total Sugars 2.8g
Protein 29.3g

Set the Instant Pot to Sauté and melt the oil. Mix the garlic salt, red pepper, basil, kosher salt, black pepper, and tomatoes in a medium bowl.

Pour bone broth into the Instant Pot, then add the brisket, and top with the premixed sauce. Close the lid, set the pressure release to Sealing, and hit Cancel to stop the current program. Select Manual/Pressure Cook, set the Instant Pot to 75 minutes on high pressure, and let cook.

Once cooked, carefully switch the pressure release to Venting. Open the Instant Pot, and serve. You can pour remaining sauce over brisket, if desired.

CRAB BISQUE

Serves 4

Prep Time: 5 minutes, Cook Time: 3 minutes, Total Time: 8 minutes, Pressure: Low, Release: Quick

Gluten Free, Soy Free, 10 Minutes or Less

Crab bisque—is there anything more delicious (and nutritious) for dinner? I frequently pair this with fresh asparagus, or some steamed broccoli. Try garnishing the bisque with a pinch of tarragon or paprika, for even more taste.

4 tablespoons grass-fed butter, softened

3 cups grass-fed bone broth

8 ounces full-fat cream cheese, softened

2 stalks celery, chopped

1 pound frozen crab meat, thawed

1 teaspoon Old Bay seasoning

1/2 teaspoon cayenne pepper, ground

1/2 teaspoon freshly ground black pepper

1/2 teaspoon kosher salt

1/4 cup bell peppers, chopped

1/4 cup heavy whipping cream

1/4 (4-ounce) small onion, thinly sliced

1 (14-ounce) can sugar-free or low-sugar crushed tomatoes

Set the Instant Pot to Sauté. Add the butter, melting it gently.

Pour in the bone broth, then mix in the cream cheese, celery, crab, Old Bay, cayenne pepper, black pepper, salt, bell peppers, whipping cream, onion, and tomatoes. Close the lid, set the pressure release to Sealing, and select Manual/Pressure Cook. Set the Instant Pot to 3 minutes on low pressure and let cook.

When cooking is complete, perform a quick release by carefully switching the pressure valve to Venting. For a smoother soup, briefly use an immersion blender, until desired consistency is reached.

Remove the bisque, serve, and enjoy!

Nutrition Facts
Amount per serving
Calories 415
Total Fat 35.1g
Total Carbohydrate 10.7g
Dietary Fiber 1.6g
Total Sugars 4.1g
Protein 13g

9-MINUTE MAHI MAHI

Serves 4

Prep Time: 5 minutes, Cook Time: 4 minutes, Total Time: 9 minutes, Pressure: Low, Release: Quick

Gluten Free, Dairy Free, Soy Free, 10 Minutes or Less, Kid Friendly

Mahi mahi is one of my favorites, and this recipe is very easy to make. The Instant Pot makes cooking fish a breeze, and you can prepare some asparagus, mashed cauliflower, or a side salad, while the mahi mahi cooks. Serve with lemon, butter, or garlic, if you want an even richer taste.

3 tablespoons grass-fed butter, softened

1 piece ginger, grated

½ lime, juiced

½ lemon, juiced

½ teaspoon basil, dried

½ teaspoon freshly ground black pepper

½ teaspoon kosher salt

½ teaspoon garlic, minced

4 mahi mahi fillets

Nutrition Facts
Amount per serving
Calories 310
Total Fat 11.4g
Total Carbohydrate 1.3g
Dietary Fiber 0.3g
Total Sugars 0.2g
Protein 47.4g

Pour ½ cup filtered water into the Instant Pot, then insert the trivet. In a large bowl, combine the butter, ginger, lime juice, lemon juice, basil, black pepper, salt, and garlic. Mix thoroughly. Coat the mahi mahi filets with this mixture, then place the filets into a well-greased, Instant Pot–friendly dish.

Place the dish onto the trivet, and cover loosely with aluminum foil. Close the lid, set the pressure release to Sealing and select Manual/Pressure Cook. Set the Instant Pot to 4 minutes on low pressure, and let cook.

Once cooked, perform a quick release by carefully switching the pressure valve to Venting. Open the Instant Pot, and remove the filets. Serve, and enjoy!

HIGH-PROTEIN MEATZA CASSEROLE

Serves 4

**Prep Time: 5 minutes, Cook Time: 20 minutes, Total Time: 25 minutes,
Pressure: High, Release: Natural**

Gluten Free, Soy Free, 25 Minutes or Less, Kid Friendly

There is nothing easier or more delicious for dinner than a meatza! Instead of a pizza, you can get more protein, by using meat as your "crust." However, this meatza is more like a casserole, and the Instant Pot makes cooking this a breeze. The options to customize this to your liking are also truly endless. I personally like to add some crushed red pepper to the finished dish, but you can add bacon, more cheese, or any other keto-friendly toppings.

16 pepperoni slices, uncured

1 cup mozzarella cheese, shredded

1 cup full-fat Cheddar cheese, shredded

1 pound chicken, ground

1 egg

1 teaspoon garlic, minced

½ cup full-fat Parmesan cheese, grated

½ teaspoon parsley, dried

½ teaspoon thyme, ground

½ teaspoon basil, dried

½ teaspoon freshly ground black pepper

½ teaspoon crushed red pepper

½ teaspoon oregano, dried

1 (14-ounce) can sugar-free or low-sugar fire roasted tomatoes

Nutrition Facts
Amount per serving
Calories 538
Total Fat 30.9g
Total Carbohydrate 4.9g
Dietary Fiber 0.8g
Total Sugars 1.8g
Protein 57.9g

Pour 1 cup of filtered water into the inner pot of the Instant Pot, then insert the trivet. In a large bowl combine pepperoni slices, mozzarella, Cheddar, chicken, egg, garlic, Parmesan, parsley, thyme, basil, black pepper, red pepper, oregano, and tomatoes. Mix thoroughly. Transfer this mixture into a well-greased, Instant Pot–friendly dish.

Place the dish onto the trivet, and cover loosely with aluminum foil. Close the lid, set the pressure release to Sealing, and select Manual/Pressure Cook. Set the Instant Pot to 20 minutes on high pressure, and let cook.

Once cooked, let the pressure naturally disperse from the Instant Pot for about 10 minutes, then carefully switch the pressure release to Venting.

Open the Instant Pot, and remove the dish. Let cool, serve, and enjoy!

FAST AND EASY CHICKEN ESCABÈCHE

Recipe courtesy of True Fare

Serves 4

Prep Time: 5 minutes, Cook Time: 15 minutes, Total Time: 20 minutes, Pressure: High, Release: Natural

Gluten Free, Dairy Free, Soy Free, 25 Minutes or Less, Kid Friendly

This chicken dish is traditionally popular in France and Spain, but the Instant Pot version is far faster. I like serving this dinner with collard greens, though any greens would be a good choice. To get even more nutritional benefits, drink a warm mug of bone broth with this protein-rich meal.

3 garlic cloves, smashed

2 bay leaves

1 pound chicken, mixed pieces

1 onion, chopped

½ cup red wine vinegar

½ teaspoon cumin, ground

½ teaspoon coriander

½ teaspoon mint, finely chopped

½ teaspoon freshly ground black pepper

½ teaspoon kosher salt

Nutrition Facts
Amount per serving
Calories 195
Total Fat 3.6g
Total Carbohydrate 4.1g
Dietary Fiber 0.8g
Total Sugars 1.3g
Protein 33.4g

Pour 1 cup of filtered water into the inner pot of the Instant Pot, then insert the trivet. In a large, Instant Pot–friendly bowl, combine the garlic, bay leaves, chicken, onion, vinegar, cumin, coriander, mint, black pepper, and salt. Mix thoroughly.

Place the bowl onto the trivet, and cover loosely with aluminum foil. Close the lid, set the pressure release to Sealing, and select Manual/Pressure Cook. Set the Instant Pot to 15 minutes on high pressure, and let cook.

Once cooked, let the pressure naturally disperse from the Instant Pot for about 10 minutes, then carefully switch the pressure release to Venting.

Open the Instant Pot, and remove the dish. Let cool, serve, and enjoy!

CREAMY CAULIFLOWER SOUP

Serves 4

Prep Time: 5 minutes, Cook Time: 20 minutes, Total Time: 25 minutes, Pressure: High, Release: Quick

Gluten Free, Soy Free, 25 Minutes or Less, Kid Friendly

Cauliflower is a great keto all-purpose substitute for potatoes, and other higher carb foods. This soup is similar in taste and texture to baked potato soup, but—crucially— it will still keep you in fat-burning ketosis. Make sure you eat it warm, as the melting cheese makes this soup absolutely mouthwatering.

2 tablespoons grass-fed butter, softened

2 cups grass-fed bone broth

6 slices no-sugar-added bacon, sliced, crumbled, cooked

1 cup full-fat Cheddar cheese, shredded

1 head cauliflower, chopped

1 cup celery, chopped

1/2 cup heavy whipping cream

1/2 cup full-fat coconut milk

1/4 cup green onion, thinly sliced

1/2 teaspoon garlic powder

1/2 teaspoon freshly ground black pepper

1/2 teaspoon kosher salt

Nutrition Facts
Amount per serving
Calories 485
Total Fat 40.1g
Total Carbohydrate 9.4g
Dietary Fiber 3.2g
Total Sugars 3.5g
Protein 22.9g

Set the Instant Pot to Sauté mode. Add the butter, melting it gently.

Pour in bone broth, then mix in bacon, cheese, cauliflower, celery, whipping cream, milk, onion, garlic powder, black pepper, salt, and 1 cup of filtered water. Close the lid, set the pressure release to Sealing, and select Manual/Pressure Cook. Set the Instant Pot to 10 minutes on high pressure and let cook.

When cooking is complete, perform a quick release. Open the lid. Using an immersion blender, blend the soup until achieving your desired consistency. Add an extra tablespoon (or two) of heavy whipping cream for a thicker texture. Serve, and enjoy!

The Essential Instant Pot® Keto Cookbook

STEAK AND CAULIFLOWER RICE

Serves 4

**Prep Time: 5 minutes, Cook Time: 20 minutes, Total Time: 25 minutes,
Pressure: High, Release: Natural**

Gluten Free, Soy Free, 25 Minutes or Less, Kid Friendly

Steak is one of the best keto foods—it is filling, loaded with protein, vitamins, and minerals—and it goes with almost anything. Cauliflower rice is filling in for the more traditional potato here, but the simplicity of the Instant Pot makes this whole recipe super easy. Pair with grilled asparagus, broccoli, Swiss chard, or a walnut salad.

1 ribeye steak

½ teaspoon paprika, fresh

½ teaspoon turmeric, ground

½ teaspoon parsley, dried

½ teaspoon cumin, ground

½ teaspoon freshly ground black pepper

½ teaspoon kosher salt

1 head cauliflower, chopped

2 tablespoons grass-fed butter, softened

1 avocado, mashed

Nutrition Facts
Amount per serving
Calories 418
Total Fat 22.1g
Total Carbohydrate 8.5g
Dietary Fiber 5.3g
Total Sugars 1.9g
Protein 54.4g

Pour 1 cup of filtered water into the inner pot of the Instant Pot, then insert the trivet. In a small bowl, mix together the paprika, turmeric, parsley, cumin, black pepper, and salt. Coat the steak evenly with this mixture.

Once coated, place the steak onto a well-greased, Instant Pot–friendly dish. Arrange the cauliflower beside the steak.

Place the dish onto the trivet, and cover loosely with aluminum foil. Close the lid, set the pressure release to Sealing, and select Manual/Pressure Cook. Set the Instant Pot to 20 minutes on high pressure, and let cook.

Once cooked, let the pressure naturally disperse from the Instant Pot for about 10 minutes, then carefully switch the pressure release to Venting.

Open the Instant Pot, and remove the dish. Add the butter to the steak, serve with the avocado, and enjoy!

FAST AND EASY CRACK CHICKEN

(IPM)

Serves 2

**Prep Time: 5 minutes, Cook Time: 15 minutes, Total Time: 20 minutes,
Pressure: High, Release: Quick**

Gluten Free, Soy Free, 25 Minutes or Less

Crack chicken has become a viral sensation, and this keto Instant Pot variation is just as addictive as the best recipes out there. Bacon, cheese, and ranch dressing are the secret ingredients that make this chicken so indescribably awesome. Try making this dish in your Instant Pot Mini, and pair it with a side salad full of dark, leafy greens.

½ cup grass-fed bone broth

¼ cup tablespoons keto-friendly ranch dressing

2 ounces cream cheese, softened

½ pound boneless, skinless chicken breasts

½ cup full-fat Cheddar cheese, shredded

3 slices bacon, cooked, chopped into small pieces

Nutrition Facts
Amount per serving
Calories 548
Total Fat 45.8g
Total Carbohydrate 2.5g
Dietary Fiber 0g
Total Sugars 0.2g
Protein 32.3g

Pour bone broth into the inner pot of the Instant Pot, then add the ranch dressing, cream cheese, and chicken. Stir thoroughly.

Close the lid, set the pressure release to Sealing, and select Manual/Pressure Cook. Set the Instant Pot to 15 minutes on high pressure and let cook.

Once cooked, perform a quick release by carefully switching the pressure valve to Venting.

Stir in the cheese and bacon, and serve.

ONE-POT SHRIMP SCAMPI

Serves 4

Prep Time: 5 minutes, Cook Time: 20 minutes, Total Time: 25 minutes, Pressure: High, Release: Natural

Gluten Free, Soy Free, 25 Minutes or Less, Kid Friendly

This simple-to-make dish is high in protein and very low in carbs. On top of that, it tastes incredible, as the Parmesan cheese provides a nice finish. Pair with cauliflower rice, kale, artichokes, asparagus, spinach, broccoli, or a side salad.

2 tablespoons grass-fed butter, softened

1 cup grass-fed bone broth

2 cups cauliflower rice

1 pound shrimp, deveined and deshelled

½ cup heavy whipping cream

½ cup full-fat Parmesan cheese, grated

½ teaspoon freshly ground black pepper

½ teaspoon kosher salt

½ teaspoon garlic, minced

½ teaspoon basil, dried

½ teaspoon parsley, dried

½ teaspoon turmeric, ground

Set Instant Pot to Sauté and melt the butter.

Pour in the bone broth, then add the cauliflower rice, shrimp, whipping cream, Parmesan, black pepper, salt, garlic, basil, parsley, and turmeric. Stir together thoroughly. Press Cancel to stop the current program, then set the Instant Pot to 20 minutes cook time, on high pressure.

Once cooked, perform a quick release by carefully switching the pressure valve to Venting.

Open the Instant Pot, serve, and enjoy!

Nutrition Facts
Amount per serving
Calories 356
Total Fat 19.5g
Total Carbohydrate 6.6g
Dietary Fiber 1.2g
Total Sugars 1g
Protein 37.5g

The Essential Instant Pot® Keto Cookbook

CHICKEN POT PIE

Serves 4

**Prep Time: 5 minutes, Cook Time: 15 minutes, Total Time: 20 minutes,
Pressure: High, Release: Natural**

Gluten Free, Soy Free, 25 Minutes or Less, Kid Friendly

Rejoice—this keto twist is far lighter than the traditional preparation!

CRUST
1 tablespoon grass-fed butter, softened

2 tablespoons sour cream, at room temperature

1 tablespoon psyllium husk

1 cup blanched almond flour

FILLING
2 cups boneless, skinless chicken breast, cubed, cooked

2 garlic cloves, minced

¼ cup green beans, cut into small pieces

½ teaspoon freshly ground black pepper

½ teaspoon kosher salt

½ teaspoon rosemary, ground

½ teaspoon thyme, ground

½ teaspoon parsley, dried

½ teaspoon basil, dried

¼ (4-ounce) small onion, thinly sliced

Nutrition Facts
Amount per serving
Calories 247
Total Fat 15.5g
Total Carbohydrate 3.7g
Dietary Fiber 1.3g
Total Sugars 0.3g
Protein 22.5g

In a large bowl, thoroughly combine all crust ingredients.

Pour 1 cup filtered water into the Instant Pot, and insert the trivet. Transfer the mixture from the bowl to a well-greased Instant Pot–friendly dish (or pan), forming a crust on the bottom and lightly on the sides. Freeze the dish for 15 minutes. While freezing, in a large bowl, mix the chicken and other filling ingredients.

Remove the dish from freezer, then pour the filling into the center of the dish. Using a sling if desired, place the dish onto the trivet, and cover loosely with aluminum foil. Close the lid, set the pressure release to Sealing, and select Manual/Pressure Cook. Set the Instant Pot to 15 minutes on high pressure, and let cook.

Once cooked, let the pressure naturally leave the Instant Pot, for about 10 minutes. Next, switch the pressure release to Venting. Open the Instant Pot, and remove the dish. Let cool, fold the crust into a covered pie (if desired), and serve.

CHEESY QUESADILLAS

Serves 4

Prep Time: 5 minutes, Cook Time: 20 minutes, Total Time: 25 minutes, Pressure: High, Release: Natural

Gluten Free, Soy Free, 25 Minutes or Less, Kid Friendly

These keto quesadillas provide all the protein and nutrition of the traditional favorite.

BASE
2 ounces full-fat cream cheese, softened

2 eggs

2 tablespoons grass-fed butter, softened

1/2 cup blanched almond flour

FILLING
1 cup full-fat Monterey Jack cheese, shredded

1 cup full-fat Cheddar cheese, shredded

1/4 cup bok choy, chopped

1/4 cup bell peppers, chopped

1/4 cup green onions, thinly sliced

1/2 teaspoon freshly ground black pepper

1/2 teaspoon kosher salt

1/2 teaspoon cilantro, dried

1/2 teaspoon cumin, ground

1/2 teaspoon curry powder

1/2 jalapeño, chopped, seeded

1/4 (4-ounce) small onion, thinly sliced

Nutrition Facts
Amount per serving
Calories 566
Total Fat 48.8g
Total Carbohydrate 8.2g
Dietary Fiber 1.7g
Total Sugars 3.4g
Protein 25.2g

In a large bowl, mix together the cream cheese, eggs, butter, and almond flour. Combine them very thoroughly, until a perfectly even mixture is obtained.

Pour 1 cup of filtered water into the Instant Pot, and insert the trivet. Transfer the mixture from the bowl into a well-greased, Instant Pot–friendly dish. Pack the mixture down firmly to create a smooth surface.

Place the dish onto the trivet, and cover loosely with aluminum foil. Close the lid, set the pressure release to Sealing, and select Manual/Pressure Cook. Set the Instant Pot to 15 minutes on high pressure, and let cook.

Once cooked, perform a quick release by carefully switching the pressure valve to Venting. Very carefully remove the aluminum foil. Pour in the Monterey Jack, Cheddar, bok choy, bell peppers, green onions, black pepper, salt, cilantro, cumin, curry powder, jalapeño, and onion. Loosely re-cover with aluminum foil, then close the lid. Set the pressure release to Sealing and select Manual/Pressure Cook. Set the

The Essential Instant Pot® Keto Cookbook

Instant Pot to 5 minutes on high pressure, and let cook.

Once cooked, let the pressure naturally disperse from the Instant Pot for about 10 minutes, then carefully switch the pressure release to Venting. Open the Instant Pot and remove the dish. Let cool, fold the quesadilla in half (if desired), and cut into 4 pieces. Serve, and enjoy!

SIMPLE BROCCOLI CHEDDAR SOUP

Recipe courtesy of Danielle Walker

(IPM)

Serves 2

**Prep Time: 5 minutes, Cook Time: 10 minutes, Total Time: 15 minutes,
Pressure: High, Release: Quick**

Gluten Free, Soy Free, 25 Minutes or Less

Broccoli Cheddar soup is a great regular keto meal choice, as it provides plenty of brain-friendly nutrients, along with bioavailable protein. It's hard to believe something this healthy for you can still taste so good! And for those cooking for just one or two—this recipe works great in your Instant Pot Mini!

2 tablespoons grass-fed butter
2 ½ cups grass-fed bone broth
1 cup broccoli, chopped
1 cup full-fat Cheddar cheese, shredded
½ teaspoon basil, fresh
salt and pepper to taste

Nutrition Facts
Amount per serving
Calories 376
Total Fat 30.9g
Total Carbohydrate 5.3g
Dietary Fiber 1.2g
Total Sugars 1.1g
Protein 19.1g

Pour all ingredients into the inner pot. Close the lid, set the pressure release to Sealing, and select Manual/Pressure Cook. Set the Instant Pot to 15 minutes on high pressure and let cook.

Once cooked, perform a quick release by carefully switching the pressure valve to Venting. Serve, and enjoy!

CLASSIC LASAGNA

Serves 4

Prep Time: 5 minutes, Cook Time: 20 minutes, Total Time: 25 minutes, Pressure: High, Release: Natural

Gluten Free, Soy Free, 25 Minutes or Less, Kid Friendly

By replacing the pasta with zucchini, we can keep our carbs down but the flavor up. I like to sprinkle some extra Parmesan cheese on top of the finished dish to give it even more taste.

2 tablespoons coconut oil

1 pound grass-fed beef, ground

1 egg

1 cup spinach, chopped

3/4 cup mozzarella cheese, shredded

1/2 cup full-fat Parmesan cheese, grated

1/2 teaspoon basil, dried

1/2 teaspoon fennel seeds

1/2 teaspoon garlic

1/2 teaspoon oregano, dried

1/2 teaspoon parsley, dried

1/4 (4-ounce) small onion, thinly sliced

1 1/2 cups whole milk ricotta cheese

1 (14-ounce) can sugar-free or low-sugar fire roasted tomatoes

Nutrition Facts
Amount per serving
Calories 533
Total Fat 35.5g
Total Carbohydrate 10.3g
Dietary Fiber 1g
Total Sugars 2.7g
Protein 43.3g

Pour 1 cup of filtered water into the inner pot of the Instant Pot, then insert the trivet. In a large bowl, combine the coconut oil, beef, egg, spinach, mozzarella, Parmesan, basil, fennel, garlic, oregano, parsley, onion, ricotta, and tomatoes. Mix thoroughly. Transfer this mixture into a well-greased, Instant Pot–friendly dish.

Place the dish onto the trivet, and cover loosely with aluminum foil. Close the lid, set the pressure release to Sealing and select Manual/Pressure Cook. Set the Instant Pot to 20 minutes on high pressure, and let cook.

Once cooked, let the pressure naturally disperse from the Instant Pot for about 10 minutes, then carefully switch the pressure release to Venting.

Open the Instant Pot, and remove the dish. Let cool, serve, and enjoy!

CAULIFLOWER "FRIED" RICE

Serves 4

**Prep Time: 5 minutes, Cook Time: 2 minutes, Total Time: 7 minutes,
Pressure: High, Release: Quick**

Gluten Free, Dairy Free, Soy Free, 10 Minutes or Less, Kid Friendly

A simple classic recipe, updated for keto and the Instant Pot. Fried rice is a
traditional Asian dish, but this variation is much lower in carbohydrates. Cauliflower
also contains almost an entire day's worth of vitamin C, as well as numerous
other vitamins and minerals.

1 (9-ounce) head cauliflower, chopped
½ teaspoon garlic powder
½ teaspoon freshly ground black pepper
½ teaspoon turmeric, ground
½ teaspoon curry powder
½ teaspoon kosher salt
½ teaspoon paprika, fresh
¼ (4-ounce) small onion, thinly sliced

Nutrition Facts
Amount per serving
Calories 24
Total Fat 0.2g
Total Carbohydrate 5g
Dietary Fiber 2.2g
Total Sugars 2g
Protein 1.6g

Pour 1 cup of filtered water into the inner pot of the Instant Pot, then insert the trivet. In a well-greased, Instant Pot–friendly dish, add the cauliflower. Sprinkle the garlic powder, black pepper, turmeric, curry powder, salt, paprika, and onion over top.

Place the dish onto the trivet, and cover loosely with aluminum foil. Close the lid, set the pressure release to Sealing and select Manual/Pressure Cook. Set the Instant Pot to 2 minutes on high pressure, and let cook.

Once cooked, perform a quick release.

Open the Instant Pot, and remove the dish. Serve, and enjoy!

The Essential Instant Pot® Keto Cookbook

Cheddar-Herbed Strata (page 7)

Chocolate Chip Mini Muffins (page 9)

Hot Chocolate Breakfast Cereal (page 11) and Fat Burning Coffee (page 12)

Traditional Coffee Cake (page 23)

Chocolate Cinnamon Roll Fat Bombs (page 25)

Easy Mug Cakes (page 34)

Sunrise Pizza (page 38)

Fast and Easy Shakshuka (page 40)

Lobster Bisque (page 61)

Crispy Bacon Chili (page 72)

Shrimp and Avocado Salad (page 86)

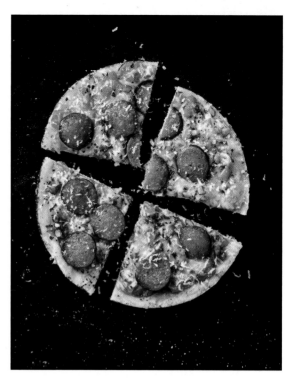

20-Minute Pepperoni Pizza (page 88)

Savory Pumpkin and Bacon Soup (page 79)

Mug Lasagna (page 107)

Clam Chowder (page 91)

Clambake (page 115) with Paprika-Lemon Brussels Sprouts (page 192)

Baby Back Ribs (page 109)

Crab Bisque (page 122)

Coconut Cake (page 152)

Mac and Cheese (page 137)

Traditional Cupcakes (page 155)

Soft and Chewy Chocolate Chip Cookie Bites (page 156)

Coconut-Crusted Chocolate Bark (page 153)

Crème Brûlée (page 160)

Antioxidant-Rich Matcha Cheesecake (page 172)

Coconut Flaked Walnut Fudge (page 181)

Chocolate Chip Cheesecake (page 188)

Loaded Cobb Salad (page 205)

from left to right: Coconut Milk Berry Smoothie (page 227); Basil-Mint Green Smoothie (page 219); and Super Fat Burning Shake (page 218)

MAC AND CHEESE

Serves 4

**Prep Time: 5 minutes, Cook Time: 5 minutes, Total Time: 10 minutes,
Pressure: High, Release: Natural**

Gluten Free, Soy Free, 10 Minutes or Less, Kid Friendly

Macaroni and cheese is a comfort food classic, and this Instant Pot keto variation will help to satisfy all those cravings. By using cauliflower instead of macaroni, we stay in ketosis, but still capture the familiar flavor and texture of the traditional dish. Try topping with a little ground turmeric, to pack in even more nutrition. Or, mix with a little bit of cooked lobster, to really add some decadence!

4 tablespoons grass-fed butter, softened

1 cup full-fat Cheddar cheese, shredded

1 cup full-fat Monterey Jack cheese, shredded

1 head cauliflower, chopped

1/2 cup heavy whipping cream

1/2 cup full-fat Parmesan cheese, grated

1/2 teaspoon cayenne pepper, ground

1/2 teaspoon freshly ground black pepper

1/2 teaspoon kosher salt

Nutrition Facts
Amount per serving
Calories 489
Total Fat 41.6g
Total Carbohydrate 5.8g
Dietary Fiber 1.8g
Total Sugars 1.9g
Protein 24.6g

Pour 2 cups of filtered water into the Instant Pot, then insert the trivet. In a large bowl, combine all ingredients, mixing thoroughly. Transfer this mixture into a well-greased, Instant Pot–friendly dish.

Place the dish onto the trivet, and cover loosely with aluminum foil. Close the lid, set the pressure release to Sealing, and select Manual/Pressure Cook. Set the Instant Pot to 5 minutes on high pressure, and let cook.

Once cooked, let the pressure naturally disperse from the Instant Pot for about 10 minutes, then carefully switch the pressure release to Venting.

Open the Instant Pot, and remove the dish. Let cool, serve, and enjoy!

NOTE: If you would like a crunchier top, carefully place the dish under a broiler for 2 to 3 minutes (or until reaching desired texture).

SPINACH CASSEROLE

Serves 4

Prep Time: 5 minutes, Cook Time: 20 minutes, Total Time: 25 minutes, Pressure: High, Release: Natural

Gluten Free, Dairy Free, Soy Free, 25 Minutes or Less, Kid Friendly

Spinach is one of the best (if not the single best) vegetable for your brain. It packs a huge antioxidant punch, and it even helps to repair your cells. This casserole tastes great, and only takes 25 minutes to make in the Instant Pot. Try pairing this casserole with some warm, cinnamon-topped coconut milk.

6 eggs

1 cup spinach, chopped

½ cup full-fat coconut milk

½ teaspoon crushed red pepper

½ teaspoon basil, dried

½ teaspoon cilantro, dried

½ teaspoon kosher salt

½ teaspoon freshly ground black pepper

Nutrition Facts
Amount per serving
Calories 168
Total Fat 13.8g
Total Carbohydrate 3g
Dietary Fiber 1.1g
Total Sugars 1.6g
Protein 9.5g

Pour 1 cup of filtered water into the inner pot of the Instant Pot, then insert the trivet. In a large bowl, combine the eggs, spinach, coconut milk, red pepper, basil, cilantro, salt, and black pepper. Mix thoroughly. Transfer this mixture into a well-greased, Instant Pot–friendly dish.

Using a sling if desired, place this dish onto the trivet, and cover loosely with aluminum foil. Close the lid, set the pressure release to Sealing, and select Manual/Pressure Cook. Set the Instant Pot to 20 minutes on high pressure, and let cook.

Once cooked, let the pressure naturally disperse from the Instant Pot for about 10 minutes, then carefully switch the pressure release to Venting.

Open the Instant Pot, serve, and enjoy!

The Essential Instant Pot® Keto Cookbook

SIMPLE KETO BRUSCHETTA CHICKEN

(IPM)

Serves 2

**Prep Time: 5 minutes, Cook Time: 20 minutes, Total Time: 25 minutes,
Pressure: High, Release: Quick**

Gluten Free, Dairy Free, Soy Free, 25 Minutes or Less

Bruschetta chicken is a cooking classic, as it's fast, easy—and always tastes delicious. This version works great in your Instant Pot Mini, and can easily be modified any which way you choose. Try adding a dash of chili powder, to add just a hint of spice.

2 boneless, skinless chicken breasts

¼ teaspoon basil, dried

1 (14-ounce) can sugar-free or low-sugar crushed tomatoes

¼ cup heavy whipping cream

½ cup full-fat Cheddar cheese, shredded

Nutrition Facts
Amount per serving
Calories 591
Total Fat 38.1g
Total Carbohydrate 5.5g
Dietary Fiber 1g
Total Sugars 3g
Protein 56.8g

Pour in ½ cup of filtered water, then add the chicken breasts, basil, and tomatoes. Close the lid, set the pressure release to Sealing, and select Manual/Pressure Cook. Set the Instant Pot to 20 minutes on high pressure and let cook.

Immediately upon cooking completion, perform a quick release by carefully switching the pressure valve to Venting, and carefully stir in the whipping cream and cheese. When cheese is melted, serve, and enjoy.

STEAK NACHOS

Serves 6

**Prep Time: 5 minutes, Cook Time: 20 minutes, Total Time: 25 minutes,
Pressure: High, Release: Natural**

Gluten Free, Soy Free, 25 Minutes or Less, Kid Friendly

This fully loaded dish is one of my personal favorites, and it is a very tasty way to get a big dose of your protein and healthy fat for the day. I sometimes like to add a little extra spice to this recipe, by mixing in a little crushed red pepper or curry powder—but be careful not to overdo it!

2 tablespoons grass-fed butter, softened

1 (14-ounce) can sugar-free or low-sugar fire roasted tomatoes, drained

1 pound beef steak, sliced into thin strips

1/2 pound cauliflower, chopped

1/2 cup full-fat Cheddar cheese, shredded

1/2 cup full-fat Monterey Jack cheese, shredded

1/2 teaspoon chili powder

1/2 jalapeño, chopped, seeded

1/2 teaspoon turmeric, ground

1/2 teaspoon cumin, ground

1/2 teaspoon curry powder

1/4 cup coconut oil

1 avocado, mashed

1/4 cup sour cream, at room temperature

Nutrition Facts
Amount per serving
Calories 449
Total Fat 32.5g
Total Carbohydrate 10g
Dietary Fiber 4.7g
Total Sugars 3.5g
Protein 30.5g

Pour 1 cup of filtered water into the inner pot of the Instant Pot, then insert the trivet. In a large bowl, combine butter, tomatoes, steak, cauliflower, Cheddar, Monterey Jack, chili powder, jalapeño, turmeric, cumin, curry powder, and coconut oil. Mix thoroughly. Transfer this mixture into a well-greased, Instant Pot–friendly dish.

Using a sling if desired, place the dish onto the trivet, and cover loosely with aluminum foil. Close the lid, set the pressure release to Sealing, and select Manual/Pressure Cook. Set the Instant Pot to 20 minutes on high pressure, and let cook.

Once cooked, let the pressure naturally disperse from the Instant Pot for about 10 minutes, then carefully switch the pressure release to Venting.

Open the Instant Pot, and remove the dish. Let cool, add the avocado and sour cream atop the nachos, and enjoy!

BALSAMIC BEEF

Serves 4

Prep Time: 5 minutes, Cook Time: 20 minutes, Total Time: 25 minutes,
Pressure: High, Release: Natural

Gluten Free, Soy Free, 25 Minutes or Less

A protein-packed dish with very few carbs, this is a solid meal to make on any day of the week. Balsamic vinegar is often underutilized, but this is a great way to cook with it. Serve with a warm mug of bone broth, if you would like to add even more skin-enhancing nutrients, like collagen.

1 pound chuck roast

2 cloves garlic, minced

1 cup grass-fed bone broth

½ teaspoon rosemary, ground

½ teaspoon freshly ground black pepper

½ teaspoon kosher salt

½ teaspoon thyme, ground

½ teaspoon crushed red pepper

¼ cup balsamic vinegar

4 tablespoons grass-fed butter, softened

1 cup broccoli, chopped

Nutrition Facts
Amount per serving
Calories 323
Total Fat 15.6g
Total Carbohydrate 3.1g
Dietary Fiber 0.9g
Total Sugars 0.5g
Protein 39.5g

Pour ½ cup filtered water into the Instant Pot, then add the chuck roast. Close the lid, set the pressure release to Sealing, and select Manual/Pressure Cook. Set the Instant Pot to 20 minutes on high pressure, and let cook.

In a large bowl, combine the garlic, bone broth, rosemary, black pepper, salt, thyme, red pepper, vinegar, and 2 tablespoons of butter. Mix thoroughly.

Once cooked, let the pressure naturally disperse from the Instant Pot for about 10 minutes, then carefully switch the pressure release to Venting.

Open the Instant Pot, and remove the dish. Set the Instant Pot to Sauté mode, add in the broccoli, and mix in 2 additional tablespoons of grass-fed butter. Cook the broccoli, stirring continuously, until cooked.

Remove the broccoli, and serve alongside the roast. Spoon your prepared sauce over both, to taste.

SESAME BEEF

Serves 4

Prep Time: 5 minutes, Cook Time: 20 minutes, Total Time: 25 minutes, Pressure: High, Release: Natural

Gluten Free, Soy Free, 25 Minutes or Less, Kid Friendly

One of my favorite meals from classic Chinese food delivery menus, this sesame beef has been enhanced and made much healthier. This is a simple (yet flavorful) recipe that you can return to time and time again. Pair with cauliflower rice to round out the meal.

½ cup grass-fed bone broth

2 tablespoons coconut oil

1 pound chuck steak, sliced

1 green onion, chopped

1 jalapeño pepper, sliced thinly

½ teaspoon garlic

½ teaspoon ginger, finely grated

½ teaspoon freshly ground black pepper

½ teaspoon kosher salt

½ teaspoon crushed red pepper

½ teaspoon parsley, dried

1 teaspoon sesame seeds

1 cup broccoli, chopped

Nutrition Facts
Amount per serving
Calories 365
Total Fat 22.2g
Total Carbohydrate 3.2g
Dietary Fiber 1.1g
Total Sugars 0.6g
Protein 36.9g

Pour the bone broth into the Instant Pot, then add the oil, steak, green onion, jalapeño, garlic, ginger, black pepper, salt, red pepper, and parsley. Close the lid, set the pressure release to Sealing, and select Manual/Pressure Cook. Set the Instant Pot to 20 minutes on high pressure, and let cook.

Once cooked, let the pressure naturally disperse from the Instant Pot for about 10 minutes, then carefully switch the pressure release to Venting.

Open the Instant Pot and remove the dish. Add broccoli, and let cook for 2 to 5 minutes (or until desired tenderness, sautéing with butter, if desired). Remove the broccoli.

Once beef is cooled, top with the sesame seeds, serve with the broccoli, and enjoy!

FAST AND EASY LASAGNA SOUP

(IPM)

Serves 2

Prep Time: 5 minutes, Cook Time: 5 minutes, Total Time: 10 minutes, Pressure: N/A, Release: N/A

Gluten Free, Soy Free, 10 Minutes or Less, Kid Friendly

A rich, creamy, and filling soup—this Instant Pot Mini favorite is a great option for a cold and rainy day. Try adding some extra Parmesan cheese to make this even more delicious.

1 cup full-fat Cheddar cheese, shredded

½ cup full-fat Parmesan cheese, grated

½ cup heavy whipping cream

½ teaspoon basil, dried

½ teaspoon oregano, dried

¼ zucchini, grated

1 (14-ounce) can sugar-free or low-sugar fire roasted tomatoes

Pour 1½ cups of filtered water into the inner pot of the Instant Pot. Then add the Cheddar, Parmesan, whipping cream, basil, oregano, zucchini, and tomatoes. Mix together thoroughly.

Set the Instant Pot to Sauté and let cook for 5 minutes (or until cheese is melted), stirring occasionally.

Nutrition Facts
Amount per serving
Calories 545
Total Fat 41.9g
Total Carbohydrate 10.3g
Dietary Fiber 1.4g
Total Sugars 4.6g
Protein 34g

BACON CHEESE "WAFFLE"

Serves 4

**Prep Time: 5 minutes, Cook Time: 20 minutes, Total Time: 25 minutes,
Pressure: High, Release: Natural**

Gluten Free, Soy Free, 25 Minutes or Less, Kid Friendly

This incredible bacon "waffle" really shows that no one is starving with a keto approach—even if they are losing a ton of weight! Try pairing with some green vegetables for an added healthy punch.

WAFFLE

2 tablespoons coconut oil

2 tablespoons full-fat Parmesan cheese, grated

2 eggs

1 cup blanched almond flour

1 cup cauliflower, chopped

½ teaspoon cinnamon, ground

½ teaspoon kosher salt

TOPPINGS

1 cup full-fat Cheddar cheese, shredded

6 slices no-sugar-added bacon, sliced into small pieces

Nutrition Facts
Amount per serving
Calories 428
Total Fat 35.3g
Total Carbohydrate 4.3g
Dietary Fiber 1.5g
Total Sugars 1.2g
Protein 24.6g

Pour 1 cup of filtered water into the Instant Pot, then insert the trivet. In a large bowl, combine the coconut oil, Parmesan, eggs, almond flour, cauliflower, cinnamon, and salt. Mix thoroughly. Transfer this mixture into a well-greased, Instant Pot–friendly dish.

Place the dish onto the trivet, and cover loosely with aluminum foil. Close the lid, set the pressure release to Sealing, and select Manual/Pressure Cook. Set the Instant Pot to 10 minutes on high pressure, and let cook.

Once cooked, perform a quick release by carefully switching the pressure valve to Venting. Top the waffle with an even layer of the Cheddar cheese, followed by the bacon. Close the lid, set the pressure valve back to Sealing, and then set the Instant Pot to 10 minutes, on high pressure. Once cooked, again perform a quick release.

Open the Instant Pot and remove the dish. Let cool, cut into quarters, and serve.

SIMPLE ROPA VIEJA

Serves 8

Prep Time: 5 minutes, Cook Time: 85 minutes, Total Time: 90 minutes, Pressure: High, Release: Natural

Gluten Free, Dairy Free, Soy Free

The keto approach is (by nature) full of meats and vegetables. This out-of-this world soup, however, feels anything but mundane. In case you were wondering about the name of this dish—it translates as "old clothes"—which is what the finished recipe sometimes looks like!

3 pounds beef roast

½ cup grass-fed bone broth

½ teaspoon cumin, ground

½ teaspoon, oregano

½ teaspoon chili powder

1 (14-ounce) can sugar-free or low-sugar crushed tomatoes

salt and pepper to taste

Nutrition Facts
Amount per serving
Calories 317
Total Fat 14.3g
Total Carbohydrate 1.5g
Dietary Fiber 0.3g
Total Sugars 0.9g
Protein 45.5g

Pour all ingredients into the inner pot of the Instant Pot. Close the lid, set the pressure release to Sealing, and select Manual/Pressure Cook. Set the Instant Pot to 85 minutes on high pressure and let cook.

Once cooked, let the pressure naturally disperse from the Instant Pot for about 10 minutes, then carefully switch the pressure release to Venting. Open the lid, shred the beef, and enjoy!

DESSERT

TRADITIONAL CHEESECAKE

Serves 5 to 6

Prep Time: 5 minutes, Cook Time: 25 minutes, Total Time: 30 minutes, Pressure: High, Release: Natural

Gluten Free, Soy Free

Yes, you really can make an entire cheesecake in the Instant Pot!

CAKE

16 ounces full-fat cream cheese, softened

1/2 cup Swerve, confectioners (or more, to taste)

4 teaspoons vanilla extract

2 eggs

TOPPINGS

1/2 cup Swerve, confectioners (or more, to taste)

2 tablespoons heavy whipping cream

1 tablespoon coconut, shredded and lightly toasted

1 tablespoon slivered almonds (or other chopped nuts), lightly toasted

2 tablespoons sugar-free chocolate chips

Nutrition Facts
Amount per serving
Calories 337
Total Fat 31.8g
Total Carbohydrate 5.6g
Dietary Fiber 0.9g
Total Sugars 0.7g
Protein 8.2g

In a large bowl, combine cream cheese, Swerve, vanilla, and eggs. Mix thoroughly. Place mixture in a well-greased springform pan.

Pour 2 cups of filtered water into the Instant Pot, then insert the trivet. Using a sling if desired, place the springform pan on top of the trivet, and cover with aluminum foil. Close the lid, set the pressure release to Sealing, and select Manual/Pressure Cook. Set the Instant Pot to 25 minutes on high pressure and let cook.

Once cooked, let pressure naturally disperse. Then remove pan, leaving foil on, and let cool for 30 minutes. For extra decadence, drizzle some extra (melted) sugar-free chocolate on top, if desired. Refrigerate for 45 minutes.

Take the cheesecake from the refrigerator, and remove the foil. Using a handheld mixer, in a small bowl, whip the Swerve and whipping cream until thickened, then spread evenly on top of the cake. Sprinkle with toasted coconut, slivered almonds, and chocolate chips, as desired. Enjoy!

DECADENT FUDGE

Serves 6

Prep Time: 5 minutes, Cook Time: 5 minutes, Total Time: 10 minutes, Pressure: N/A, Release: N/A

Gluten Free, Soy Free, 10 Minutes or Less, Kid Friendly

This fudge is a great keto dessert choice, and there are many different flavor varieties to choose from. I am personally most fond of the pecan-filled version of this fudge, but your taste preferences may vary. Try adding an extra half cup of chocolate chips for an extra chocolatey experience!

1 teaspoon grass-fed butter

1 teaspoon raw coconut butter

1 teaspoon vanilla extract

½ cup Swerve, confectioners (or more, to taste)

¼ cup full-fat coconut milk

1 cup dark sugar-free chocolate chips

FLAVOR ADD-INS

1 tablespoon avocado (or more, to taste)

½ cup pecans, chopped

⅓ cup almonds, chopped

¼ cup walnuts, chopped

¼ cup macadamia nuts

¼ cup hazelnuts, chopped

¼ cup pistachios, chopped

⅛ teaspoon peppermint extract

Set the Instant Pot to simmer by pressing Sauté and then pressing the Adjust button twice. Add all ingredients (including any desired flavors), stirring very frequently, until fudge melts together smoothly. Do not overcook.

Turn off Instant Pot and remove fudge. Cool briefly, then carefully pour it into a greased, deep glass dish.

Place into freezer for 20 minutes. Cut into 12 squares, and serve. Store leftovers in the refrigerator or freezer.

Nutrition Facts
(Base recipe only)
Calories 98
Total Fat 7.9g
Total Carbohydrate 11g
Dietary Fiber 2.8g
Total Sugars 0.2g
Protein 1.4g

The Essential Instant Pot® Keto Cookbook

CLASSIC MINT CHOCOLATE CHIP ICE CREAM

Serves 5 to 6

Prep Time: 5 minutes, Cook Time: 2 to 4 hours, Total Time: 2 to 4 hours, Pressure: High, Release: Natural

Gluten Free, Soy Free, Kid Friendly

Ice cream is one of the best desserts in the world. What is there not to love—there is sugar, fat, and an amazing texture. Switching to a ketogenic diet does not mean that you have to give up all indulgences, and this recipe will satisfy even the biggest sweet tooth—all while keeping you in fat-burning ketosis.

6 egg whites

4 teaspoons vanilla extract

1 teaspoon mint extract

1/2 cup Swerve, confectioners (or more, to taste)

1/4 cup almonds, slivered (optional)

1/4 cup coconut, shredded (optional)

2 2/3 cups heavy whipping cream

1/2 cup sugar-free chocolate chips

Nutrition Facts
Amount per serving
Calories 351
Total Fat 31.4g
Total Carbohydrate 13.7g
Dietary Fiber 3.2g
Total Sugars 0.9g
Protein 8.8g

In a large bowl, using a handheld mixer or stand mixer, beat egg whites until stiff peaks form. Gently fold in vanilla, mint, Swerve, almond, coconut, and whipping cream. Mix thoroughly. Cover and freeze for 2 to 4 hours.

When ready to eat, set the Instant Pot to simmer by pressing Sauté and then pressing the Adjust button twice. Pour in the chocolate chips, stirring very frequently, until they melt together smoothly. Do not overcook. Turn off heat, and remove melted chocolate.

Scoop the ice cream into a bowl and drizzle the melted chocolate over it. Store leftovers in freezer.

PEPPERMINT CHOCOLATE ALMOND BUTTER

Serves 6

**Prep Time: 5 minutes, Cook Time: 5 minutes, Total Time: 10 minutes,
Pressure: High, Release: Natural**

Gluten Free, Soy Free, 10 Minutes or Less, Kid Friendly

Almond butter tastes like a dessert on its own, but this recipe takes it up a notch. The melted chocolate makes this concoction even sweeter, and the peppermint adds just the right hint of flavor. Drizzle this on keto ice cream for an extra special treat.

2 tablespoons grass-fed butter, softened

¾ cup almond butter, smooth

¼ cup sugar-free chocolate chips

⅛ teaspoon peppermint extract (or to taste)

Nutrition Facts
Amount per serving
Calories 237
Total Fat 21.7g
Total Carbohydrate 10.3g
Dietary Fiber 4g
Total Sugars 1.2g
Protein 6.3g

Set the Instant Pot to Sauté and melt the butter.

Add the almond butter, chocolate chips, and peppermint to the Instant Pot. Mix thoroughly, until melted.

Remove mixture with a spoon, and place into a Mason jar.

Refrigerate until firm. Serve and enjoy! Store remaining almond butter in refrigerator, eating on its own, or using as a topping.

BACON AND CHOCOLATE COVERED BRAZIL NUTS

Serves 10

Prep Time: 5 minutes, Cook Time: 5 minutes, Total Time: 10 minutes, Pressure: High, Release: Natural

Gluten Free, Soy Free, 10 Minutes or Less, Kid Friendly

Brazil nuts are one of the healthiest nuts on the planet (they are very rich with selenium, among many other nutrients), but they still remain vastly underutilized. This ultra-simple dessert recipe may change that. To take this dish to the next level, try mixing in a spoonful or two of almond or coconut butter.

2 tablespoons grass-fed butter, softened

1 cup sugar-free chocolate chips

2 slices no-sugar-added bacon, crushed up, cooked

1 cup Brazil nuts

Nutrition Facts
Amount per serving
Calories 149
Total Fat 12.3g
Total Carbohydrate 13.2g
Dietary Fiber 3.4g
Total Sugars 0.1g
Protein 3.4g

Set the Instant Pot to Sauté and melt the butter.

Add the chocolate chips, bacon, and Brazil nuts to the Instant Pot. Mix thoroughly, until melted.

Pour mixture into a large bowl.

Refrigerate until firm. Serve, and enjoy!

COCONUT CAKE

Serves 5 to 6

**Prep Time: 5 minutes, Cook Time: 40 minutes, Total Time: 45 minutes,
Pressure: High, Release: Natural**

Gluten Free, Soy Free, Kid Friendly

This cake is light, but tasty — enjoy responsibly!

3 tablespoons sugar-free chocolate chips

2 tablespoons grass-fed butter, softened

2 eggs

1 ⅓ cup blanched almond flour

1 tablespoon arrowroot powder

1 teaspoon baking powder

1 teaspoon pumpkin purée, organic

½ cup Swerve, confectioners (or more, to taste)

½ cup unsweetened coconut flakes

½ cup heavy whipping cream

½ teaspoon nutmeg, ground

½ teaspoon cinnamon, ground

½ teaspoon vanilla extract

Nutrition Facts
Amount per serving
Calories 227
Total Fat 21.1g
Total Carbohydrate 8.8g
Dietary Fiber 2.5g
Total Sugars 0.9g
Protein 4.2g

In a large bowl, thoroughly mix together all ingredients, until a perfectly even mixture is obtained.

Next, pour 1 cup filtered water into the Instant Pot and insert the trivet.

Transfer the mixture from the bowl into a well-greased, Instant Pot–friendly pan (or dish).

Using a sling if desired, place the pan onto the trivet, and cover loosely with aluminum foil. Close the lid, set the pressure release to Sealing, and select Manual/Pressure Cook. Set the Instant Pot to 40 minutes on high pressure, and let cook.

Once cooked, let the pressure naturally disperse from the Instant Pot for about 10 minutes, then carefully switch the pressure release to Venting.

Open the Instant Pot and remove the pan. Allow to cool completely before serving. Add any desired toppings on top of the finished dessert, serve, and enjoy!

The Essential Instant Pot® Keto Cookbook

COCONUT-CRUSTED CHOCOLATE BARK

Serves 20

Prep Time: 5 minutes, Cook Time: 20 minutes, Total Time: 25 minutes, Pressure: High, Release: Natural

Gluten Free, Dairy Free, Soy Free, 25 Minutes or Less, Kid Friendly

Dark chocolate is a favorite healthy indulgence, and this recipe provides a nice crunch along with it. This chocolatey bark will help you stave off any sugar cravings and keep you on the fat-burning path. Try adding in a tiny bit of peppermint extract to the mixture.

16 ounces raw dark chocolate, raw

3 tablespoons raw coconut butter

2 tablespoons coconut oil

2 cups macadamia nuts, chopped

1 tablespoon almond butter, smooth

½ teaspoon salt

⅓ cup Swerve, confectioners (or more, to taste)

Nutrition Facts
Amount per serving
Calories 258
Total Fat 22g
Total Carbohydrate 14.8g
Dietary Fiber 2.8g
Total Sugars 10.3g
Protein 2g

In a large bowl, mix together the chocolate, coconut butter, coconut oil, macadamia nuts, almond butter, salt, and Swerve. Combine them very thoroughly, until a perfectly even mixture is obtained.

Pour 1 cup of filtered water into the Instant Pot, and insert the trivet. Transfer the mixture from the bowl into a well-greased, Instant Pot–friendly dish.

Place the dish onto the trivet, and cover loosely with aluminum foil. Close the lid, set the pressure release to Sealing, and select Manual/Pressure Cook. Set the Instant Pot to 20 minutes on high pressure, and let cook.

Once cooked, let the pressure naturally disperse from the Instant Pot for about 10 minutes, then carefully switch the pressure release to Venting.

Open the Instant Pot and remove the dish. Cool in the refrigerator until set. Break into pieces, serve, and enjoy! Store remaining bark in the refrigerator or freezer.

ICE CREAM BITES

Serves 7

**Prep Time: 5 minutes, Cook Time: 5 minutes, Total Time: 10 minutes,
Pressure: High, Release: Natural**

Gluten Free, Soy Free, 10 Minutes or Less, Kid Friendly

These keto-friendly bites will hit all the right spots when you are craving something sweet on a hot day, but will not bring any of the guilt with them. Try mixing some coconut flakes on top of your finished bites for even more guilt-free indulgence.

6 tablespoons sugar-free chocolate chips

4 ounces full-fat cream cheese, softened

½ cup full-fat coconut milk

1 cup heavy whipping cream

½ cup Swerve, confectioners (or more, to taste)

½ teaspoon vanilla extract

Nutrition Facts
Amount per serving
Calories 170
Total Fat 16g
Total Carbohydrate 5.7g
Dietary Fiber 0.7g
Total Sugars 4.1g
Protein 2.1g

Pour 1 cup of filtered water into the inner pot of the Instant Pot, then insert the trivet. In a large bowl, combine the chocolate chips, cream cheese, coconut milk, whipping cream, Swerve, and vanilla. Mix thoroughly and transfer into well-greased egg bites molds.

Place molds on top of the trivet, stacking on top of each other, if needed. Cover loosely with aluminum foil. Close the lid, set the pressure release to Sealing, and select Manual/Pressure Cook. Set the Instant Pot to 5 minutes on high pressure, and let cook.

Once cooked, let the pressure release naturally, for about 10 minutes. Then, switch the pressure release to Venting. Open the Instant Pot, and remove the molds. Freeze for at least 1 hour, then serve. Keep uneaten bites stored in freezer.

The Essential Instant Pot® Keto Cookbook

TRADITIONAL CUPCAKES

Serves 7

Prep Time: 5 minutes, Cook Time: 30 minutes, Total Time: 35 minutes, Pressure: High, Release: Natural

Gluten Free, Soy Free, Kid Friendly

Keto cupcakes are a delicious no-brainer.

CAKE

2 cups blanched almond flour

2 tablespoons grass-fed butter, softened

2 eggs

1/2 cup unsweetened almond milk

1/2 cup Swerve, confectioners (or more, to taste)

1/2 teaspoon nutmeg, ground

1/2 teaspoon baking powder

FROSTING

4 ounces full-fat cream cheese, softened

4 tablespoons grass-fed butter, softened

2 cups heavy whipping cream

1 teaspoon vanilla extract

1/2 cup Swerve, confectioners (or more, to taste)

6 tablespoons sugar-free chocolate chips (optional)

Nutrition Facts
Amount per serving (2)
Calories   219
Total Fat 22.3g
Total Carbohydrate 2.8g
Dietary Fiber 0.8g
Total Sugars 0.6g
Protein 3.3g

Pour 1 cup of filtered water into the inner pot of the Instant Pot, then insert the trivet. In a large bowl, combine the flour, butter, eggs, almond milk, Swerve, nutmeg, and baking powder. Mix thoroughly. Working in batches if needed, transfer this mixture into a well-greased, Instant Pot–friendly muffin (or egg bites) mold.

Place the molds onto the trivet, and cover loosely with aluminum foil. Close the lid, set the pressure release to Sealing, and select Manual/Pressure Cook. Set the Instant Pot to 30 minutes on high pressure, and let cook.

While you wait, in a large bowl, combine the cream cheese, butter, whipping cream, vanilla, Swerve, and chocolate chips. Use an electric hand mixer until you achieve a light and fluffy texture. Place frosting in refrigerator.

Once the cupcakes are cooked, let the pressure release naturally, for about 10 minutes. Then, switch the pressure release to Venting. Open the Instant Pot, and remove the food. Let cool, top each cupcake evenly with a scoop of frosting.

SOFT AND CHEWY CHOCOLATE CHIP COOKIE BITES

Serves 7

Prep Time: 5 minutes, Cook Time: 20 minutes, Total Time: 25 minutes, Pressure: High, Release: Natural

Gluten Free, Soy Free, 25 Minutes or Less, Kid Friendly

These chocolate chip cookies are an addictive treat—yet they are still healthy. By replacing the traditional sugar with Swerve, and using almond flour instead of wheat flour, you still get all of the taste, but none of the sugar and carbs. To make crunchier cookies, add some chopped walnuts or pecans to the batter.

8 tablespoons sugar-free chocolate chips

2 tablespoons grass-fed butter, softened

2 cups blanched almond flour

1 egg

½ cup Swerve, confectioners (or more, to taste)

¼ teaspoon baking soda

Nutrition Facts
Amount per serving (1)
Calories 124
Total Fat 11.5g
Total Carbohydrate 6.5g
Dietary Fiber 1.8g
Total Sugars 0.2g
Protein 2.2g

Pour 1 cup water into the Instant Pot, then insert the trivet. In a large bowl, combine the chocolate chips, butter, almond flour, egg, Swerve, and baking soda. Mix until a soft dough forms. Once mixed thoroughly, transfer into a well-greased, Instant Pot–friendly egg bites mold. Work in batches, if needed. I prefer to stack 2 egg bites molds on top of each other, separated by Mason jar lids (or similar dividers).

Cover loosely with aluminum foil. Close the lid, set the pressure release to Sealing, and select Manual/Pressure Cook. Set the Instant Pot to 20 minutes on high pressure, and let cook.

Once cooked, let the pressure naturally disperse from the Instant Pot for about 10 minutes, then carefully switch the pressure release to Venting.

Open the Instant Pot, and remove the pan. Let cool, serve, and enjoy!

The Essential Instant Pot® Keto Cookbook

CAKE BALLS

IPM

Serves 6

**Prep Time: 5 minutes, Cook Time: 5 minutes, Total Time: 10 minutes,
Pressure: N/A, Release: N/A**

Gluten Free, Soy Free, 10 Minutes or Less, Kid Friendly

A wonderful treat to make quickly after dinner, this rich recipe is easily made in an Instant Pot Mini. Oftentimes I like to mix things up, and try a variety of different flavor combinations with these (coconut, almond, walnut—anything you can dream up!).

4 tablespoons grass-fed butter

⅓ cup almond butter, fresh

¼ cup blanched almond flour

¼ cup unsweetened cocoa powder

¼ cup sugar-free chocolate chips

⅓ cup Swerve, confectioners (or more, to tastep)

Nutrition Facts
Amount per serving
Calories 130
Total Fat 12.2g
Total Carbohydrate 7.7g
Dietary Fiber 2.6g
Total Sugars 0.1g
Protein 1.8g

Spread the butter evenly inside the inner pot and then set the Instant Pot to Sauté.

Add the almond butter, flour, cocoa powder, chocolate chips, and Swerve to the Instant Pot. Mix thoroughly, until melted together evenly (about 5 minutes).

Using a spatula to help scrape the sides of the bowl, pour mixture into a silicone mini muffin (or egg bites) mold. Freeze until firm.

Sprinkle cake balls with additional Swerve (if desired) before serving, and enjoy! Store leftovers in the freezer.

CLASSIC BROWNIES

Serves 5

**Prep Time: 5 minutes, Cook Time: 40 minutes, Total Time: 45 minutes,
Pressure: High, Release: Natural**

Gluten Free, Soy Free, Kid Friendly

When made traditionally, brownies are loaded with gluten, and contain enough sugar for an entire day. However, these keto Instant Pot brownies have none of the bad stuff, but retain that perfect texture and chocolatey taste.

8 tablespoons sugar-free chocolate chips

3 tablespoons unsweetened cocoa powder

2 tablespoons grass-fed butter, softened

½ cup walnuts, chopped (optional)

1 egg

½ cup Swerve, confectioners (or more, to taste)

1 cup blanched almond flour

½ teaspoon salt

½ teaspoon vanilla extract

Nutrition Facts
Amount per serving
Calories 162
Total Fat 14.3g
Total Carbohydrate 8.9g
Dietary Fiber 3.1g
Total Sugars 0.3g
Protein 5g

Pour 1 cup of filtered water into the inner pot of the Instant Pot, then insert the trivet. Using an electric mixer, combine chocolate chips, cocoa powder, butter, walnuts, egg, Swerve, almond flour, salt, and vanilla extract. Mix thoroughly. Transfer this mixture into a well-greased, Instant Pot–friendly dish.

Place the dish onto the trivet, and cover loosely with aluminum foil. Close the lid, set the pressure release to Sealing and select Manual/Pressure Cook. Set the Instant Pot to 40 minutes on high pressure, and let cook.

Once cooked, let the pressure naturally disperse from the Instant Pot for about 10 minutes, then carefully switch the pressure release to Venting.

Open the Instant Pot, and remove the dish.

Let cool, slice into 10 pieces, serve, and enjoy!

HOLIDAY PUMPKIN PIE

Serves 5 to 6

Prep Time: 5 minutes, Cook Time: 40 minutes, Total Time: 45 minutes, Pressure: High, Release: Natural

Gluten Free, Soy Free, Kid Friendly

Save yourself the carbs and sugar—make this pumpkin pie instead!

BASE
2 tablespoons grass-fed butter, softened
1 cup blanched almond flour
½ cup pecans, chopped

TOPPING
½ cup Swerve, confectioners (or more, to taste)
⅓ cup heavy whipping cream
½ teaspoon cinnamon, ground
½ teaspoon ginger, finely grated
½ teaspoon nutmeg, ground
½ teaspoon cloves, ground
1 (14-ounce) can organic pumpkin purée
1 egg

Nutrition Facts
Amount per serving
Calories 152
Total Fat 13.5g
Total Carbohydrate 6.1g
Dietary Fiber 2.1g
Total Sugars 2.2g
Protein 3.1g

Pour 1 cup of filtered water into the inner pot of the Instant Pot, then insert the trivet. Using an electric mixer, combine the butter, almond flour, and pecans. Mix thoroughly. Transfer this mixture into a well-greased, Instant Pot–friendly pan, and form a crust at the bottom of the pan, with a slight coating of the mixture also on the sides. Freeze for 15 minutes. In a large bowl, thoroughly combine the topping ingredients.

Take the pan from the freezer, add the topping evenly, and then place the pan onto the trivet. Cover loosely with aluminum foil. Close the lid, set the pressure release to Sealing, and select Manual/Pressure Cook. Set the Instant Pot to 40 minutes on high pressure, and let cook.

Once cooked, let the pressure naturally disperse from the Instant Pot for about 10 minutes, then carefully switch the pressure release to Venting.

Open the Instant Pot and remove the pan. Cool in the refrigerator for 4 to 5 hours, serve, and enjoy!

CRÈME BRÛLÉE

Serves 5

Prep Time: 5 minutes, Cook Time: 6 minutes, Total Time: 11 minutes, Pressure: High, Release: Natural

Gluten Free, Soy Free, 25 Minutes or Less, Kid Friendly

This classic French dessert is one of my all-time favorites, and serves as the perfect end to a romantic dinner. While traditional crème brûlée is very high in sugar, this keto adaptation has none. Serve with a few dark berries to add in some extra antioxidants.

2 egg yolks

1 cup heavy whipping cream

1 teaspoon vanilla extract

½ cup Swerve, confectioners (or more, to taste)

⅛ teaspoon salt

Nutrition Facts
Amount per serving
Calories 110
Total Fat 10.6g
Total Carbohydrate 0.9g
Dietary Fiber 0g
Total Sugars 0.3g
Protein 2.7g

Pour 1 cup of filtered water into the inner pot of the Instant Pot, then insert the trivet. In a large bowl, combine egg yolks, whipping cream, vanilla, Swerve, and salt. Mix thoroughly. Once mixed, evenly pour into 5 well-greased, Instant Pot–friendly ramekins.

Place the ramekins on the trivet, and cover each loosely with aluminum foil. Close the lid, set the pressure release to Sealing, and select Manual/Pressure Cook. Set the Instant Pot to 6 minutes on high pressure, and let cook.

Once cooked, let the pressure naturally disperse from the Instant Pot for about 10 minutes, then carefully switch the pressure release to Venting. Open the Instant Pot, and remove the ramekins. Let cool, serve and enjoy!

NOTE: If you would like a crunchier top to the crème brûlée, carefully place the ramekins under a broiler for 2 to 3 minutes (or until reaching desired texture).

COCONUT WHIPPED CREAM

Serves 5 to 6

**Prep Time: 5 minutes, Cook Time: 5 minutes, Total Time: 10 minutes,
Pressure: High, Release: Natural**

Gluten Free, Soy Free, 10 Minutes or Less, Kid Friendly

This unique keto coconut whipped cream works very well on its own. It can also be used for keto frostings, as well as to drizzle on top of cakes. As an added bonus, just like coconut oil, coconut milk contains medium chain triglycerides (MCTs), which aid in fat-burning.

1 (14-ounce) can full-fat coconut milk, refrigerated

½ cup heavy whipping cream

½ teaspoon vanilla extract

⅓ cup Swerve, confectioners (or more, to taste)

Nutrition Facts
Amount per serving
Calories 220
Total Fat 22.8g
Total Carbohydrate 4.8g
Dietary Fiber 1.8g
Total Sugars 2.7g
Protein 2g

With a large spoon, carefully scoop out the cream portion of the coconut milk, discarding the remaining liquid.

In a small bowl, mix the coconut milk with the heavy whipping cream, vanilla, and Swerve and stir until combined.

Set the Instant Pot to Sauté and pour in the mixture. Melt together for one minute, stirring thoroughly.

Remove cream mixture from the Instant Pot and whip with an electric mixer, until reaching desired consistency. Refrigerate until ready to serve.

SUGAR-FREE KEY LIME PIE

Serves 5 to 6

**Prep Time: 5 minutes, Cook Time: 40 minutes, Total Time: 45 minutes,
Pressure: High, Release: Natural**

Gluten Free, Soy Free, Kid Friendly

Try adding a hint of lemon juice to the filling to try a slighter different taste.

BASE
1 tablespoon grass-fed butter, softened
1 tablespoon coconut oil
1 cup blanched almond flour

TOPPING
3 key limes, juiced
1 cup heavy whipping cream
½ cup sour cream
½ cup Swerve, confectioners (or more, to taste)

Nutrition Facts
Amount per serving
Calories 305
Total Fat 30.1g
Total Carbohydrate 7.5g
Dietary Fiber 2.3g
Total Sugars 2.3g
Protein 5.3g

Pour 1 cup of filtered water into the inner pot of the Instant Pot, then insert the trivet. Using an electric mixer, thoroughly combine base ingredients. Transfer this mixture into a well-greased, Instant Pot–friendly pan, and form a crust at the bottom of the pan, with a slight coating of the mixture also on the sides. Freeze for 15 minutes. Meanwhile, thoroughly mix topping ingredients in a large bowl.

Remove the pan from the freezer, and pour the topping mixture evenly into the middle of the crust. Using a sling if desired, place the pan onto the trivet, and cover loosely with aluminum foil. Close the lid, set the pressure release to Sealing, and select Manual/Pressure Cook. Set the Instant Pot to 40 minutes on high pressure, and let cook.

Once cooked, let the pressure naturally disperse from the Instant Pot for about 10 minutes, then carefully switch the pressure release to Venting. Remove the dish and refrigerate for at least 3 to 4 hours, before serving.

The Essential Instant Pot® Keto Cookbook

TINY PUMPKIN CHEESECAKES

Serves 4

Prep Time: 5 minutes, Cook Time: 25 minutes, Total Time: 30 minutes, Pressure: High, Release: Natural

Gluten Free, Soy Free, Kid Friendly

Cheesecake is one of the best parts about making the switch to a ketogenic lifestyle, and these tiny pumpkin-tinged cakes add even more variety. Try sprinkling some shredded coconut to the top of each tiny cake to add even more flavor!

CAKE

8 ounces full-fat cream cheese, softened

½ cup organic pumpkin purée

⅓ cup Swerve, confectioners (or more, to taste)

2 teaspoons vanilla extract

1 egg

TOPPING

¼ cup sugar-free chocolate chips

Nutrition Facts
Amount per serving
Calories 285
Total Fat 25g
Total Carbohydrate 12.3g
Dietary Fiber 2.9g
Total Sugars 1.5g
Protein 7g

Combine the cream cheese, pumpkin, Swerve, vanilla, and egg, in a large bowl. Mix thoroughly. Place mixture into ramekins, then cover each ramekin with aluminum foil.

Pour 1 cup of filtered water into the inner pot of the Instant Pot, then insert the trivet, placing your covered ramekins on top. Move the valve to Sealing and close the lid.

Cook for 25 minutes at high pressure. Let pressure naturally disperse. Then remove ramekins, and let cool on the countertop, uncovered, for 30 minutes. Move ramekins to the refrigerator and allow to completely chill, about 45 minutes.

Take the desserts from the refrigerator. Sprinkle each cheesecake with chocolate chips, serve, and enjoy.

CANNOLI BITES

Serves 5 to 6

Prep Time: 5 minutes, Cook Time: 20 minutes, Total Time: 25 minutes, Pressure: High, Release: Natural

Gluten Free, Soy Free, 25 Minutes or Less

Cannoli are one of the best Italian culinary exports, and this keto recipe will let you get all the flavor, without the sugar. These cannoli bites also work perfectly for the endcap to a romantic dinner. Try a soft sprinkling of coconut flakes on the finished bites, to add even more decadence.

3 tablespoons sugar-free chocolate chips

2 tablespoons coconut oil

1 egg

½ cup blanched almond flour

½ teaspoon vanilla extract

½ cup Swerve, confectioners (or more, to taste)

1 (15-ounce) container whole milk ricotta cheese

Nutrition Facts
Amount per serving
Calories 189
Total Fat 14g
Total Carbohydrate 8.2g
Dietary Fiber 1.3g
Total Sugars 0.4g
Protein 10g

Pour 1 cup of filtered water into the inner pot of the Instant Pot, then insert the trivet. In a large bowl, combine the chocolate chips, coconut oil, egg, almond flour, vanilla, Swerve, and ricotta. Mix thoroughly. Once mixed, evenly pour this mixture into 6 well-greased, Instant Pot–friendly ramekins (or use an egg bites mold).

Place the ramekins on the trivet, and cover each loosely with aluminum foil. Close the lid, set the pressure release to Sealing, and select Manual/Pressure Cook. Set the Instant Pot to 20 minutes on high pressure, and let cook.

Once cooked, let the pressure naturally disperse from the Instant Pot for about 10 minutes, then carefully switch the pressure release to Venting.

Open the Instant Pot, and remove the ramekins. Place in the refrigerator for at least 20 minutes. Let cool, serve, and enjoy!

The Essential Instant Pot® Keto Cookbook

DECADENT CHOCOLATE MOUSSE

Serves 5 to 6

Prep Time: 5 minutes, Cook Time: 5 minutes, Total Time: 10 minutes, Pressure: N/A, Release: N/A

Gluten Free, Soy Free, Less Than 10 Minutes, Kid Friendly

Chocolate mousse is one of my all-time favorite desserts. This keto-friendly recipe lets you taste all of the chocolate, but without any of the downsides. Try adding some almonds or walnuts on top of your finished mousse for a bit of a crunch.

2 tablespoons grass-fed butter, softened

¼ cup sugar-free chocolate chips

1 cup full-fat cream cheese, softened

1 tablespoon raw cacao nibs

½ teaspoon vanilla extract

½ cup Swerve, confectioners (or more, to taste)

⅓ cup unsweetened cocoa powder

½ cup heavy whipping cream

Nutrition Facts
Amount per serving
Calories 119
Total Fat 11g
Total Carbohydrate 8.3g
Dietary Fiber 2.8g
Total Sugars 0.1g
Protein 1.8g

Set the Instant Pot to Sauté and melt the butter. Add the chocolate chips, cream cheese, cacao nibs, vanilla, Swerve, and cocoa powder to the Instant Pot. Stir continuously for 5 minutes.

Once thoroughly mixed, hit Cancel to stop the current program. Remove the inner pot from the Instant Pot, and refrigerate for at least 20 minutes.

Whisk (or use an electric mixer) to beat the heavy whipping cream, until stiff peaks form.

Using a spatula, gently fold the whipped cream into the cooled chocolate mixture. Serve, and enjoy!

CHOCOLATE ALMOND SQUARES

Serves 8

Prep Time: 5 minutes, Cook Time: 40 minutes, Total Time: 45 minutes, Pressure: High, Release: Natural

Gluten Free, Soy Free, Kid Friendly

Chocolate squares are a very common dessert, but making them keto is not always easy. Fortunately, this recipe is simple to follow, contains no sugar, and almost no carbohydrates—but you would never guess it by their amazing taste!

1 cup almond flour

6 tablespoons sugar-free chocolate chips

¼ cup unsweetened cocoa powder

2 tablespoons coconut oil

2 eggs

2 tablespoons cacao nibs, raw

1 cup almonds, chopped

½ cup Swerve, confectioners (or more, to taste)

¼ cup full-fat coconut milk

½ teaspoon vanilla extract

½ teaspoon salt

Nutrition Facts
Amount per serving
Calories 213
Total Fat 18.1g
Total Carbohydrate 13.1g
Dietary Fiber 5.5g
Total Sugars 1.2g
Protein 6g

In a large bowl, mix together the chocolate chips, cocoa powder, coconut oil, eggs, cacao nibs, almonds, Swerve, coconut milk, vanilla, and salt. Combine them very thoroughly.

Pour 1 cup of filtered water into the inner pot of the Instant Pot, and insert the trivet. Transfer the chocolate mixture from the bowl into a well-greased, Instant Pot–friendly dish.

Place the dish onto the trivet, and cover loosely with aluminum foil. Close the lid, set the pressure release to Sealing and select Manual/Pressure Cook. Set the Instant Pot to 40 minutes on high pressure, and let cook.

Once cooked, let the pressure naturally leave the Instant Pot, for about 10 minutes. Next, switch the pressure release to Venting.

Open the Instant Pot, and remove the dish. Refrigerate for at least 20 minutes (or until firm). Once sufficiently firm, cut into 8 squares, serve, and enjoy!

The Essential Instant Pot® Keto Cookbook

CHOCOLATE COCONUT BUTTER

Serves 16

**Prep Time: 5 minutes, Cook Time: 10 minutes, Total Time: 15 minutes,
Pressure: High, Release: Natural**

Gluten Free, Soy Free, 25 Minutes or Less, Kid Friendly

Coconut butter is a hidden gem among foodies, and this recipe takes it one step further. By combining the natural sweetness of coconut with the decadence of chocolate, we create an entirely new taste sensation. And since coconut is loaded with fat-burning medium chain triglycerides (MCTs), this dessert not only tastes like chocolate—it helps to burn away body fat.

4 tablespoons grass-fed butter, softened

1 cup raw coconut butter

2 tablespoons cacao nibs, raw

1/2 cup sugar-free chocolate chips

1/2 teaspoon vanilla extract

1/2 teaspoon salt

1/2 cup Swerve, confectioners (or more, to taste)

Nutrition Facts
Amount per serving
Calories 182
Total Fat 19.3g
Total Carbohydrate 4.8g
Dietary Fiber 1.5g
Total Sugars 0.1g
Protein 0.6g

In a large bowl, mix together the butter, coconut butter, cacao nibs, chocolate chips, vanilla, salt, and Swerve. Whisk or stir until the mixture reaches a smooth consistency.

Pour 1 cup of filtered water into the inner pot of the Instant Pot, and insert the trivet. Transfer the mixture from the bowl into a well-greased, Instant Pot–friendly dish.

Place the dish onto the trivet, and cover loosely with aluminum foil. Close the lid, set the pressure release to Sealing, and select Manual/Pressure Cook. Set the Instant Pot to 10 minutes on high pressure, and let cook.

Once cooked, let the pressure naturally disperse from the Instant Pot for about 10 minutes, then carefully switch the pressure release to Venting.

Open the Instant Pot, and remove the dish. Once sufficiently cooled, cut into 16 bars, serve, and enjoy!

TRADITIONAL PECAN PIE

Serves 7 to 8

**Prep Time: 5 minutes, Cook Time: 40 minutes, Total Time: 45 minutes,
Pressure: High, Release: Natural**

Gluten Free, Soy Free, Kid Friendly

Pecan pie is a holiday indulgence that is usually filled with tons of sugar and gluten.
However, this keto Instant Pot version retains the essence of the pie (whole pecans),
but substitutes in healthier alternatives—so you can indulge without being
knocked out of fat-burning ketosis. Try mixing in a little bit of chocolate chips
(sugar free) for an added twist.

CRUST

2 tablespoons grass-fed butter, softened

1 teaspoon vanilla extract

2 teaspoons unsweetened almond milk

¼ cup Swerve, confectioners (or more, to taste)

1 cup blanched almond flour

TOPPING

2 cups pecans, chopped

¾ cup heavy whipping cream

½ cup Swerve, confectioners (or more, to taste)

½ cup sugar-free maple syrup

Nutrition Facts
Amount per serving
Calories 254
Total Fat 25.3g
Total Carbohydrate 3.8g
Dietary Fiber 1.2g
Total Sugars 1.1g
Protein 4.2g

Pour 2 cups filtered water into the Instant Pot, and insert the trivet. To make the crust, in a large bowl mix together the butter, vanilla, almond milk, Swerve, and almond flour. Combine thoroughly until the crust reaches a uniform texture.

Transfer the mixture from the bowl into a well-greased, Instant Pot–friendly pan (or dish). Use a spatula to firmly press the crust into the base of the pan, with a slight coating on the sides. Freeze for 15 minutes. Meanwhile, stir together pecans, whipping cream, Swerve, and sugar-free maple syrup in a large bowl.

Remove the pan from the freezer, and pour in the topping, being careful not to overfill. Place the pan onto the trivet, and cover loosely with aluminum foil. Close the lid, set the pressure release to Sealing, and select Manual/Pressure Cook. Set the Instant Pot to 40 minutes on high pressure, and let cook.

The Essential Instant Pot® Keto Cookbook

Once the crust is cooked, let the pressure naturally leave the Instant Pot, for about 10 minutes. Next, switch the pressure release to Venting. Open the Instant Pot, and remove the pie. Allow to cool completely on the counter, before serving.

5-INGREDIENT MINI CHOCOLATE CAKES

IPM

Serves 4

**Prep Time: 5 minutes, Cook Time: 20 minutes, Total Time: 25 minutes,
Pressure: High, Release: Quick**

Gluten Free, Dairy Free, Soy Free, 25 Minutes or Less, Kid Friendly

These tiny cakes are a perfect bite-size dessert, and they are done in almost no time at all! The Instant Pot Mini cooks these up beautifully, and you can even add a drizzle of extra melted sugar-free chocolate over the finished cakes, if you are feeling adventurous.

1 egg
1 cup blanched almond flour
½ cup sugar-free chocolate chips
¼ teaspoon baking soda
¼ cup unsweetened cocoa powder

Nutrition Facts
Amount per serving
Calories 158
Total Fat 11.5g
Total Carbohydrate 19.8g
Dietary Fiber 6g
Total Sugars 0.3g
Protein 5.1g

Pour 1 cup of filtered water into the inner pot, then insert the trivet. Using an electric hand mixer, combine egg, almond flour, chocolate chips, baking soda, and cocoa powder.

Transfer batter evenly into 4 well-greased ramekins. Cover with aluminum foil. Place the ramekins on top of the trivet.

Close the lid, set the pressure release to Sealing, and select Manual/Pressure Cook. Set the Instant Pot to 20 minutes on high pressure and let cook.

Once cooked, perform a quick release by carefully switching the pressure valve to Venting, and carefully remove the ramekins. Let the cakes cool, then serve, and enjoy!

EASY PECAN COOKIE BARS

Serves 5 to 6

Prep Time: 5 minutes, Cook Time: 40 minutes, Total Time: 45 minutes, Pressure: High, Release: Natural

Gluten Free, Soy Free, Kid Friendly

Pecan cookies are a childhood favorite of mine. This keto adaptation will truly blow your mind, as they absolutely do not taste like they are healthy—yet they are. If I have leftover keto fudge, sometimes I will melt a bit, and drizzle it over these already-luscious goodies.

1 cup blanched almond flour

2 tablespoons butter, softened

½ cup Swerve, confectioners (or more, to taste)

½ cup pecans, chopped

½ teaspoon vanilla extract

½ teaspoon cinnamon, ground

½ teaspoon nutmeg, ground

¼ teaspoon baking soda

Nutrition Facts
Amount per serving
Calories 147
Total Fat 15.6g
Total Carbohydrate 1.6g
Dietary Fiber 0.9g
Total Sugars 0.4g
Protein 1.4g

In a large bowl, mix together almond flour and butter. Add Swerve, pecans, vanilla, cinnamon, nutmeg, and baking soda, and stir until an evenly textured dough forms.

Add one cup filtered water into the Instant Pot, and insert the trivet.

Transfer the mixture from the bowl into a well-greased, Instant Pot–friendly dish or pan.

Place the dish onto the trivet, and cover loosely with aluminum foil. Close the lid, set the pressure release to Sealing, and select Manual/Pressure Cook. Set the Instant Pot to 40 minutes on high pressure, and let cook.

Once cooked, let the pressure naturally leave the Instant Pot, for about 10 minutes. Next, switch the pressure release to Venting.

Open the Instant Pot, and remove the dish. Once sufficiently cooled, cut into bars, serve, and enjoy!

ANTIOXIDANT-RICH MATCHA CHEESECAKE

Serves 8

**Prep Time: 5 minutes, Cook Time: 40 minutes, Total Time: 45 minutes,
Pressure: High, Release: Natural**

Gluten Free, Soy Free, Kid Friendly

Matcha is one of the more popular new trends to emerge in recent years, as it has numerous reported health benefits. This Instant Pot cheesecake features all the benefits of matcha, and is also wonderfully easy to make.

BASE

16 ounces full-fat cream cheese, softened

3 teaspoons blanched almond flour

3 tablespoons heavy cream

2 eggs

1 tablespoon matcha powder

1/2 teaspoon vanilla extract

TOPPING

2/3 cup Swerve, confectioners (or more, to taste)

1/2 cup sour cream, at room temperature

1/2 cup sugar-free chocolate chips

Nutrition Facts
Amount per serving
Calories 325
Total Fat 31.2g
Total Carbohydrate 4.6g
Dietary Fiber 1.3g
Total Sugars 0.6g
Protein 8.6g

Combine the cream cheese, almond flour, heavy cream, eggs, matcha powder, and vanilla in a large bowl. Mix thoroughly. Place mixture in springform pan, then loosely cover with aluminum foil.

Pour 2 cups filtered water into Instant Pot, then add trivet, placing the springform pan atop the rack. Move the valve to Sealing and close the lid of the Instant Pot.

Set to Manual/Pressure Cook, and let cook for 40 minutes at high pressure. Once cooked, let the pressure naturally disperse from the Instant Pot for about 10 minutes, then carefully switch the pressure release to Venting.

Remove pan, and let cool for 30 minutes. Then refrigerate for at least 45 minutes (a few hours is preferable).

Remove foil. Mix together the Swerve and sour cream in a small bowl, then spread evenly on the cake before serving and sprinkle with chocolate chips. Store any remaining cheesecake in the refrigerator.

COCONUT COOKIE BITES

Serves 5 to 6

Prep Time: 5 minutes, Cook Time: 20 minutes, Total Time: 25 minutes, Pressure: High, Release: Natural

Gluten Free, Soy Free, 25 Minutes or Less, Kid Friendly

Simple, tasty, and healthy—the perfect keto treat.

2 tablespoons grass-fed butter, softened

2 eggs

1 cup blanched almond flour

3/4 cup unsweetened coconut flakes

1/2 cup Swerve, confectioners (or more, to taste)

1/2 cup almond butter, smooth

1/2 teaspoon baking powder

1/2 teaspoon vanilla extract

1/2 teaspoon salt

Nutrition Facts
Amount per serving
Calories 129
Total Fat 11.9g
Total Carbohydrate 3.1g
Dietary Fiber 1.5g
Total Sugars 1g
Protein 3.5g

In a large bowl, mix together the butter, eggs, almond flour, coconut, Swerve, almond butter, baking powder, vanilla, and salt. Combine until ingredients are fully incorporated.

Pour 1 cup of filtered water into the inner pot of the Instant Pot, and insert the trivet. Transfer the mixture from the bowl into a well-greased, Instant Pot–friendly egg bites pan. Work in batches, if need be. I prefer to stack 2 egg bites molds on top of each other, separated by Mason jar lids (or similar dividers).

Place the dish onto the trivet, and cover loosely with aluminum foil. Close the lid, set the pressure release to Sealing, and select Manual/Pressure Cook. Set the Instant Pot to 20 minutes on high pressure, and let cook.

Once cooked, let the pressure naturally leave the Instant Pot, for about 10 minutes. Next, switch the pressure release to Venting.

Open the Instant Pot, and remove the dish. Once sufficiently cooled, serve, and enjoy!

LUSCIOUS LEMON SQUARES

Serves 5 to 6

**Prep Time: 5 minutes, Cook Time: 40 minutes, Total Time: 45 minutes,
Pressure: High, Release: Natural**

Gluten Free, Soy Free, Kid Friendly

If you need lemon squares for a social function or work party, these are your new
go-to. They are very low in carbs and sugar, and yet pack in all the traditional flavor of
lemon squares that you are used to. A tart and tasty keto dessert, par excellence.

3 eggs

2 tablespoons grass-fed butter, softened

½ cup full-fat coconut milk

½ teaspoon baking powder

½ teaspoon vanilla extract

**½ cup Swerve, confectioners (or more,
to taste)**

¼ cup lemon juice

1 cup blanched almond flour

Nutrition Facts
Amount per serving
Calories 166
Total Fat 14.8g
Total Carbohydrate 2.8g
Dietary Fiber 1g
Total Sugars 1.4g
Protein 6.2g

In a large bowl, mix together the eggs,
butter, coconut milk, baking powder,
vanilla, Swerve, lemon juice, and flour. Stir
thoroughly, until a perfectly even mixture
is obtained.

Next, pour 1 cup filtered water into the
Instant Pot, and insert the trivet. Transfer
the mixture from the bowl into a well-
greased, Instant Pot–friendly pan (or dish).

Using a sling if desired, place the
dish onto the trivet, and cover loosely
with aluminum foil. Close the lid, set
the pressure release to Sealing, and select
Manual/Pressure Cook. Set the Instant
Pot to 40 minutes on high pressure, and
let cook.

Once cooked, let the pressure
naturally disperse from the Instant Pot for
about 10 minutes, then carefully switch the
pressure release to Venting.

Open the Instant Pot, and remove the
dish. Let cool, cut into 6 squares, serve,
and enjoy!

SAVORY CHOCOLATE CASHEWS

Serves 6

**Prep Time: 5 minutes, Cook Time: 5 minutes, Total Time: 10 minutes,
Pressure: High, Release: Natural**

Gluten Free, Soy Free, 10 Minutes or Less, Kid Friendly

Cashews are one of my favorite nuts. They are surprisingly high in copper,
phosphorus, and manganese. This recipe infuses cashews with a healthy dose of
butter and chocolate (who is going to complain about that?). The coconut adds a
nice texture and flavor to complement the crunchiness of the nuts.

2 tablespoons grass-fed butter, softened

¼ cup sugar-free chocolate chips

2 teaspoons coconut, shredded (optional)

¾ cup cashews, chopped

Nutrition Facts
Amount per serving
Calories 203
Total Fat 17.7g
Total Carbohydrate 12.1g
Dietary Fiber 2.6g
Total Sugars 1.2g
Protein 3.6g

Set the Instant Pot to Sauté and melt the
butter.

Add chocolate chips, shredded
coconut (if using), and cashews to the
Instant Pot, and mix thoroughly until
chocolate is melted.

Pour mixture into a large bowl and
refrigerate until firm. Break into pieces
and serve.

SUPER FUDGE FAT BOMBS

Serves 7 to 8

**Prep Time: 5 minutes, Cook Time: 5 minutes, Total Time: 10 minutes,
Pressure: N/A, Release: N/A**

Gluten Free, Soy Free, 10 Minutes or Less, Kid Friendly

Fat bombs are one of the best parts about going keto, and these do not disappoint.
You will get some healthy fats (which keep you in ketosis), but you will also truly feel
like you are indulging. And because these are low carb, you can get away with having
one of these as an occasional snack.

2 tablespoons coconut oil

1 cup sugar-free chocolate chips

2 teaspoons coconut, shredded (optional)

1 cup raw coconut butter

½ cup nuts, chopped (optional)

Nutrition Facts
Amount per serving
Calories 342
Total Fat 35.8g
Total Carbohydrate 10.2g
Dietary Fiber 2.8g
Total Sugars 0.4g
Protein 2.5g

Set the Instant Pot to Sauté and melt the oil.

Add the chocolate chips, coconut, coconut butter, and nuts to the Instant Pot. Mix thoroughly, until melted.

Pour mixture into a silicone mini-muffin mold.

Refrigerate until firm. Serve, and enjoy! Store leftover fudge in the refrigerator or freezer.

The Essential Instant Pot® Keto Cookbook

CLASSIC BLONDIES

Serves 8

Prep Time: 5 minutes, Cook Time: 40 minutes, Total Time: 45 minutes, Pressure: High, Release: Natural

Gluten Free, Soy Free, Kid Friendly

All the taste of the classic, with none of the sugar.

1 cup blanched almond flour

1 cup pecans, chopped

1/2 cup macadamia nuts

2 eggs

4 tablespoons heavy cream

2 tablespoons grass-fed butter, softened

1 tablespoon erythritol powder

1/2 teaspoon baking powder

1/2 teaspoon vanilla extract

1/2 teaspoon cinnamon, ground

1/2 teaspoon salt

Nutrition Facts
Amount per serving
Calories 298
Total Fat 29.1g
Total Carbohydrate 3.9g
Dietary Fiber 1.6g
Total Sugars 1g
Protein 7.6g

In a large bowl, mix together the eggs, flour, pecans, macadamia nuts, heavy cream, butter, erythritol powder, baking powder, vanilla, cinnamon, and salt. Combine until the mixture is even and fully incorporated.

Pour 1 cup of filtered water into the inner pot of the Instant Pot, and insert the trivet. Transfer the mixture from the bowl into a well-greased, Instant Pot–friendly pan (or dish).

Using a sling if desired, place the dish onto the trivet, and cover loosely with aluminum foil. Close the lid, set the pressure release to Sealing, and select Manual/Pressure Cook. Set the Instant Pot to 40 minutes on high pressure, and let cook.

Once cooked, let the pressure naturally disperse from the Instant Pot for about 10 minutes, then carefully switch the pressure release to Venting.

Open the Instant Pot, and remove the dish. Remove the foil and allow the blondies to cool completely on the counter. Cut into 8 bars, serve, and enjoy!

MIXED CANDIED NUTS

Serves 8

Prep Time: 5 minutes, Cook Time: 15 minutes, Total Time: 20 minutes, Pressure: High, Release: Quick

Gluten Free, Dairy Free, Soy Free, 25 Minutes or Less, Kid Friendly

Making keto-friendly desserts in the Instant Pot is always fun, and these candied nuts are a personal favorite. Despite tasting like they are loaded with waistline-increasing sugar, they contain virtually none. Great for parties, as well as after-dinner coffee.

1 cup pecan halves

1 cup walnuts, chopped

⅓ cup Swerve, confectioners (or more, to taste)

⅓ cup grass-fed butter

1 teaspoon cinnamon, ground

Nutrition Facts
Amount per serving
Calories 122
Total Fat 11.7g
Total Carbohydrate 2.4g
Dietary Fiber 1.5g
Total Sugars 0.3g
Protein 4g

Preheat your oven to 350°F, and line a baking sheet with aluminum foil.

While your oven is warming, pour ½ cup of filtered water into the inner pot of the Instant Pot, followed by the pecans, walnuts, Swerve, butter, and cinnamon. Stir nut mixture, close the lid, and then set the pressure valve to Sealing. Use the Manual/Pressure Cook mode to cook at high pressure, for 5 minutes.

Once cooked, perform a quick release by carefully switching the pressure valve to Venting, and strain the nuts. Pour the nuts onto the baking sheet, spreading them out in an even layer. Place in the oven for 5 to 10 minutes (or until crisp, being careful not to overcook). Cool before serving. Store leftovers in the refrigerator or freezer.

The Essential Instant Pot® Keto Cookbook

10-MINUTE CHOCOLATE MACADAMIA BUTTER

Serves 8

Prep Time: 5 minutes, Cook Time: 5 minutes, Total Time: 10 minutes, Pressure: High, Release: Natural

Gluten Free, Soy Free, 10 Minutes or Less, Kid Friendly

Macadamia butter has to be one of the best-kept secrets in the nutrition universe. It is rich, creamy, and full of healthy fat—yet hardly anyone talks about it. This concoction of coconut, chocolate, and macadamia butter will satisfy anyone looking for a sugar fix—all while still keeping you on the keto path.

2 tablespoons coconut oil

1 cup macadamia butter

½ cup sugar-free chocolate chips

2 teaspoons coconut, shredded (optional)

Nutrition Facts
Amount per serving
Calories 111
Total Fat 9.2g
Total Carbohydrate 6.8g
Dietary Fiber 0.7g
Total Sugars 5.6g
Protein 1.3g

Set the Instant Pot to Sauté and melt the oil.

Add macadamia butter, chocolate chips, and shredded coconut (if using) to the Instant Pot. Cook, and continue to mix until melted and smooth.

Remove mixture with a spoon, and place into a Mason jar.

Refrigerate until firm. Serve on its own, or use to top other baked goods. Store remaining macadamia butter in refrigerator.

MILLION-DOLLAR POUND CAKE

Serves 8

**Prep Time: 5 minutes, Cook Time: 40 minutes, Total Time: 45 minutes,
Pressure: High, Release: Natural**

Gluten Free, Soy Free, Kid Friendly

This is an after-dinner classic. Try serving with warm, organic coffee.

3 eggs

1 cup blanched almond flour

2/3 cup Swerve, confectioners (or more, to taste)

1/4 cup heavy cream

4 ounces full-fat cream cheese, softened

2 tablespoons grass-fed butter, softened

1/2 teaspoon baking powder

1/2 teaspoon vanilla extract

1/2 teaspoon salt

Nutrition Facts
Amount per serving
Calories 213
Total Fat 20.2g
Total Carbohydrate 2.1g
Dietary Fiber 0.4g
Total Sugars 0.4g
Protein 6.5g

In a large bowl, whisk together eggs, almond flour, Swerve, and heavy cream. Stir in cream cheese, butter, baking powder, vanilla, and salt. Continue to stir for several minutes, until the mixture is well-combined and even in texture.

Pour 1 cup of filtered water into the inner pot of the Instant Pot, and insert the trivet. Transfer the mixture from the bowl into a well-greased, Instant Pot–friendly pan (or dish).

Using a sling if desired, place the pan onto the trivet, and cover loosely with aluminum foil. Close the lid, set the pressure release to Sealing, and select Manual/Pressure Cook. Set the Instant Pot to 40 minutes on high pressure, and let cook.

Once cooked, let the pressure naturally leave the Instant Pot, for about 10 minutes. Next, switch the pressure release to Venting.

Open the Instant Pot, and remove the pan. If desired, remove aluminum foil, and finish the cake for 2 to 5 minutes in the oven at 350°F., to brown the top. Let cool, slice, serve, and enjoy!

The Essential Instant Pot® Keto Cookbook

COCONUT FLAKED WALNUT FUDGE

Serves 4

Prep Time: 5 minutes, Cook Time: 5 minutes, Total Time: 10 minutes, Pressure: N/A, Release: N/A

Gluten Free, Soy Free, 10 Minutes or Less, Kid Friendly

Fudge is hands-down one of my favorite desserts from childhood. This keto fudge is healthier than the classic recipe, and the walnuts provide lots of omega-3 fatty acids, copper, manganese, and biotin. For a slightly different twist, omit the coconut flakes, and instead dip each finished piece of fudge into a bowl filled with shredded coconut.

2 tablespoons coconut oil

1 cup sugar-free chocolate chips

½ cup full-fat coconut milk

½ cup walnuts, chopped (or more, to taste)

2 tablespoons unsweetened coconut flakes (or more, to taste)

2 tablespoons grass-fed butter, softened

1 teaspoon vanilla extract

Nutrition Facts
Amount per serving
Calories 152
Total Fat 13.4g
Total Carbohydrate 11.4g
Dietary Fiber 3.1g
Total Sugars 0.2g
Protein 2.7g

Set the Instant Pot to Sauté and melt the oil.

Stir in the chocolate chips, coconut milk, walnuts, coconut flakes, butter, and vanilla. Mix thoroughly, until melted.

Remove the inner pot from the Instant Pot and carefully pour the fudge into a greased, deep glass dish. Smooth the surface with a spatula so the fudge is evenly distributed in the dish.

Freeze until firm, about 30 minutes. Slice into squares, serve, and enjoy!

EASY ALMOND BUTTER MINI CAKES

(IPM)

Serves 6

Prep Time: 5 minutes, Cook Time: 30 minutes, Total Time: 35 minutes, Pressure: High, Release: Natural

Gluten Free, Soy Free, Kid Friendly

These light cakes provide a light and summery alternative to their heavier chocolate cousins. These mini delicacies work perfectly for after-dinner coffee, and can also easily be made in your Instant Pot Mini.

1 egg
½ cup almond flour
¼ cup almond butter
¼ teaspoon baking soda
⅓ cup Swerve, confectioners

Nutrition Facts
Amount per serving
Calories 196
Total Fat 17.5g
Total Carbohydrate 7.1g
Dietary Fiber 3.1g
Total Sugars 3g
Protein 6.4g

Mix the egg, flour, almond butter, baking soda, and Swerve in a large bowl. Use an electric mixer, until a smooth consistency is obtained. Pour this mixture evenly into ramekins.

Pour 1 cup of filtered water into the Instant Pot, then insert the trivet.

Working in batches if needed, cover the ramekins with aluminum foil, and place on top of the trivet. Close the lid, set the pressure release to Sealing, and select Manual/Pressure Cook. Set the Instant Pot to 30 minutes on high pressure and let cook.

Once cooked, let the pressure naturally disperse, then remove the mini cakes, and let cool. If desired, brown cakes in the oven at 350°F for 2 to 3 minutes, to finish.

The Essential Instant Pot® Keto Cookbook

HOLIDAY GINGER COOKIE BITES

Serves 4

**Prep Time: 5 minutes, Cook Time: 20 minutes, Total Time: 25 minutes,
Pressure: High, Release: Natural**

Gluten Free, Soy Free, 25 Minutes or Less, Kid Friendly

Gingerbread cookies are a classic holiday treat. This recipe will give you equally flavorful results, without all the gluten.

1 cup blanched almond flour

½ cup Swerve, confectioners (or more, to taste)

1 egg

1 tablespoon grass-fed butter

1 teaspoon ginger, finely grated

½ teaspoon cloves, ground

½ teaspoon nutmeg, ground

½ teaspoon cinnamon, ground

½ teaspoon salt

½ teaspoon vanilla extract

Nutrition Facts
Amount per serving
Calories 89
Total Fat 7.8g
Total Carbohydrate 2.5g
Dietary Fiber 1.1g
Total Sugars 0.5g
Protein 3g

In a large bowl, mix together the flour, Swerve, egg, butter, ginger, cloves, nutmeg, cinnamon, salt, and vanilla extract. Continue stirring until a perfectly even mixture is obtained.

Next, pour 1 cup of filtered water into the Instant Pot and insert the trivet. Transfer the mixture from the bowl into a well-greased, Instant Pot–friendly egg bites pan. Work in batches, if need be. I prefer to stack two egg bites molds on top of each other, separated by Mason jar lids (or similar dividers).

Using a sling if desired, place the pan onto the trivet, and cover loosely with aluminum foil. Close the lid, set the pressure release to Sealing, and select Manual/Pressure Cook. Set the Instant Pot to 40 minutes on high pressure, and let cook.

Once cooked, let the pressure naturally disperse from the Instant Pot for about 10 minutes, then carefully switch the pressure release to Venting.

Open the Instant Pot, and remove the pan. Once cooled, serve, and enjoy!

TRADITIONAL CHOCOLATE PIE

Serves 5 to 6

Prep Time: 5 minutes, Cook Time: 40 minutes, Total Time: 45 minutes, Pressure: High, Release: Natural

Gluten Free, Soy Free, Kid Friendly

It doesn't get more decadent than this—and it's still keto!

CRUST

1 cup blanched almond flour

1 egg

1/2 cup unsweetened cocoa powder

1/2 teaspoon salt

1/2 teaspoon vanilla extract

1/4 teaspoon baking soda

FILLING

8 ounces full-fat cream cheese, softened

8 tablespoons sugar-free chocolate chips

1/4 cup raw cacao nibs

1/4 cup heavy whipping cream

2 tablespoons grass-fed butter, softened

2/3 cup Swerve, confectioners (or more, to taste)

Nutrition Facts
Amount per serving
Calories 322
Total Fat 21g
Total Carbohydrate 18.3g
Dietary Fiber 8g
Total Sugars 1.2g
Protein 8.1g

Pour 1 cup of filtered water into the inner pot of the Instant Pot, and insert the trivet. To make the crust, mix together flour, cocoa powder, egg, salt, vanilla, and baking soda in a large bowl. Transfer the mixture from the bowl into a well-greased, Instant Pot–friendly pan (or dish), pressing down with a spatula to create a smooth crust. Coat the sides of the pan slightly, as well. Freeze for 15 minutes.

Mix all filling ingredients evenly in a large bowl. Remove the pan from the freezer, and pour in filling evenly. Do not overfill. Place the pan onto the trivet, and cover loosely with aluminum foil. Close the lid, set the pressure release to Sealing, and select Manual/Pressure Cook. Set the Instant Pot to 40 minutes on high pressure, and let cook.

Once cooked, let the pressure naturally disperse from the Instant Pot for about 10 minutes, then carefully switch the pressure release to Venting. Remove the pan, and let cool for at least 3 to 4 hours in the refrigerator, before serving.

EASY COCONUT MACAROONS

Serves 5 to 6

**Prep Time: 5 minutes, Cook Time: 20 minutes, Total Time: 25 minutes,
Pressure: High, Release: Natural**

Gluten Free, Soy Free, 25 Minutes or Less, Kid Friendly

Macaroons are definitely not typically thought of as a health food. With this recipe, I have taken all the sugary goodness, and kept all the flavor—but removed almost all the carbs. Serve with some keto hot chocolate, if desired.

BASE
2 cups blanched almond flour

1 egg white

½ cup Swerve, confectioners (or more, to taste)

¼ cup unsweetened coconut flakes

1 teaspoon vanilla extract

½ teaspoon salt

TOPPING
6 tablespoons sugar-free chocolate chips

Nutrition Facts
Amount per serving
Calories 106
Total Fat 8.2g
Total Carbohydrate 9.6g
Dietary Fiber 2.8g
Total Sugars 0.5g
Protein 3g

Pour 1 cup of filtered water into the inner pot of the Instant Pot, then insert the trivet. In a large bowl, combine almond flour, egg white, Swerve, coconut flakes, vanilla, and salt and mix well. Transfer this mixture into a well-greased, Instant Pot–friendly egg bites mold, working in batches if needed.

Place the dish onto the trivet, and cover loosely with aluminum foil. Close the lid, set the pressure release to Sealing, and select Manual/Pressure Cook. Set the Instant Pot to 20 minutes on high pressure, and let cook.

Once cooked, let the pressure naturally disperse from the Instant Pot for about 10 minutes, then carefully switch the pressure release to Venting.

Open the Instant Pot, and remove the dish. Melt the chocolate chips in a medium microwave-safe bowl in the microwave for about 20 seconds. Once melted, drizzle evenly over the macaroons. Once completely cooled, serve, and enjoy!

Dessert

CLASSIC CHOCOLATE CAKE

Serves 5 to 6

**Prep Time: 5 minutes, Cook Time: 40 minutes, Total Time: 45 minutes,
Pressure: High, Release: Natural**

Gluten Free, Soy Free, Kid Friendly

This truly tasty treat is very easy to make and can be topped with coconut flakes (or melted dark chocolate). Try adding the optional chocolate chips to the batter for a bit of texture and extra indulgence.

¼ cup sugar-free chocolate chips

2 tablespoons grass-fed butter, softened

¼ cup raw cacao nibs

3 eggs

2 tablespoons coconut oil

1 cup blanched almond flour

2/3 cup Swerve, confectioners (or more, to taste)

½ teaspoon vanilla extract

½ cup unsweetened cocoa powder

¼ cup sour cream, at room temperature

¼ teaspoon baking soda

Nutrition Facts
Amount per serving
Calories 255
Total Fat 22g
Total Carbohydrate 14.9g
Dietary Fiber 6.6g
Total Sugars 1.2g
Protein 6.4g

In a large bowl mix together the chocolate chips, butter, cacao nibs, eggs, coconut oil, almond flour, Swerve, vanilla, cocoa powder, sour cream, and baking soda. Mix until batter is smooth.

Pour 1 cup of filtered water into the inner pot of the Instant Pot, and insert the trivet.

Transfer the mixture from the bowl into a well-greased, Instant Pot–friendly pan (or dish).

Place the pan onto the trivet, and cover loosely with aluminum foil. Close the lid, set the pressure release to Sealing and select Manual/Pressure Cook. Set the Instant Pot to 40 minutes on high pressure, and let cook.

Once cooked, let the pressure naturally disperse from the Instant Pot for about 10 minutes, then carefully switch the pressure release to Venting.

Open the Instant Pot and remove the pan. Let cool, serve, and enjoy!

MINI LAVA CAKES

(IPM)

Serves 5 to 6

Prep Time: 5 minutes, Cook Time: 35 minutes, Total Time: 40 minutes, Pressure: High, Release: Quick

Gluten Free, Soy Free, Kid Friendly

These delicious lava cakes are overflowing with chocolatey goodness, but they're still good for you.

2 tablespoons grass-fed butter, softened

2 eggs

½ cup sugar-free chocolate chips

½ cup unsweetened cocoa powder

2 ½ cups blanched almond flour

¼ teaspoon baking soda

⅓ cup Swerve, confectioners (or more, to taste)

coconut oil (to grease)

Nutrition Facts
Amount per serving
Calories 165
Total Fat 13.4g
Total Carbohydrate 11.4g
Dietary Fiber 2.9g
Total Sugars 0.3g
Protein 5.5g

Mix the butter, eggs, chocolate chips, cocoa powder, almond flour, baking soda, and Swerve in a large bowl. Stir until batter is smooth.

Grease smaller, Instant Pot–friendly bowls or ramekins with coconut oil. Transfer batter evenly into these bowls, working in batches if needed.

Pour 1 cup of filtered water into the Instant Pot, then insert the trivet. Place your bowls gently on top of the trivet.

Close the lid, set the pressure release to Sealing, and select Manual/Pressure Cook. Set the Instant Pot to 35 minutes on high pressure, and let cook.

Once cooked, immediately switch the pressure release to Venting (do this carefully, to avoid steam).

Cook some additional chocolate chips in the microwave for 20 seconds (or until they melt).

Turn each bowl upside down, allowing cake to come out. Drizzle melted chocolate chips over each cake, and enjoy!

CHOCOLATE CHIP CHEESECAKE

Serves 5 to 6

**Prep Time: 5 minutes, Cook Time: 25 minutes, Total Time: 30 minutes,
Pressure: High, Release: Natural**

Gluten Free, Soy Free, Kid Friendly

Cheesecake is a great indulgence, but this chocolate chip keto cheesecake is much healthier, as it cuts out all the sugar. With only 5 ingredients, it is also a treat you should be able whip up at almost any time—no complicated shopping list required. The Instant Pot makes preparing this classic recipe much faster too; you will be done in just 30 minutes.

CAKE
16 ounces full-fat cream cheese, softened

½ cup Swerve, confectioners (or more, to taste)

2 eggs

4 teaspoons vanilla extract

TOPPING
5 tablespoons sugar-free chocolate chips

Nutrition Facts
Amount per serving
Calories 339
Total Fat 31.2g
Total Carbohydrate 9.1g
Dietary Fiber 1.7g
Total Sugars 0.6g
Protein 8.4g

Combine cream cheese, Swerve, eggs, and vanilla together in a large bowl, and mix thoroughly. Pour mixture in a well-greased springform pan, then cover with aluminum foil.

Pour 2 cups of filtered water into the Instant Pot, then insert the trivet, placing your covered pan on top. Move the valve to Sealing and close the lid.

Use Manual/Pressure Cook mode, to set the timer for 25 minutes, at high pressure. Let pressure naturally disperse. Then remove pan and let cool for 30 minutes. Refrigerate until completely chilled, about 45 minutes.

Take the cheesecake from the refrigerator, and remove the foil. Sprinkle and evenly distribute the chocolate chips over the top of the cake, slice, serve, and enjoy!

CHOCOLATE-COVERED PUMPKIN SEEDS

Serves 5 to 6

**Prep Time: 5 minutes, Cook Time: 5 minutes, Total Time: 10 minutes,
Pressure: High, Release: Natural**

Gluten Free, Soy Free, 10 minutes or less, Kid Friendly

Pumpkin seeds are a surprisingly dense source of nutrients. They have a wide range of antioxidants, as well as minerals. This a very simple dessert recipe that is easily multiplied (so you can store a lot for later), if so desired.

2 tablespoons coconut oil

½ cup sugar-free chocolate chips

½ cup pumpkin seeds

½ teaspoon salt (optional)

Nutrition Facts
Amount per serving
Calories 175
Total Fat 15.1g
Total Carbohydrate 12.7g
Dietary Fiber 3.1g
Total Sugars 0.1g
Protein 4.2g

Set the Instant Pot to Sauté and melt the oil.

Add chocolate chips, pumpkin seeds, and salt to the Instant Pot, and mix thoroughly, until chocolate is melted.

Using a spatula, scrape mixture into a large bowl or a cookie sheet in a single layer.

Refrigerate until firm. Serve, and enjoy! Store leftovers in the refrigerator or freezer.

SIDES

SMOKY BACON SLIDERS

Serves 4 to 5

**Prep Time: 5 minutes, Cook Time: 10 minutes, Total Time: 15 minutes,
Pressure: High, Release: Natural**

Gluten Free, Soy Free, 25 Minutes or Less, Kid Friendly

Perfect for parties—or for an at-home movie night.

2 tablespoons coconut oil

½ pound no-sugar-added bacon, sliced into small pieces

1 pound grass-fed beef, ground

½ teaspoon black ground pepper

½ teaspoon kosher salt

½ teaspoon chili powder

½ teaspoon crushed red pepper

½ teaspoon cayenne pepper, ground

1 cup full-fat Cheddar cheese, shredded

1 cup full-fat mozzarella cheese, shredded

Nutrition Facts
Amount per serving
Calories 526
Total Fat 41.1g
Total Carbohydrate 1.4g
Dietary Fiber 0.1g
Total Sugars 0.2g
Protein 36.3g

Set the Instant Pot to Sauté, and gently melt the coconut oil. Add the bacon and cook until crisp. Remove bacon and drain on a paper towel–lined plate. Set aside.

Meanwhile, in a large bowl, combine the beef with pepper and salt, chili powder, red pepper, and cayenne pepper, until the spices are evenly distributed throughout the beef. Avoid overmixing, as this might cause the patties to become tough.

In a greased, Instant Pot–friendly dish, mold the beef mixture into 4 to 5 thin, flat sliders.

Pour ¾ cup of filtered water into the Instant Pot, then insert the trivet. Set the dish with the sliders on top of the trivet. Close the Instant Pot, set the pressure release to Sealing, and select Manual/Pressure Cook. Set the Instant Pot to 10 minutes on high pressure and let cook.

Once cooked, let the pressure naturally disperse for 5 to 10 minutes. Open the lid and remove the food. In a small bowl, mix the cheeses. Sprinkle the cheeses and cooked bacon over the sliders, and enjoy!

PAPRIKA-LEMON BRUSSELS SPROUTS

Serves 4

**Prep Time: 5 minutes, Cook Time: 3 minutes, Total Time: 8 minutes,
Pressure: Low, Release: Quick**

Gluten Free, Dairy Free, Soy Free, 10 Minutes or Less, Kid Friendly

Brussels sprouts are one of the most nutrient-dense vegetables on the planet. Scientific research has even shown that Brussels sprouts help to block sulphotransferase enzymes. This is important because these enzymes have a negative impact on our cells, sometimes even being linked to cancer. This recipe pairs great with any protein-based dinner or breakfast, or works just as well on its own.

2 tablespoons extra-virgin olive oil

1 pound Brussels sprouts, outer leaves removed, and washed

1 lemon, juiced

1/2 teaspoon kosher salt

1/2 teaspoon black ground pepper

1/2 teaspoon paprika, fresh

1 cup grass-fed bone broth

Nutrition Facts
Amount per serving
Calories 121
Total Fat 7.5g
Total Carbohydrate 12.3g
Dietary Fiber 4.8g
Total Sugars 2.8g
Protein 5.3g

Set the Instant Pot to Sauté, and gently heat the extra-virgin olive oil. Add the Brussels sprouts, followed by the lemon juice, salt, pepper, and paprika.

Cook for 1 minute, then pour in the bone broth.

Close the Instant Pot, set the pressure release to Sealing, and select Manual/Pressure Cook. Set the Instant Pot to 3 minutes on low pressure and let cook.

Once cooked, carefully release the pressure. Open the lid, remove the Brussels sprouts, and enjoy!

EXTRA CRISPY PARMESAN CRISPS

Serves 7 to 8

Prep Time: 5 minutes, Cook Time: 4 minutes, Total Time: 9 minutes, Pressure: High, Release: Quick

Gluten Free, Soy Free, 10 Minutes or Less, Kid Friendly

These crunchy chips will have you feeling like you are cheating on keto, but the good news is—you won't be. For gatherings you can serve these with guacamole.

6 slices no-sugar-added bacon, sliced into small pieces
2 cups full-fat Parmesan cheese, grated
1 cup full-fat Cheddar cheese, shredded
½ teaspoon paprika, fresh
½ teaspoon chili powder
½ teaspoon freshly ground black pepper
½ teaspoon kosher salt

Nutrition Facts
Amount per serving
Calories 315
Total Fat 22.7g
Total Carbohydrate 2.6g
Dietary Fiber 0.1g
Total Sugars 0.1g
Protein 26.9g

Set the Instant Pot to Sauté, and add the bacon to cook. In a large bowl, mix the Parmesan and Cheddar, paprika, chili powder, and salt and pepper. Using a spoon, transfer cheese mixture into a greased, Instant Pot–friendly dish.

Make sure bacon is cooked, then press Cancel. Briefly drain the bacon on a paper towel–lined plate, break into large pieces, and divide evenly over the cheese.

Pour 1 cup of filtered water into the inner pot of the Instant Pot, then insert the trivet. Place the dish with the cheese and bacon on top of the trivet. Close the Instant Pot, set the pressure release to Sealing, and select Manual/Pressure Cook. Set the Instant Pot to 4 minutes on high pressure and let cook.

Once cooked, quickly release the pressure. Use a spatula to transfer crisp mixture to a baking sheet, and separate into 7 or 8 individual crisps. Finish the crisps on the baking sheet in the oven at 350°F for about 5 to 7 minutes (or until crunchy). Let cool, and enjoy!

TURMERIC EGG SALAD

Serves 2

Prep Time: 5 minutes, Cook Time: 7 minutes, Total Time: 12 minutes, Pressure: High, Release: Natural

Gluten Free, Dairy Free, Soy Free, 25 Minutes or Less, Kid Friendly

Egg salad is a healthy keto dish, and provides plenty of protein and brain-friendly nutrients. This recipe works great with breakfast, lunch, or dinner. Be sure to use a keto-friendly mayonnaise, and try using a hint of curry powder if you want to spice things up.

6 eggs

¼ cup keto mayonnaise

½ teaspoon paprika, fresh

½ teaspoon freshly ground black pepper

½ teaspoon turmeric, ground

½ teaspoon kosher salt

¼ cup green onions, thinly sliced

Nutrition Facts
Amount per serving
Calories 398
Total Fat 37.3g
Total Carbohydrate 2.9g
Dietary Fiber 0.8g
Total Sugars 1.4g
Protein 17g

Crack the eggs in an Instant Pot–friendly bowl, and scramble. Pour 1 cup of filtered water into the inner pot of the Instant Pot, then insert the trivet. Place the bowl with the eggs on top of the trivet.

Close the lid, set the pressure release to Sealing, and select Manual/Pressure Cook. Set the Instant Pot to 7 minutes on high pressure and let cook.

Once cooked, let the pressure naturally disperse from the Instant Pot for about 10 minutes, then carefully switch the pressure release to Venting.

Meanwhile, in a small bowl, mix together mayonnaise, paprika, black pepper, turmeric, and salt, until well combined.

Open the lid, remove the eggs, and allow to cool. Stir in the mayo mixture and serve with the green onions on top.

The Essential Instant Pot® Keto Cookbook

CLASSIC GINGER ALE SODA

Serves 4

Prep Time: 5 minutes, Cook Time: 25 minutes, Total Time: 30 minutes, Pressure: High, Release: Natural

Gluten Free, Dairy Free, Soy Free, Kid Friendly

Ginger is a spice that is great for many gastrointestinal issues, and also works well any time you are feeling under the weather. But ginger ale (to most of us) is mostly familiar as a carbonated, sugary beverage. However, this refreshing Instant Pot version has no sugar, no carbs, no calories—and is a perfect drink for any occasion.

2 lemons, juiced

1/4 cup ginger, diced

1/4 lime, juiced

1/2 teaspoon lavender, dried

1/2 teaspoon mint, finely chopped

4 cups carbonated water

1 cup erythritol, powder (or more, to taste)

Nutrition Facts
Amount per serving
Calories 30
Total Fat 0.4g
Total Carbohydrate 7.4g
Dietary Fiber 1.7g
Total Sugars 1.1g
Protein 0.9g

In a blender, blend the lemon juice, ginger, lime, lavender, and mint, until it becomes a purée.

Pour the carbonated water and erythritol into the Instant Pot, then add the purée.

Close the lid, set the pressure release to Sealing, and select Manual/Pressure Cook. Set the Instant Pot to 25 minutes on high pressure and let cook.

Once cooked, let the pressure naturally disperse, strain the ginger ale, then refrigerate until ready to serve.

CAULIFLOWER MASHED "POTATOES"

(IPM)

Serves 4

Prep Time: 5 minutes, Cook Time: 4 minutes, Total Time: 9 minutes, Pressure: High, Release: Quick

Gluten Free, Soy Free, 10 Minutes or Less, Kid Friendly

This keto version of a comfort food classic works perfectly in an Instant Pot Mini, and will have you reminiscing about many past holiday seasons. Sprinkle some garlic in, to get a slightly different flavor profile. Or, try adding 2 extra tablespoons of butter, to make these mashed "potatoes" even richer.

1 head cauliflower, broken into florets

2 tablespoons grass-fed butter

¼ cup heavy whipping cream

pinch of kosher salt

pinch of freshly ground black pepper

¼ cup full-fat Cheddar cheese, shredded

Nutrition Facts
Amount per serving
Calories 126
Total Fat 11.2g
Total Carbohydrate 3.8g
Dietary Fiber 1.7g
Total Sugars 1.6g
Protein 3.2g

Pour 1 cup of filtered water into the inner pot of the Instant Pot, then add the cauliflower. Move the valve to Sealing and close the lid.

Cook for 4 minutes at high pressure, then perform a quick release. Using a potato masher, mash cauliflower carefully, while inside inner pot. Strain out excess liquid, if desired.

Once mashed, mix in butter, and whipping cream, and season with salt and pepper. Gently stir, until a uniform texture forms. Transfer to a serving bowl, sprinkle cheese on top, and serve.

The Essential Instant Pot® Keto Cookbook

MINI PIZZA BITES

Serves 4 to 5

**Prep Time: 5 minutes, Cook Time: 5 minutes, Total Time: 10 minutes,
Pressure: High, Release: Natural**

Gluten Free, Soy Free, 10 Minutes or Less, Kid Friendly

These keto pizza bites are a great way to stay in fat-burning mode, while still feeling like you are indulging. These little guys will also work great at any work gatherings, family functions, or big parties. Try sprinkling a little crushed red pepper on top of the finished bites to add a little more spice!

2 cups full-fat mozzarella cheese, shredded

1 (14-ounce) can sugar-free or low-sugar diced tomatoes, drained

1 cup full-fat Parmesan cheese, grated

16 uncured pepperoni slices, cut in half

1 teaspoon basil, dried

1 teaspoon oregano, dried

Nutrition Facts
Amount per serving
Calories 328
Total Fat 24.8g
Total Carbohydrate 6.2g
Dietary Fiber 1.5g
Total Sugars 2.7g
Protein 22.3g

Pour 1 cup of filtered water into the inner pot of the Instant Pot, then insert the trivet. In a large bowl, combine the mozzarella, tomatoes, Parmesan, pepperoni, basil, and oregano. Mix thoroughly. Transfer this mixture into a well-greased, Instant Pot–friendly egg bites mold. Work in batches, if needed. I prefer to stack 2 egg bites molds on top of each other, separated by Mason jar lids (or similar dividers).

Place the molds onto the trivet, and cover loosely with aluminum foil. Close the lid, set the pressure release to Sealing, and select Manual/Pressure Cook. Set the Instant Pot to 5 minutes on high pressure, and let cook.

Once cooked, let the pressure release naturally, for about 10 minutes. Then, switch the pressure release to Venting. Open the Instant Pot, and remove the molds. Serve warm, and enjoy!

CALIFORNIA CAULIFLOWER SALAD

Recipe courtesy of Dr. Robin Berzin

Serves 4

**Prep Time: 5 minutes, Cook Time: 10 minutes, Total Time: 15 minutes,
Pressure: High, Release: Natural**

Gluten Free, Dairy Free, Soy Free, 15 Minutes or Less, Kid Friendly

I like to add this cauliflower salad as a side dish to many of my lunches and dinners. It is simple, easy to make, and loaded with nutrients. Try adding some keto-friendly nuts to the finished salad, or drizzle some extra-virgin olive oil or avocado oil, on top.

2 tablespoons coconut oil

2 cups boneless, skinless chicken breasts, cubed

1 cup broccoli, chopped

1 cup cauliflower, chopped

2 eggs, hard-boiled and sliced

1 avocado, mashed

¼ cup green onions, thinly sliced

½ teaspoon turmeric, ground

½ teaspoon nutmeg, ground

½ teaspoon sage, dried

½ teaspoon freshly ground black pepper

2 tablespoons extra-virgin olive oil

Nutrition Facts
Amount per serving
Calories 409
Total Fat 31.3g
Total Carbohydrate 9.3g
Dietary Fiber 5.3g
Total Sugars 1.9g
Protein 25.5g

Set the Instant Pot to Sauté. Add the coconut oil, melting it gently.

Mix in chicken, along with 1 cup filtered water. Close the lid, set the pressure release to Sealing, and select Manual/Pressure Cook. Set the Instant Pot to 10 minutes on high pressure and let cook.

Meanwhile, in a large bowl, mix together eggs, avocado, green onions, turmeric, nutmeg, sage, and black pepper. Stir until seasoning is well-distributed.

When the chicken is finished, perform a quick release. Gently add the broccoli and cauliflower into the Instant Pot, re-cover, and leave in for 1 to 2 minutes. Press Cancel and remove the inner pot carefully, using oven mitts.

Drain out any excess liquid from the chicken and vegetable mixture, and allow to cool before adding to the prepared salad. Drizzle salad with the olive oil, and enjoy!

The Essential Instant Pot® Keto Cookbook

ARTICHOKE WITH BUTTERY GARLIC DIPPING SAUCE

IPM

Serves 2

Prep Time: 5 minutes, Cook Time: 5 minutes, Total Time: 10 minutes, Pressure: N/A, Release: N/A

Gluten Free, Soy Free, 10 Minutes or Less, Kid Friendly

Making vegetables in the Instant Pot is extremely fast and easy. The artichokes in this recipe come out beautiful-looking, and are a good introductory and demonstrative recipe to show someone what the Instant Pot can really do. This recipe also works great in any Instant Pot Mini model. Likewise, if you're serving a larger crowd, this recipe is easily doubled or tripled.

1 artichoke, fresh

5 tablespoons salted grass-fed butter

1 teaspoon garlic, minced

¼ teaspoon lime juice, fresh

¼ teaspoon cilantro, dried

¼ teaspoon oregano, dried

Nutrition Facts
Amount per serving
Calories 289
Total Fat 28.9g
Total Carbohydrate 7.8g
Dietary Fiber 3.6g
Total Sugars 0.8g
Protein 2.5g

Prepare the artichoke by removing the stem, top, and thorns. Pour ½ cup of filtered water into the Instant Pot, then insert the trivet. Place the artichoke on the trivet, then set the valve to Sealing and close the lid. Use the Manual/Pressure Cook setting, and set the cook time for 5 minutes. Let cook.

Immediately, when cooking is complete, perform a quick release by carefully switching the pressure valve to Venting, and remove the artichoke. Mix butter, garlic, lime juice, cilantro, and oregano in a small bowl, and microwave briefly, until melted, about 30 to 40 seconds. Serve the sauce alongside the artichoke for dipping, and enjoy!

10-MINUTE KALE CHIPS

Serves 4

Prep Time: 5 minutes, Cook Time: 5 minutes, Total Time: 10 minutes, Pressure: N/A, Release: N/A

Gluten Free, Soy Free, 10 Minutes or Less, Kid Friendly

Kale is loaded with tons of vitamin A, vitamin K, vitamin C, and many more nutrients. As such, kale chips are an increasingly popular healthy indulgence. Sprinkle some crumbled bacon or Parmesan cheese on top of these chips to make them even more flavorful.

½ cup extra-virgin olive oil

4 tablespoons grass-fed butter, softened

4 cups kale, in large pieces, washed and dried, stems removed

½ cup full-fat Parmesan cheese, grated

½ teaspoon freshly ground black pepper

½ teaspoon kosher salt

Nutrition Facts
Amount per serving
Calories 215
Total Fat 19.8g
Total Carbohydrate 7.3g
Dietary Fiber 1.1g
Total Sugars 0g
Protein 3.2g

Set the Instant Pot to Sauté mode. Add the oil and grass-fed butter, melting it gently, and mix together.

Insert the trivet, and place the kale on top of it. In a small dish, mix together the Parmesan cheese, black pepper, and salt; then sprinkle mixture over the kale.

After 5 minutes, remove the chips. Finish the chips on a baking sheet in the oven at 350°F, for about 5 to 7 minutes (or until crisp). Allow to cool before enjoying.

BACON-LIME GUACAMOLE

Serves 8

Prep Time: 5 minutes, Cook Time: 10 minutes, Total Time: 15 minutes, Pressure: High, Release: Natural

Gluten Free, Dairy Free, Soy Free, 25 Minutes or Less, Kid Friendly

Guacamole is a delicious side, and this version takes it up a notch. Loaded with tons of healthy fats, the avocado in this guacamole will fulfill many important nutrient requirements. The bacon, on the other hand, will provide protein, and delight your taste buds!

2 tablespoons avocado oil

1/2 pound no-sugar-added bacon, sliced into small pieces

1/4 (4-ounce) small onion, thinly sliced

1 avocado, mashed

1/2 teaspoon kosher salt

1/4 teaspoon cilantro, dried

1 tablespoon lime juice

Nutrition Facts
Amount per serving
Calories 237
Total Fat 20.1g
Total Carbohydrate 3.4g
Dietary Fiber 1.8g
Total Sugars 0.4g
Protein 11g

Set the Instant Pot to Sauté mode. Add the oil to the Instant Pot, melting it gently.

Add the bacon, and cook until crisp. Once cooked, remove the bacon with tongs, and drain on a paper towel–lined plate. Sprinkle the onion into the Instant Pot and let cook for 1 minute (or until translucent). Hit Cancel on the Instant Pot.

Spoon the onion into a large bowl, along with the avocado, salt, and cilantro. Crumble the cooled bacon into the bowl, then mix in the lime juice. Stir thoroughly, until desired consistency is reached.

The Essential Instant Pot® Keto Cookbook

ZERO CALORIE ICED TEA

Serves 4

**Prep Time: 5 minutes, Cook Time: 5 minutes, Total Time: 10 minutes,
Pressure: High, Release: Natural**

Gluten Free, Dairy Free, Soy Free, 10 Minutes or Less, Kid Friendly

Iced tea—a true summer classic. This "set it, and forget it" recipe is so easy, it's ridiculous. Add in any creative ideas you like —this drink is endlessly customizable.

½ cup Swerve, confectioners (or more, to taste)

3 to 4 of your favorite flavor tea bags

⅛ teaspoon mint extract

⅛ teaspoon vanilla extract

4 lemon wedges, to serve

Nutrition Facts
Amount per serving
Calories 0
Total Fat 0g
Total Carbohydrate 0g
Dietary Fiber 0g
Total Sugars 0g
Protein 0g

Inside the inner pot, pour in 4 cups of filtered water, then add the Swerve, followed by the tea bags, mint, and vanilla.

Close the lid, set the pressure release to Sealing, and select Manual/Pressure Cook. Set the Instant Pot to 5 minutes on high pressure and let cook.

Once cooked, let the pressure naturally disperse from the Instant Pot for about 10 minutes, then carefully switch the pressure release to Venting.

Open the lid, let cool, then remove tea bags with a ladle. Pour tea into a glass filled with ice, top with lemon wedges, and enjoy!

CUCUMBER-TURMERIC WELLNESS TONIC

Serves 4

Prep Time: 5 minutes, Cook Time: 6 minutes, Total Time: 11 minutes, Pressure: High, Release: Natural

Gluten Free, Soy Free, 15 Minutes or Less, Kid Friendly

There are few things more soothing than a warm beverage when you are feeling sick. This warm mixture is both soothing and healing. Try adding a touch of coconut milk to thicken, or serve cold, with ice cubes.

1 tablespoon grass-fed butter

1 teaspoon turmeric, ground

1/2 teaspoon ginger, finely grated

1/2 teaspoon lavender, dried

1/2 teaspoon cinnamon, ground

1/2 teaspoon vanilla extract

1/4 cucumber, peeled, thinly sliced

1/2 cup Swerve, confectioners (or more, to taste)

Nutrition Facts
Amount per serving
Calories 35
Total Fat 3.1g
Total Carbohydrate 1.5g
Dietary Fiber 0.4g
Total Sugars 0.4g
Protein 0.2g

Set the Instant Pot to Sauté mode. Add the grass-fed butter, melting it gently.

Mix in the turmeric, ginger, lavender, cinnamon, vanilla, and cucumber. Add 4 cups of carbonated water, then the Swerve. Stir. Close the lid, set the pressure release to Sealing, cancel the current program, and select Manual/Pressure Cook. Set the Instant Pot to 6 minutes on high pressure and let cook.

When cooking is complete, let the pressure naturally disperse, for about 10 minutes. Open the lid, and remove the tonic.

Strain the liquid into a bowl or pitcher. Serve with lemon or lime slices (if desired), and enjoy!

The Essential Instant Pot® Keto Cookbook

LOADED COBB SALAD

Recipe courtesy of Dr. David Perlmutter

Serves 1

**Prep Time: 5 minutes, Cook Time: 5 minutes, Total Time: 10 minutes,
Pressure: High, Release: Natural**

Gluten Free, Dairy Free, Soy Free, 10 Minutes or Less, Kid Friendly

The Cobb salad is an American classic, but few people know that it is also very healthy. This keto specialty is also loaded with some extra bacon and eggs, upping the protein and nutrient content. If you double the quantities found in this recipe, this salad can also easily become a full-blown lunch or dinner.

2 tablespoons avocado oil

3 slices no-sugar-added bacon

¼ pound boneless, skinless chicken breasts, cubed

2 eggs, hard-boiled

1 cup spinach, chopped

1 teaspoon turmeric, ground

½ avocado, mashed

½ teaspoon freshly ground black pepper

½ teaspoon kosher salt

Nutrition Facts
Amount per serving
Calories 553
Total Fat 44.1g
Total Carbohydrate 6.7g
Dietary Fiber 4.1g
Total Sugars 0.7g
Protein 34g

Set the Instant Pot to Sauté mode. Add the oil, warming it gently.

Mix in bacon and chicken. Stir thoroughly and continuously.

Once bacon is crisp and chicken is cooked through, remove them from the Instant Pot and hit Cancel. In a large salad bowl, mix together spinach, eggs, turmeric, avocado, and salt and pepper.

Crumble the bacon, then add to the salad along with the chicken. Serve and enjoy!

CONDIMENTS, DIPS & SAUCES

CLASSIC BBQ SAUCE

Serves 7 to 8

Prep Time: 5 minutes, **Cook Time:** 5 minutes, **Total Time:** 10 minutes,
Pressure: N/A, **Release:** N/A

Gluten Free, Dairy Free, Soy Free, 10 Minutes or Less, Kid Friendly

Barbecue sauce works great for summertime grilling, but is traditionally very high in sugar. This keto version retains all the spicy and smoky flavor, but leaves out all the carbs. Try coating this on keto baby back ribs or beef for a real treat!

1 (14-ounce) can sugar-free or low-sugar diced tomatoes

4 tablespoons no-sugar-added ketchup

2 tablespoons Worcestershire sauce

½ teaspoon paprika, fresh

½ teaspoon chili powder

½ teaspoon cayenne pepper, ground

½ teaspoon cumin, ground

½ teaspoon garlic, minced

½ teaspoon freshly ground black pepper

½ teaspoon kosher salt

¼ cup sugar-free or low-sugar tomato purée

¼ cup Swerve, confectioners

½ teaspoon onion powder

Preheat the Instant Pot by turning on Sauté mode.

Add the tomatoes to the Instant Pot, then pour in the ketchup, Worcestershire sauce, paprika, chili powder, cayenne pepper, cumin, garlic, black pepper, salt, tomato purée, Swerve, and onion powder.

Stir continuously, until an even texture is obtained. For a smoother sauce, briefly blend using an immersion blender (about 20 seconds).

Hit Cancel and pour the BBQ sauce into a storage container. Refrigerate until ready for use.

Nutrition Facts
Amount per serving
Calories 23
Total Fat 0.1g
Total Carbohydrate 5.1g
Dietary Fiber 1.2g
Total Sugars 2.9g
Protein 0.7g

ROSEMARY-DIJON MAYO

Serves 7 to 8

**Prep Time: 5 minutes, Cook Time: 5 minutes, Total Time: 10 minutes,
Pressure: N/A, Release: N/A**

Gluten Free, Dairy Free, Soy Free, 10 Minutes or Less, Kid Friendly

Mayo has become increasingly popular in the keto world over the past few years, and it is easy to understand why. This mayo packs quite a bit of flavor into very few calories, and works great with many different dishes.

1 teaspoon vinegar

¾ cup extra-virgin olive oil

1 teaspoon Dijon mustard

1 egg

1 tablespoon lemon juice

½ teaspoon rosemary, ground

Nutrition Facts
Amount per serving
Calories 171
Total Fat 19.5g
Total Carbohydrate 0.2g
Dietary Fiber 0.1g
Total Sugars 0.1g
Protein 0.7g

Preheat the Instant Pot by turning on Sauté mode.

Add the vinegar to the Instant Pot, then pour in olive oil, mustard, egg, lemon juice, and rosemary.

Whisk continuously, until an even texture is obtained. For a smoother sauce, briefly blend using an immersion blender.

Hit Cancel and pour the mayo into a storage container. Refrigerate for at least 1 hour, until ready for use.

The Essential Instant Pot® Keto Cookbook

HOTTER THAN HOT SAUCE

Serves 40

Prep Time: 5 minutes, Cook Time: 5 minutes, Total Time: 10 minutes, Pressure: N/A, Release: N/A

Gluten Free, Dairy Free, Soy Free, 10 Minutes or Less

I know I am not the only one who tries to put hot sauce on literally everything. This homemade version can be as spicy or as mild as you like, and is also easily customizable. Try adding a tiny pinch of curry powder to really give it some extra bite.

½ cup white vinegar

2 poblano peppers, finely chopped

2 cloves garlic, minced

½ pound cayenne peppers, finely chopped

1 habanero pepper, finely chopped

½ teaspoon freshly ground black pepper

Nutrition Facts
Amount per serving
Calories 9
Total Fat 0.4g
Total Carbohydrate 1.6g
Dietary Fiber 0.6g
Total Sugars 0.4g
Protein 0.3g

Preheat the Instant Pot by turning on Sauté mode.

Add the vinegar to the Instant Pot, then add in the poblano peppers, garlic, cayenne peppers, habanero pepper, and black pepper.

Whisk continuously until an even texture is obtained. For a smoother sauce, briefly blend using an immersion blender.

Hit Cancel and pour the hot sauce into a storage container. Refrigerate until ready for use.

Condiments, Dips, & Sauces

HOMEMADE KETCHUP

Serves 20

**Prep Time: 5 minutes, Cook Time: 5 minutes, Total Time: 10 minutes,
Pressure: N/A, Release: N/A**

Gluten Free, Dairy Free, Soy Free, 10 Minutes or Less, Kid Friendly

Leave the French fries behind and use this keto ketchup for any meat or protein you like. I like putting it on a keto-friendly burger, or on a hot dog. You can even use this ketchup for dipping your favorite veggies or low-carb chips.

1 (14-ounce) can sugar-free or low-sugar tomato purée

1 teaspoon garlic, minced

1/2 teaspoon cloves, ground

1/2 teaspoon kosher salt

1/2 teaspoon freshly ground pepper

1/4 (4-ounce) small onion, thinly sliced

1/3 cup Swerve, confectioners (or more, to taste)

Preheat the Instant Pot by turning on Sauté mode.

Add the tomato purée to the Instant Pot, then add in garlic, cloves, salt, black pepper, onion, and Swerve.

Stir continuously, until an even texture is obtained. Blend with an immersion blender until smooth (about 20 seconds).

Hit Cancel and pour the ketchup into a storage container. Refrigerate until ready for use.

Nutrition Facts
Amount per serving
Calories 9
Total Fat 0.1g
Total Carbohydrate 2.1g
Dietary Fiber 0.5g
Total Sugars 1.1g
Protein 0.4g

The Essential Instant Pot® Keto Cookbook

10-MINUTE BACON SPINACH DIP

Serves 5

**Prep Time: 5 minutes, Cook Time: 5 minutes, Total Time: 10 minutes,
Pressure: N/A, Release: N/A**

Gluten Free, Soy Free, 10 Minutes or Less, Kid Friendly

It is rare that a simple dip gets much attention. This dip, however, will have you coming back for seconds—and thirds. This gooey recipe is so versatile that it works with almost any keto-friendly food. Crumble a little extra bacon on top of the finished dish to add even more texture and crunch.

½ cup full-fat cream cheese, softened

6 slices no-sugar-added bacon, crumbled and cooked

½ cup sour cream, at room temperature

½ cup spinach, chopped

½ teaspoon turmeric, ground

¼ (4-ounce) small onion, thinly sliced

¼ cup garlic, minced

Nutrition Facts
Amount per serving
Calories 89
Total Fat 7.5g
Total Carbohydrate 1.7g
Dietary Fiber 0.1g
Total Sugars 0.1g
Protein 3.8g

Preheat the Instant Pot by turning on Sauté mode.

Add the cream cheese to the Instant Pot, then add in the bacon, sour cream, spinach, turmeric, onion, and garlic.

Stir continuously, until cheese is melty and sauce is smooth. For a smoother sauce, briefly blend using an immersion blender.

Press Cancel and pour the dip into a storage container. Refrigerate until ready for use.

THREE-CHEESE QUESO DIP

Serves 15

**Prep Time: 5 minutes, Cook Time: 5 minutes, Total Time: 10 minutes,
Pressure: N/A, Release: N/A**

Gluten Free, Soy Free, 10 Minutes or Less, Kid Friendly

This queso dip is extremely easy to make and works with a wide range of foods. It makes plain broccoli easier to eat, and goes perfectly with keto mac and cheese. Try topping with some roasted garlic, and sprinkle a touch of cayenne pepper on top.

1 cup heavy whipping cream

2 tablespoons grass-fed butter, softened

1 cup full-fat Cheddar cheese, shredded

1/2 cup full-fat mozzarella cheese, shredded

1/2 cup full-fat Gruyère cheese, thinly sliced

1/2 cup chili peppers, chopped

1/2 teaspoon cumin, ground

1/2 teaspoon cilantro, dried

1/2 teaspoon freshly ground black pepper

1/2 teaspoon kosher salt

1/4 jalapeño, chopped, seeded

Preheat the Instant Pot by turning on Sauté mode.

Add the heavy whipping cream to the Instant Pot, then add in butter, Cheddar, mozzarella, Gruyère, chili peppers, cumin, cilantro, black pepper, salt, and jalapeño.

Stir continuously, until cheese is melted and smooth. For a smoother sauce, briefly blend using an immersion blender.

Press Cancel and pour the dip into a storage container. Refrigerate until ready for use.

Nutrition Facts
Amount per serving
Calories 92
Total Fat 8.3g
Total Carbohydrate 1.6g
Dietary Fiber 0.4g
Total Sugars 0.9g
Protein 3.1g

CREAMY PARMESAN ALFREDO SAUCE

Serves 15

**Prep Time: 5 minutes, Cook Time: 5 minutes, Total Time: 10 minutes,
Pressure: N/A, Release: N/A**

Gluten Free, Soy Free, 10 Minutes or Less, Kid Friendly

This alfredo sauce is extremely good to use with your favorite iteration of zucchini noodles. It also works great with any keto-friendly pizza. Try adding some extra garlic into the mix for even more flavor.

2 cups heavy whipping cream

3 cloves garlic, minced

2 tablespoons grass-fed butter, softened

1 tablespoon extra-virgin olive oil

½ cup full-fat Parmesan cheese, grated

½ cup full-fat mozzarella cheese, shredded

½ teaspoon freshly ground black pepper

½ teaspoon kosher salt

Nutrition Facts
Amount per serving
Calories 106
Total Fat 10.2g
Total Carbohydrate 1g
Dietary Fiber 0g
Total Sugars 0g
Protein 3.1g

Preheat the Instant Pot by turning on Sauté mode.

Add the heavy whipping cream to the Instant Pot, then add in the garlic, butter, olive oil, Parmesan, mozzarella, black pepper, and salt.

Stir continuously, until a smooth, even texture is obtained. For a smoother sauce, briefly blend using an immersion blender.

Press Cancel and pour the sauce into a storage container. Use immediately or refrigerate until ready for use.

GARLIC-RED PEPPER MARINARA SAUCE

Serves 10

**Prep Time: 5 minutes, Cook Time: 5 minutes, Total Time: 10 minutes,
Pressure: N/A, Release: N/A**

Gluten Free, Dairy Free, Soy Free, 10 Minutes or Less, Kid Friendly

Marinara sauce is extremely versatile, and this keto adaptation is even healthier than more traditional versions. Try pouring this over eggs, or use it for the base sauce for any keto pizzas. You can even get more creative, and use this with more diverse dishes, like roasted eggplant.

1 (14-ounce) can sugar-free or fire-roasted tomatoes

2 cloves garlic, minced

1 teaspoon kosher salt

½ cup extra-virgin olive oil

½ teaspoon crushed red pepper

½ teaspoon oregano, dried

Nutrition Facts
Amount per serving
Calories 93
Total Fat 10.1g
Total Carbohydrate 1.3g
Dietary Fiber 0.3g
Total Sugars 0.6g
Protein 0.1g

Preheat the Instant Pot by turning on Sauté mode.

Add the tomatoes to the Instant Pot, then add in garlic, salt, olive oil, red pepper, and oregano.

Stir continuously, until a smooth, even texture is obtained. For a smoother sauce, briefly blend using an immersion blender.

Press Cancel and pour the sauce into a storage container. Refrigerate until ready for use.

TRADITIONAL GHEE

Serves 20

Prep Time: 5 minutes, Cook Time: 10 minutes, Total Time: 15 minutes, Pressure: N/A, Release: N/A

Gluten Free, Soy Free, 25 Minutes or Less, Kid Friendly

Ghee—a true superstar of the new health movement. Loaded with fat-soluble vitamins, ghee also works with a wide variety of dishes from breakfast to dinner, and even to dessert! Even cinnamon goes with ghee—try mixing a touch in to add yet more flavor to this healthy, fat-filled indulgence!

1 pound grass-fed butter, softened

Nutrition Facts
Amount per serving
Calories 176
Total Fat 19.2g
Total Carbohydrate 0g
Dietary Fiber 0g
Total Sugars 0g
Protein 0g

Preheat the Instant Pot by turning on Sauté mode.

Add the butter and set the Instant Pot for 10 minutes. Stir occasionally.

Press Cancel and let the butter cool.

Strain the butter using a cheesecloth (or other fine-mesh filter).

Store the ghee in a container, and enjoy!

NOTE: Ghee does not need to be refrigerated and can be stored out of the light for roughly three months. If refrigerated, it can be used for up to one year.

SHAKES &
SMOOTHIES

PERFECT BREAKFAST SHAKE

Serves 3

**Prep Time: 5 minutes, Cook Time: 5 minutes, Total Time: 10 minutes,
Pressure: N/A, Release: N/A**

Gluten Free, Soy Free, 10 Minutes or Less

There is no faster way to start your morning than with a nutrient-dense shake.
This breakfast shake has all the right ingredients to keep you in ketosis, and will keep
you burning fat all day long. Try adding an extra serving of MCT oil to ramp up your
fat-burning capabilities even more.

2 tablespoons grass-fed butter, softened

½ cup full-fat coconut milk

10 drops liquid stevia

1 tablespoon pecans, chopped

1 tablespoon cashews, chopped

1 tablespoon macadamia nuts

½ teaspoon cinnamon, ground

½ teaspoon turmeric, ground

¼ cup heavy whipping cream

**¼ cup mixed dark berries (blueberries,
strawberries, blackberries, raspberries)**

2 scoops grass-fed whey protein powder

ice cubes, to serve

Nutrition Facts
Amount per serving
Calories 333
Total Fat 26.3g
Total Carbohydrate 8.3g
Dietary Fiber 1.9g
Total Sugars 3.6g
Protein 18.1g

Start by pouring 1½ cups filtered water into a blender. Depending on personal taste, you can use less water, to achieve a thicker consistency.

Set the Instant Pot to Sauté and melt the butter.

Pour in the coconut milk, then add the stevia, pecans, cashews, macadamia nuts, cinnamon, turmeric, whipping cream, and berries. Stir continuously.

Once thoroughly mixed, hit Cancel to stop the current program. Remove the inner pot from the Instant Pot, and carefully pour this mixture into your blender.

Add in the protein powder, then blend until desired consistency. Serve in a tall, ice-filled glass. Store extra servings in the refrigerator, for up to two days.

SUPER FAT BURNING SHAKE

Serves 3

Prep Time: 5 minutes, Cook Time: 5 minutes, Total Time: 10 minutes, Pressure: N/A, Release: N/A

Gluten Free, Soy Free, 10 Minutes or Less

The keto approach works wonderfully because it cuts sugar almost completely out of your diet. This easy to assemble shake is low in carbs, but high in ingredients that will help you lose the extra pounds. Try an additional serving of coconut oil for some extra fat-shedding fuel.

2 tablespoons grass-fed butter, softened

¾ cup full-fat coconut milk

10 drops liquid stevia

3 tablespoons unflavored MCT oil

2 tablespoons pecans, chopped

2 tablespoons walnuts, chopped

2 tablespoons sugar-free chocolate chips

1 tablespoon coconut oil

½ teaspoon vanilla extract

½ teaspoon turmeric, ground

½ teaspoon mint, finely chopped

2 scoops grass-fed whey protein powder

ice cubes, to serve

Nutrition Facts
Amount per serving
Calories 434
Total Fat 45.1g
Total Carbohydrate 5.4g
Dietary Fiber 1.9g
Total Sugars 2.5g
Protein 10.8g

Pour 1¼ cups of filtered water into a blender. Depending on personal taste, you can use less water to achieve a thicker consistency.

Set the Instant Pot to Sauté and melt the butter.

Pour in the coconut milk, then add the stevia, MCT oil, pecans, walnuts, chocolate chips, coconut oil, vanilla, turmeric, and mint to the Instant Pot. Stir continuously.

Once thoroughly mixed, hit Cancel to stop the current program. Remove the inner pot from the Instant Pot and carefully pour this mixture into your blender.

Add in the protein powder, then blend until desired consistency. Serve in a tall, ice-filled glass. Store extra servings in the refrigerator, for up to two days.

BASIL-MINT GREEN SMOOTHIE

Serves 3

Prep Time: 5 minutes, Cook Time: 5 minutes, Total Time: 10 minutes, Pressure: N/A, Release: N/A

Gluten Free, Soy Free, 10 Minutes or Less

Nutrient-dense vegetables (like kale and spinach) are one of the key ingredients missing from the Standard American Diet. This smoothie is absolutely loaded with these beneficial veggies, and as such, contains large amounts of beneficial antioxidants and brain-friendly phytonutrients.

2 tablespoons grass-fed butter, softened
½ cup full-fat coconut milk
10 drops stevia liquid
2 tablespoons coconut oil
½ teaspoon turmeric, ground
½ teaspoon mint, finely chopped
½ teaspoon basil, dried
½ teaspoon parsley, dried
¼ cup heavy whipping cream
¼ avocado, mashed
¼ cup spinach, chopped
¼ cup kale, chopped
¼ cup bok choy, chopped
¼ cup broccoli, chopped
2 scoops grass-fed whey protein powder
ice cubes, to serve

Pour 1½ cups of filtered water into a blender. Depending on personal taste, you can use less water to achieve a thicker consistency.

Set the Instant Pot to Sauté and melt the butter.

Pour in the coconut milk, then add the stevia, oil, turmeric, mint, basil, parsley, whipping cream, avocado, spinach, kale, bok choy, and broccoli. Stir continuously.

Once thoroughly mixed, hit Cancel to stop the current program. Remove the inner pot from the Instant Pot, and carefully pour this mixture into your blender.

Add in the protein powder, then blend until desired consistency. Serve in a tall, ice-filled glass. Store extra servings in the refrigerator, for up to two days.

Nutrition Facts
Amount per serving
Calories 360
Total Fat 34g
Total Carbohydrate 6.5g
Dietary Fiber 2.5g
Total Sugars 2g
Protein 10g

COCONUT CHOCOLATE WHIPPED CREAM SMOOTHIE

Serves 3

Prep Time: 5 minutes, Cook Time: 5 minutes, Total Time: 10 minutes, Pressure: N/A, Release: N/A

Gluten Free, Soy Free, 10 Minutes or Less, Kid Friendly

This is one of my all-time favorite smoothies. It is absolutely loaded with flavor, and yet still contains hardly any carbs or sugar. Add a pinch of cinnamon to the finished smoothie (or drizzle on some melted keto fudge) to really put the flavor over the top.

2 tablespoons grass-fed butter, softened

1/2 cup full-fat coconut milk

10 drops liquid stevia

2 tablespoons unflavored MCT oil

2 tablespoons unsweetened coconut flakes

2 tablespoons flax seeds, soaked

2 tablespoons raw cacao nibs

2 tablespoons sugar-free chocolate chips

1/2 teaspoon vanilla extract

1/4 cup heavy whipping cream

ice cubes, to serve

Nutrition Facts
Amount per serving
Calories 280
Total Fat 31.7g
Total Carbohydrate 3.1g
Dietary Fiber 1.2g
Total Sugars 1.7g
Protein 1.2g

Start by pouring 1½ cups of filtered water into a blender. Depending on personal taste, you can use less water, to achieve a thicker consistency.

Set the Instant Pot to Sauté and melt the butter.

Pour in the coconut milk, then add the stevia, MCT oil, coconut, flax seeds, cacao nibs, chocolate chips, vanilla, and whipping cream to the Instant Pot. Stir continuously.

Once thoroughly mixed, hit Cancel to stop the current program. Remove the inner pot from the Instant Pot, and carefully pour this mixture into your blender.

Blend until desired consistency is reached. Serve in a tall, ice-filled glass. Store extra servings in the refrigerator, for up to two days.

The Essential Instant Pot® Keto Cookbook

CASHEW CREAM SMOOTHIE

Serves 2

Prep Time: 5 minutes, Cook Time: 5 minutes, Total Time: 10 minutes,
Pressure: N/A, Release: N/A

Gluten Free, Soy Free, 10 Minutes or Less, Kid Friendly

Cashew cream is a true keto delight, and this smoothie packs a ton of flavor into just one glass. Cashews are surprisingly high in copper, phosphorus, and magnesium—especially for a food so small in size. Try mixing a little coconut milk or keto whipped cream on top of this smoothie to add a small, even more flavorful touch.

2 tablespoons grass-fed butter, softened

¼ cup full-fat coconut milk

2 tablespoons sugar-free chocolate chips

1 tablespoon unflavored MCT oil

½ teaspoon nutmeg, ground

½ teaspoon lavender, dried

¼ cup cashew cream, refrigerated

¼ cup mixed dark berries (blueberries, strawberries, blackberries, raspberries)

1 scoop grass-fed whey protein powder (optional)

Nutrition Facts
Amount per serving
Calories 442
Total Fat 38g
Total Carbohydrate 17.9g
Dietary Fiber 2.1g
Total Sugars 9.2g
Protein 13.3g

Pour ¾ cup of filtered water into a blender. Depending on personal taste, you can use less water, to achieve a thicker consistency.

Set the Instant Pot to Sauté and melt the butter.

Pour in the coconut milk, then add the chocolate chips, MCT oil, nutmeg, lavender, cashew cream, and dark berries to the Instant Pot. Stir continuously.

Once thoroughly mixed, hit Cancel to stop the current program. Remove the inner pot from the Instant Pot, and pour this mixture into your blender.

Add in the protein powder, then blend until desired consistency. Serve in a tall, ice-filled glass. Store extra serving in the refrigerator, for up to two days.

The Essential Instant Pot® Keto Cookbook

CHOCOLATE MACADAMIA BUTTER SMOOTHIE

Serves 3

Prep Time: 5 minutes, Cook Time: 5 minutes, Total Time: 10 minutes, Pressure: N/A, Release: N/A

Gluten Free, Soy Free, 10 Minutes or Less, Kid Friendly

This drink is one of my favorite ways to start the day, because it truly tastes like a decadent treat. Try adding one spoonful of grass-fed butter to add some extra richness and creaminess.

2 tablespoons grass-fed butter, softened

½ cup full-fat coconut milk

10 drops liquid stevia (or more, to taste)

2 tablespoons sugar-free chocolate chips

4 tablespoons macadamia butter

2 tablespoons coconut oil

2 tablespoons raw cacao nibs

½ cup heavy whipping cream

½ teaspoon vanilla extract

½ teaspoon cinnamon, ground

½ teaspoon nutmeg, ground

2 scoops grass-fed whey protein powder

2 tablespoons unsweetened cocoa powder

ice cubes, to serve

Nutrition Facts
Amount per serving
Calories 544
Total Fat 46.8g
Total Carbohydrate 13.9g
Dietary Fiber 3.3g
Total Sugars 2.3g
Protein 21.8g

Start by pouring 1½ cups of filtered water into a blender. Depending on personal taste, you can use less water, to achieve a thicker consistency.

Set the Instant Pot to Sauté and melt the grass-fed butter.

Pour in the coconut milk, then add the stevia, chocolate chips, macadamia butter, oil, cacao nibs, whipping cream, vanilla, cinnamon, and nutmeg to the Instant Pot. Stir continuously.

Once thoroughly mixed, hit Cancel to stop the current program. Remove the inner pot from the Instant Pot, and carefully pour this mixture into your blender.

Add the protein powder and cocoa powder, then blend until desired consistency. Serve in a tall, ice-filled glass. Store extra servings in the refrigerator, for up to two days.

CHOCOLATE MOCHA COCONUT BUTTER SMOOTHIE

Serves 3

Prep Time: 5 minutes, Cook Time: 5 minutes, Total Time: 10 minutes, Pressure: N/A, Release: N/A

Gluten Free, Soy Free, 10 Minutes or Less

For even more flavor, add some keto whipped cream on top, or a sprinkle of cinnamon.

2 tablespoons grass-fed butter, softened

1/2 cup full-fat coconut milk

10 drops liquid stevia

5 tablespoons raw coconut butter

2 tablespoons sugar-free chocolate chips

2 tablespoons unflavored MCT oil

2 tablespoons raw cacao nibs

1 teaspoon cold brew coffee

1/2 cup heavy whipping cream

1/2 teaspoon turmeric, ground

1/2 teaspoon cinnamon, ground

1/2 teaspoon erythritol, powder (or more, to taste)

2 scoops grass-fed whey protein powder

2 tablespoons unsweetened cocoa powder

ice cubes, to serve

Pour 1½ cups of filtered water into a blender. Depending on personal taste, you can use less water, to achieve a thicker consistency.

Set the Instant Pot to Sauté and melt the grass-fed butter. Pour in the coconut milk, then add the stevia, coconut butter, chocolate chips, MCT oil, cacao nibs, coffee, whipping cream, turmeric, cinnamon, and erythritol to the Instant Pot, stirring continuously.

Once thoroughly mixed, hit Cancel to stop the current program. Remove the inner pot from the Instant Pot, and carefully pour this mixture into your blender.

Add in the protein powder and cocoa powder, then blend until desired consistency. Serve in a tall, ice-filled glass. Store extra servings in the refrigerator, for up to two days.

Nutrition Facts
Amount per serving
Calories 637
Total Fat 62.1g
Total Carbohydrate 14g
Dietary Fiber 4.6g
Total Sugars 5.8g
Protein 16.4g

CREAMY CHOCOLATE ALMOND BUTTER SHAKE

Serves 3

Prep Time: 5 minutes, Cook Time: 5 minutes, Total Time: 10 minutes, Pressure: N/A, Release: N/A

Gluten Free, Soy Free, 10 Minutes or Less, Kid Friendly

Try sprinkling some ground cinnamon or halved pecans on top of this finished shake.

2 tablespoons grass-fed butter, softened

1/2 cup full-fat coconut milk

10 drops liquid stevia

4 tablespoons almond butter, smooth

2 tablespoons sugar-free chocolate chips

2 tablespoons unflavored MCT oil

2 tablespoons raw cacao nibs

1/2 cup heavy whipping cream

1/2 teaspoon vanilla extract

1/2 teaspoon cinnamon, ground

1/2 teaspoon nutmeg, ground

1/2 teaspoon erythritol powder (or more, to taste)

2 scoops grass-fed whey protein powder

2 tablespoons unsweetened cocoa powder

ice cubes, to serve

Nutrition Facts
Amount per serving
Calories 588
Total Fat 53.5g
Total Carbohydrate 20.7g
Dietary Fiber 7.4g
Total Sugars 6.9g
Protein 18.9g

Start by pouring 1½ cups filtered water into a blender. Depending on personal taste, you can use less water, to achieve a thicker consistency.

Set the Instant Pot to Sauté and melt the grass-fed butter. Pour in the coconut milk, then add the stevia, almond butter, chocolate chips, MCT oil, cacao nibs, whipping cream, vanilla, cinnamon, nutmeg, and erythritol to the Instant Pot. Stir continuously.

Once thoroughly mixed, hit Cancel to stop the current program. Remove the inner pot from the Instant Pot, and carefully pour this mixture into your blender.

Add in the protein powder and cocoa powder, then blend until desired consistency. Serve in a tall, ice-filled glass. Store extra servings in the refrigerator, for up to two days.

FALL PUMPKIN CINNAMON SHAKE

Serves 3

**Prep Time: 5 minutes, Cook Time: 5 minutes, Total Time: 10 minutes,
Pressure: N/A, Release: N/A**

Gluten Free, Soy Free, 10 Minutes or Less, Kid Friendly

This fall favorite tastes like a treat, but is packed with seriously healthy ingredients. The coconut milk is loaded with healthy fat, which will help you stay in fat-burning ketosis. I also recommend sprinkling a few cashews on top, to add some crunchy flavor.

4 tablespoons grass-fed butter, softened
1/2 cup full-fat coconut milk
10 drops liquid stevia (or more, to taste)
1 cup organic pumpkin purée
1/2 cup heavy whipping cream
1/2 teaspoon vanilla extract
1/2 teaspoon nutmeg, ground
1/2 teaspoon cinnamon, ground
1/2 teaspoon cloves, ground
2 scoops grass-fed whey protein powder
ice cubes, to serve

Nutrition Facts
Amount per serving
Calories 421
Total Fat 34.7g
Total Carbohydrate 14.2g
Dietary Fiber 4.3g
Total Sugars 5.6g
Protein 15.6g

Pour 1½ cups of filtered water into a blender. Depending on personal taste, you can use less water, to achieve a thicker consistency.

Set the Instant Pot to Sauté and melt the butter. Pour in the coconut milk, then add the stevia, pumpkin purée, whipping cream, vanilla, nutmeg, cinnamon, and cloves to the Instant Pot. Stir continuously.

Once thoroughly mixed, hit Cancel to stop the current program. Remove the inner pot from the Instant Pot, and carefully pour this mixture into your blender.

Add in the protein powder, then blend until desired consistency. Serve in a tall, ice-filled glass. Store extra servings in the refrigerator, for up to two days.

COCONUT MILK BERRY SMOOTHIE

Serves 3

**Prep Time: 5 minutes, Cook Time: 5 minutes, Total Time: 10 minutes,
Pressure: N/A, Release: N/A**

Gluten Free, Soy Free, 10 Minutes or Less

Dark berries are by far the healthiest fruit for us. This is due not only to their high levels of vitamins, but also because they contain many anti-inflammatory phytonutrients. Try adding some keto whipped cream to thicken up this smoothie, and you'll feel like you are indulging—all while consuming the world's healthiest fruits.

2 tablespoons grass-fed butter, softened

3/4 cup full-fat coconut milk

10 drops liquid stevia

2 tablespoons unflavored MCT oil

2 tablespoons flax seeds, soaked

2 tablespoons sugar-free chocolate chips (optional)

1/2 teaspoon turmeric, ground

1/2 teaspoon nutmeg, ground

1/4 cup heavy whipping cream

1/4 cup mixed dark berries (blueberries, strawberries, blackberries, raspberries)

2 scoops grass-fed whey protein powder

ice cubes, to serve

Nutrition Facts
Amount per serving
Calories 431
Total Fat 39.7g
Total Carbohydrate 13.1g
Dietary Fiber 4.4g
Total Sugars 3.4g
Protein 14.6g

Start by pouring 1¼ cups filtered water into a blender. Depending on personal taste, you can use less water, to achieve a thicker consistency.

Set the Instant Pot to Sauté and melt the butter.

Pour in the coconut milk, then add the stevia, MCT oil, flax seeds, chocolate chips, turmeric, nutmeg, whipping cream, and dark berries to the Instant Pot, stirring continuously.

Once thoroughly mixed, hit Cancel to stop the current program. Remove the inner pot from the Instant Pot, and carefully pour this mixture into your blender.

Add in the protein powder, then blend until desired consistency. Serve in a tall, ice-filled glass. Store extra servings in the refrigerator, for up to two days.

BENEFICIAL RESOURCES

Abel James (FatBurningMan.com) is a bestselling author, a Top 10 app developer on iTunes, award-winning talk show host, and serial entrepreneur. He stars on ABC's *My Diet Is Better Than Yours*.

Adam Bornstein (BornFitness.com) is an award-winning fitness and nutrition writer and editor. Formerly the editorial director for Livestrong.com and fitness editor for *Men's Health*, Adam has contributed to and been featured in the *New York Times*, *Fast Company*, and *GQ*.

Against All Grain (AgainstAllGrain.com) is one of the most popular paleo blogs in the world. Founder Danielle Walker is also the author and photographer of the *New York Times* bestselling cookbook *Against All Grain*.

Amy Myers, MD, (AmyMyersMD.com) is a renowned leader in functional medicine and the *New York Times* bestselling author of *The Autoimmune Solution* and *The Thyroid Connection*.

Authority Nutrition (www.healthline.com/nutrition) is one of the largest websites centered around nutrition in the world. Evidence-backed, and easy to understand. A go-to source.

Bare Bones Broth (BareBonesBroth.com) is one of the best bone broths in terms of nutrition. It is organic, paleo, non-GMO, and Whole30® approved. Highly recommended.

Big Commerce (BigCommerce.com) is the best e-commerce platform for growing brands. Stores powered by Big Commerce grow 200 percent faster than the industry average.

Big Tree Farms (BigTreeFarms.com) creates world-class products sourced with the highest ethical and social standards, including the best coconut sugar and coco aminos!

Bill and Hayley Mason (PrimalPalate.com) are the co-authors of four paleo cookbooks, and the inventors of the delicious Primal Palate Organic Spices—the highest quality on the market today.

The Body Book (OurBodyBook.com) was founded by actress Cameron Diaz, and is helping women learn the facts about health, then helping them turn knowledge into action.

Bonafide Provisions (BonafideProvisions.com) provides slow-cooked, hand-crafted organic bone broth and drinkable veggies. Their protein and collagen-rich broth is the top-selling organic bone broth on the market.

The Box (**TheBoxMag.com**) is the first print magazine that features cutting-edge training and nutrition—made by the CrossFit community, for the CrossFit community.

Breaking Muscle (**BreakingMuscle.com**) is the fitness world's preeminent destination for timely, high-quality information on exercise, fitness, health, and nutrition.

Brooklyn Biltong (**BrooklynBiltong.com**) is similar to beef jerky but different. It offers dried beef that has a chewier texture, and is a great source of clean protein for paleo diets, as well as Whole30®.

Bulletproof (**Bulletproof.com**) makes a wide variety of beneficial health products, like butter coffee and collagen supplements. Truly a one-stop shop for anyone curious about healthy supplements.

Butcher Box (**ButcherBox.com**) is grass-fed beef, free-range chicken, and heritage pork delivered directly to your door. All meat is also free of antibiotics and hormones.

BuzzFeed (**BuzzFeed.com**) is a globally distributed digital media powerhouse read by seventy-nine million people every month. Stories, news, commentary, quizzes—everything in one place.

Caveman Cookies (**CavemanCookies.com**) are healthy cookies made with ingredients that cavemen had access to: nuts, honey, and berries. Caveman Cookies are all natural, gluten free, chewy, and delicious, and make a great snack for on the go.

Choffy (**Choffy.com**) is a 100 percent natural dark-chocolate drink, made with cocoa beans that are roasted, ground, and packaged so you can brew it just like coffee. However, you get all the benefits (and taste) of dark chocolate, instead.

Chomps (**Chomps.com**) are 100 percent grass-fed beef jerky sticks. They are Whole30®, gluten free, paleo friendly, and perfect for anyone who wants to stay healthy on the go.

Chris Kresser (**ChrisKresser.com**) is a globally recognized leader in the fields of ancestral health, paleo nutrition, and functional and integrative medicine. He is the creator of ChrisKresser.com, one of the top twenty-five natural-health sites in the world, and the author of the *New York Times* bestseller *Your Personal Paleo Code*.

Crio Bru (**CrioBru.com**) is not coffee, it's cacao! Roasted, ground, and brewed just like coffee, Crio Bru has the amazing flavor and aroma of pure dark chocolate.

David Perlmutter, MD, (DrPerlmutter.com) is the *New York Times* bestselling author of *Grain Brain, Whole Life Plan* and *Brain Maker*, and a world-renowned neurologist.

Diane Sanfilippo, BS, NC (BalancedBites.com) is a certified nutrition consultant who specializes in blood-sugar regulation and digestive health. She is also the *New York Times* bestselling author of *Practical Paleo: A Customized Approach to Health and a Whole-Foods Lifestyle.*

DNX Bar (DNXBar.com) is a great-tasting, paleo and keto protein bar. DNX is a whole-food protein bar that is also Whole30® approved.

Eddie Williams (ExNihiloHealth.com) is a former five-year NFL player, and the founder of Ex Nihilo Health. While playing for the Seattle Seahawks and Cleveland Browns, Eddie honed his passion and knowledge for health and wellness, and now leads others on their journey to healthier lives.

Elana Amsterdam (Elana's Pantry) is the *New York Times* bestselling author of *Paleo Cooking from Elana's Pantry*. She writes cookbooks for gluten-free cooking, using almond flour and coconut flour as an alternative to wheat flour.

Emily Deans, MD, (@EvolutionaryPsy) is a Harvard-educated psychiatrist, searching for evolutionary solutions to twenty-first century general and mental health problems.

Emily Schromm (EmilySchromm.com) is a leading health and wellness expert, who has appeared on MTV's *The Real World*, *Good Morning America*, and more. She has an Instagram following of more than 250,000 fans.

EPIC Bars (EpicBar.com) are 100 percent grass-fed animal-based protein bars designed as nature intended: paleo, gluten free, and low in sugar.

Fatworks (FatWorksFoods.com) is the best lard, grass-fed tallow, and duck fat you can buy.

Vani Hari (FoodBabe.com) is an American author and activist who criticizes the food industry. She started the *Food Babe* blog in 2011, and it received more than fifty-four million views in 2014.

Four Sigmatic (FourSigmatic.com) specializes in superfoods, functional mushrooms, and adaptogenic herbs.

Goop (Goop.com) is a modern lifestyle brand, founded by Gwyneth Paltrow. It offers cutting-edge wellness advice from doctors and experts, vetted travel recommendations, and a curated shop of clean beauty.

Grandcestors Meals (Grandcestors.com) is a high-quality paleo meal delivery service, specializing in meals with no grains, dairy, soy, legumes, or artificial sugars. Whole30® approved and delicious!

Great Lakes Gelatin (GreatLakesGelatin.com) makes a variety of pasture-raised gelatin and collagen products, which help to heal the gut and make your skin positively glow. Great Lakes is also certified paleo friendly and completely gluten free.

Greatist (Greatist.com) covers all things healthy, providing the most trusted and fun fitness, health, and happiness content on the Web.

Hint Water (DrinkHint.com) contains only water and delicious natural flavors. No sugar. No diet sweeteners. Whole30® approved and available nationwide.

The Honest Bison (TheHonestBison.com) stands for exactly what their name suggests: grass-fed bison meat. They also offer bison bone broth, in addition to other grass-fed products.

Jen Fisch (KetointheCity.com) is the author of the internationally bestselling book *The Easy 5-Ingredient Ketogenic Diet Cookbook*. She is also the creator of the blog *Keto in the City*. She is passionate about offering simple solutions for following the ketogenic lifestyle.

Jen Sinkler (JenSinkler.com) is a fitness-magazine writer, personal trainer, and former American women's national team rugby player for the sevens and fifteens. She has written for *Shape, Men's Health, Women's Health,* and *Experience Life.*

Jennifer Fugo (GlutenFreeSchool.com) founded this online community of like-minded, gluten-free women looking to get informed, empowered, and inspired.

John Romaniello (RomanFitnessSystems.com) is one of the most highly regarded experts in the fitness industry. He has written for publications from *Men's Health* to *Fast Company* and has been featured on programs such as *Good Morning America.*

Julian Bakery (JulianBakery.com) is the largest dedicated low-carb, gluten-free, grain-free, GMO-free, paleo food manufacturer.

Julie Foucher, MD, MS, (JulieFoucher.com) is an American CrossFit athlete and medical doctor. She has competed in the CrossFit Games four times, and has historically been one of the most successful women in the sport.

Kasandrinos (Kasandrinos.com) makes exceptionally good quality olive oil, perfect for any paleo or primal need. It is keto certified, certified organic, and delicious!

Kasie Hunt (MSNBC.com/Kasie-DC) is the host of *Kasie DC*, a weekly two-hour show on MSNBC. She has been an NBC News Capitol Hill correspondent for more than four years, covering Congress across all NBC News and MSNBC platforms.

Kellyann Petrucci, MS, ND, (DrKellyann.com) is a *New York Times* bestselling author, and is a regular guest on *The Dr. Oz Show*. She has also appeared on *Good Morning America*, and has been featured in *Time*, the *Wall Street Journal*, and more.

Ketogains (KetoGains.com) is a community-driven exploration into the pursuit of physical excellence via ketosis. Learn how to achieve an optimal body recomposition by following a program that involves a diet of whole, mostly unprocessed foods.

Kettle and Fire (KettleandFire.com) is premium, 100 percent grass-fed bone broth. Made with all organic ingredients and bones from 100 percent grass-fed cows.

Klean Kanteen (KleanKanteen.com) offers insulated water bottles, mugs, cups, tumblers, growlers, food containers, and steel straws. BPA-free, high-quality, durable, reusable stainless steel solutions since 2002.

LaCroix (LaCroixWater.com) is a healthy beverage choice. LaCroix is natural, calorie free, sugar free, sodium free, and contains no artificial sweeteners.

Laurel Randolph (LaurelRandolph.com) is a Los Angeles–based food writer and recipe developer who has contributed food articles to *Paste Magazine*, *Wise Bread*, and *Serious Eats*. She is also the author of *The Instant Pot® Electric Pressure Cooker Cookbook: Easy Recipes for Fast & Healthy Meals*, #1 bestseller on Amazon, and *The Instant Pot® No-Pressure Cookbook*.

Leanne Vogel (HealthfulPursuit.com) is a four-time bestselling author, including national and international bestseller, *The Keto Diet*. She is also the host of *The Keto Diet Podcast* (ranked #3 in fitness and nutrition and #10 in all health podcasts on iTunes in the United States and Canada), and the owner of the largest keto resource on YouTube.

Loren Cordain, PhD, (ThePaleoDiet.com) is the world's foremost authority on the evolutionary basis of diet and disease. Featured on *Dateline*, the front page of the *Wall Street Journal*, and in the *New York Times*, Dr. Loren Cordain is widely acknowledged as one of the world's leading experts on the natural human diet of our Stone Age ancestors.

Mark Hyman, MD, (DrHyman.com) is an American physician, scholar, and *New York Times* bestselling author. He is the founder and medical director of the UltraWellness Center and a columnist for the *Huffington Post*.

Max Velocity Fitness (MaxVelocityFitness.com) was founded by former CBS Sports reporter Ken Berger, and is redefining fitness with movement, nutrition, and training.

MindBodyGreen (MindBodyGreen.com) is a lifestyle media brand dedicated to inspiring you to live your best life—mentally, physically, spiritually, emotionally, and environmentally.

Nick's Sticks (Nicks-Sticks.com) are beef sticks made with 100 percent grass-fed beef or free-range turkey, and are seasoned with Redmond organic season salt.

Nom Nom Paleo (NomNomPaleo.com) is paleo, gluten-free, grain-free, dairy-free, and Whole30®-friendly recipes from *New York Times* bestselling author Michelle Tam.

Nutpods (Nutpods.com) are a portable, dairy-free half-and-half alternative, made from heart-healthy almonds and MCT-rich coconuts. They are paleo, Whole30®, vegan, and sold in a convenient, easy-to-use box (which is perfect for travel).

NuttZo (NuttZo.com) is a gourmet seven–nut-and-seed butter—one of the healthiest and most unique products in the space.

OMGhee (OMGhee.com) is perfect for those with lactose intolerance, and is used by many high-level athletes, nutritionists, chefs, and health-food enthusiasts. If you're looking for ghee, this is it, as OMGhee is certified organic, as well as certified kosher.

Ora Wellness (OraWellness.com) offers holistic solutions for your oral health. Tongue cleaner, dental floss, teeth-whitening powder—all natural.

The Osso Good Co. (OssoGoodBones.com) makes non-GMO, hormone-free, and organic bone broths. They also have delicious, Whole30®-approved soups, and always use ingredients that are paleo and keto friendly.

Paleo Leap (PaleoLeap.com) is one of the largest paleo websites in the world. Paleo Leap's mission is to take seemingly complicated diets and lifestyle and nutrition subjects and break them down into easily applicable nuggets of information.

Paleo Magazine (PaleoMagOnline.com) is dedicated to providing readers with the information they need to live healthy lives! With content from leaders in the Paleo community like Mark Sisson, Melissa Joulwan, Stephanie Gaudreau, Sarah Ballantyne, Darryl Edwards, Emily Schromm, you're guaranteed to find something you like!

PaleOMG (PaleOMG.com) was founded by Juli Bauer, *New York Times* bestselling co-author of *The Paleo Kitchen*. Juli is a very well-known paleo cook, who creates meals that are sure to please the whole family.

Parsley Health (ParsleyHealth.com) was founded by Robin Berzin, MD. Parsley is a high-tech modern medical practice putting the patient first. It is also the only medical practice with a whole-body approach to long-term health.

Pat Flynn (ChroniclesofStrength.com) is the author of several books, and is the co-author of *Paleo Workouts For Dummies* and *Fast Diets For Dummies*. He is the founder of the blog *Chronicles Of Strength*, and is also a leading world expert in the art of exercising with kettlebells.

Perfect Health Diet (PerfectHealthDiet.com) is a diet for healing chronic conditions, restoring youthful vitality, and achieving long life—written by two Harvard scientists.

Perfect Keto (PerfectKeto.com) raises blood ketone levels up to 1.5 mmol, while tasting better and being more affordable than similar products.

Pete Evans (PeteEvans.com) is an Australian chef, author, and television personality, as well as the creator of ThePaleoWay.com. He has written more than seven bestselling books.

Picnik (PicnikAustin.com) makes bottled butter coffee—you're welcome. This is one of my new favorite products on the market, and just one sip will have you hooked.

PopSugar. (PopSugar.com) delivers the biggest moments, the hottest trends, and the best tips in entertainment, fashion, beauty, fitness, and food, and the ability to shop for it all in one place.

Primitive Feast (PrimitiveFeast.com) is revolutionizing frozen foods. Their entrees bring great flavors, real ingredients, and convenience to busy, health-conscious consumers. Gluten free, milk free, soy free—and delicious.

Quinn Mulhern (Former UFC Fighter) is a retired American professional mixed–martial artist who most recently competed in the Welterweight division of the Ultimate Fighting Championship. A professional competitor from 2007 until 2014, Mulhern also competed for Strikeforce, King of the Cage, and is the former King of the Cage Welterweight Champion.

Refinery29 (Refinery29.com) is a modern woman's destination for how to live a stylish, well-rounded life. Featuring breaking entertainment news, fashion tips, health, and more.

Robb Wolf (**RobbWolf.com**) is a legend in the paleo community. Robb is a former research biochemist, health expert, and two-time *New York Times* bestselling author.

RxBar (**RxBar.com**) is a whole-food protein bar, made with egg whites, dates, nuts, and other natural ingredients. There are no fillers, and only natural foods like cacao or blueberries are added to these delicious bars. Perfect for home or traveling.

Sarah Ballantyne, PhD, (**ThePaleoMom.com**) is the blogger behind the award-winning blog *The Paleo Mom*. Dr. Ballantyne is also a three-time *New York Times* bestselling author.

The School of Greatness (**LewisHowes.com**) podcast has grown rapidly to be one of the top-ranked business and self-development podcasts on iTunes. It regularly appears in the Top 50 of all iTunes podcasts, and gets downloaded more than one million times per month.

SeaSnax (**SeaSnax.com**) are vegan, gluten-free, paleo-friendly seaweed snacks for kids and grown-ups.

SFH (**SFH.com**) applies science and clinical testing to the design of natural products that benefit wellness and fitness. Since 2010, SFH has been committed to the philosophy that nutritionally balanced food, frequent exercise, and clean supplementation are the keys to a healthy life.

Spindrift (**SpindriftFresh.com**) is America's first and only line of sparkling beverages made with real squeezed fruit. All products are made without the use of artificial sweeteners, natural flavors, or added sugar.

Spoon University (**SpoonUniversity.com**) is a food publication by and for this generation. It features recipes, restaurant reviews, personal stories, and hacks to help you "adult."

The Stash Plan (**TheStashPlan.com**) was created by actress Laura Prepon, and is an exciting 21-day plan combining the latest in food science with ancient dietary wisdom, to help shed stubborn weight for good, and achieve overall wellness.

Steph Gaudreau (**StupidEasyPaleo.com**) is an award-winning paleo- and gluten-free-recipe creator, and author of *The Performance Paleo Cookbook*.

Swerve Sweetener (**SwerveSweet.com**) is a natural zero-calorie sweetener. Swerve measures cup-for-cup just like sugar and is diabetes friendly, as well as being non-GMO.

Terry Wahls, MD, (TerryWahls.com) overcame multiple sclerosis to develop a diet and lifestyle program that has helped millions of people around the world.

Tessemae's (Tessemaes.com) offers the nation's best tasting, #1 selling, organic salad dressing and condiments. Whole30® approved, low sugar—and absolutely delicious.

Thomas DeLauer (ThomasDeLauer.com) is a personal trainer and writer for *Muscle & Fitness* magazine, and has more than half a million Facebook fans. He is one of the leading experts in the world on the keto diet, as well as on weight loss, muscle building, and personal training.

Thrive Market (ThriveMarket.com) is an American e-commerce membership-based retailer offering natural and organic food products at reduced costs. Since its founding in 2014, Thrive has raised more than $110 million in funding, and become the leading destination in the space.

Tim Ferriss (Tim.blog) has been listed as one of *Fast Company*'s Most Innovative Business People and one of *Fortune*'s 40 under 40. Tim is the author of four #1 *New York Times* bestsellers, and the host of *The Tim Ferriss Show* podcast, the first business/interview podcast to exceed one hundred million downloads.

Tin Star Ghee (TinStarFoods.com) is an Austin, Texas-based manufacturer of the highest quality grass-fed cultured ghee on the market. The brown butter variety is especially delicious!

True Fare (TrueFare.com) offers easy to prepare, home delivered meals. Founded by Chef Richard Bradford, who created the delicious recipes for the bestselling book *The Whole30®*, True Fare offers the healthiest meal delivery options for any diet.

The Ultimate Health Podcast (UltimateHealthPodcast.com) is the leading health and wellness podcast, with guests such as Ariana Huffington, James Altucher, Carrie-Anne Moss, Dr. Anthony Gustin, Chris Kresser, and many, many more!

US Wellness Meats (GrassLandBeef.com) is the best source on the planet for grass-fed meat—including lamb, bison, pork, poultry—and even seafood! In business for almost twenty years, they know meat inside and out.

Vital Proteins (VitalProteins.com) offers a variety of grass-fed collagen products—helping to protect your hair, skin, and nails, while optimizing your healthy lifestyle.

Well + Good (WellandGood.com) offers millennials wellness news, boutique fitness studios, yoga classes, wellness experts, healthy recipes, green juices, smoothies, health facts—and much more.

Wellness Mama (WellnessMama.com) is a highly trafficked website, and its creator, Katie Wells, was named as one of *Greatist*'s Top 100 Most Influential People in Health and Wellness. She is also the author of *The Wellness Mama Cookbook*.

Wild Zora Foods (WildZora.com) offers Whole30®-approved meat and veggie bars made with 100 percent grass-fed beef, free-range turkey, or natural lamb. Perfect for traveling!

Your Health Solution (YourHealthSolution.com) is a self-care website, designed to empower patients to be in control of their own health. Founder Chris Conway has been interviewed by Dr. Oz, and has founded multiple businesses.

Zupa (DrinkZupa.com) is a drinkable superfood product, offering high-quality vegetables, collagen, and other Whole30®-approved ingredients in a simple, ready-to-drink bottle.

SPECIAL THANKS TO

LT—JT—MN—CN—AS
DS—LC—RW—MH—JM
BB—ND—MS—BK—CD
MP—LA—SA—KA—SJ
RS—SS—NT—JH

Anna Di Meglio (InstantPot.com)
Bryan Azur (PaleoMagOnline.com)
Cain Credicott (PaleoMagOnline.com)
Dr. Loren Cordain (ThePaleoDiet.com)
Judy Linden (Stonesong.com)
Melissa Hartwig (Whole30.com)
Morgan Hedden (GrandCentralLifeandStyle.com)
Ellen Scordato and Alyssa Jennette (Stonesong.com)
Stan Madaloni (studio2pt0.com)

PHOTOGRAPHY CREDITS

INDEX

The Essential Instant Pot® Keto Cookbook

C

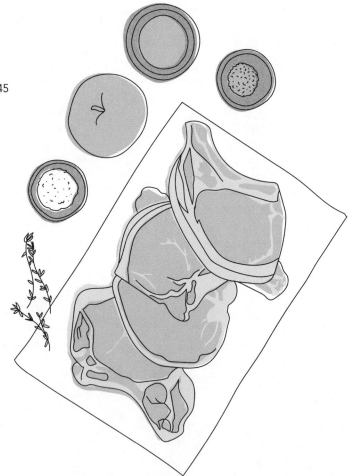

NOTES

ABOUT THE AUTHOR

CASEY THALER, NASM-CPT, FNS *has written over two hundred articles on health, science, fitness, and nutrition. As a National Academy of Sports Medicine certified personal trainer and fitness nutrition specialist, he has also helped thousands of people lose weight, look younger, and live their healthiest lives.*

Casey has been writing regularly for the founder of the paleo diet, Dr. Loren Cordain, for the past four years, publishing over fifty deeply-researched articles exploring the biochemistry and science of nutrition. He is also a former fitness model, athlete, and regular contributor to Paleo Magazine. *He has written for* Greatist, Paleohacks, Breaking Muscle, *and* MindBodyGreen online, *and currently serves as an advisor for a number of small startup companies in the health and wellness space.*